SNOW WHITE'S PEOPLE: VOLUME TWO

An Oral History of the Disney Film
Snow White and the Seven Dwarfs

DAVID JOHNSON

Theme Park Press
www.ThemeParkPress.com

Editor: Bob McLain
Layout: Artisanal Text
Cover Photo: Courtesy of Bob Cowan

The cover photo, from the Ingeborg Willy collection, depicts Marge Champion, Disney's live-action reference for Snow White.

ISBN 978-1-68390-120-4
Printed in the United States of America

Theme Park Press | www.ThemeParkPress.com
Address queries to bob@themeparkpress.com

Contents

Contents

Foreword

It took me a little longer than planned to edit the interviews for this second and final volume of *Snow White's People*. You will probably agree with me that the wait was worth it. Through the testimonies of many of the artists who worked on Walt's first feature-length cartoon we get a fascinating glimpse at the Disney studio in the mid-1930s and at life during the Great Depression in the US. A time of hardships and excitement. A time of struggles and of great achievements.

Sadly, as I mentioned in the first volume of this short series, not all of David Johnson's original interviews survived. Some of the recordings were preserved in their entirety, some only as excerpts. All of them contain information that is of utmost value to understand the making of *Snow White and the Seven Dwarfs*.

One note of caution before turning the page: while reading these testimonies, it is important to always keep in mind that no statement from any interview should ever be considered as the absolute truth, as the interviewee might have misremembered the facts, may have seen only part of the project described, or may have his own personal reasons for representing reality in a certain way. Hence the importance of the various perspectives provided in these books.

With this in mind, you are now ready to start your journey, to look behind the curtain and to meet more of "Snow White's people."

Didier Ghez
Coral Gables
August 2017

Adriana Caselotti (1916–1997)

Interview date unknown.

Adriana Caselotti was the voice of Snow White. She died at her home in Los Angeles on January 18, 1997, aged 80, of respiratory failure from lung cancer.

ADRIANA CASELOTTI: When I first went there, it was for an audition in 1935. I was then eighteen years old. So it has to have been before May 6, 1935.

DAVID JOHNSON: Because that's when you turned nineteen.

AC: Yes, nineteen. So I would say it was like March. I seem to remember March for some reason.

DJ: You went to audition, but as soon as you were there, didn't they give you the part right then?

AC: Oh no, my God.

DJ: That's the story that I hear. Walt said. "That's Snow White!"

AC: He did. He did. I heard about a year later from Frank Churchill, the musical director, that Walt said [when he was sitting behind the screen] after I finished, he said, "She's the first one we've tried, but I feel certain that this is our Snow White. But I'm not going to go with this until we really find out definitely." He said, "We're going to try out as many more as we can."

DJ: You mean you were the first one?

AC: I was the first one.

DJ: Because that's not in any of the books either. All the books talk about Deanna Durbin and many others.

AC: They were way after me. I was the first one. Deanna Durbin was much later.

DJ: Did they scout, for months and months and months?

AC: A year. A whole year. They tried out 148 other girls. I was the first; after me came 148, that makes 149, doesn't it? And I was then the 150th because they called me back. That's exactly it. I was the first and the 150th.

DJ: So it was in 1936 when they called you back.

AC: Yeah. It was definitely '36. I thought they'd forgotten. I didn't even know it was going to be a regular real motion picture. I thought it was going to be a little short, maybe fifteen minutes longer than the others, or something like that. They didn't tell me what they were doing. I knew *nothing*. In fact, halfway in between this whole thing, the whole production was stopped because he ran out of money. And when he ran out of money nobody knew we'd ever be there again. I figured the thing was finished. I didn't even know because they didn't let me hear any of the rush. I didn't see or anything. I didn't know what was going on. I was a punk kid. I was very smart, but I wasn't interested in anything except myself, and so I didn't care what was going on. I didn't know and I didn't want to know. I just went along with it.

DJ: Now, getting back to the first audition, way back in '35, did they have you do dialogue as well as songs?

AC: I just had to do some high notes; I just went through a few high notes for him and he *knew*. And what really hit it now, is this: that when Frank Churchill, the musical director, said, "I have a manuscript here, would you please hold this? We haven't really decided that this is going to be the exact song, but I'd like you to just hold it, and I will go to the piano, little girl [he's calling me "little girl"], and when I get there I'm going to play it a couple of times for you so that you'll be able to sing it. Just hum the things if you can't sing the songs, though the words are the same thing." So I waited. I didn't even let him get to the piano and I looked at it and I said [sings], "Some Day My Prince Will Come." He said, "Oh my God, the kid reads!"

DJ: Did you have perfect pitch?

AC: You can hand me a piece of music and I'll sing it to you without ever having heard it. This is what the point was.

DJ: So you do have perfect pitch and relative pitch and all that stuff and you can sing a B flat.

AC: No, the perfect pitch I may miss a half note. But what I'm telling you is that I can read the music without having heard it. What was important to him was that I could read this thing without having to have him play it for me first because I'd never heard it.

DJ: And you recall that it was "Some Day My Prince Will Come."

AC: It was definitely "Some Day My Prince Will Come." So then he said, "Oh my God, the kid reads, let's go through it." Then I just went straight through this. Of course I didn't meet Walt Disney. He's in back of the screen, because he didn't want to see me, he didn't want to be influenced by my looks.

DJ: So practically a year went by and you didn't hear a word.

AC: I didn't hear a damn thing.

DJ: And you were practicing your scales and your coloratura scales and...

AC: Yeah. My father wanted me to be an opera singer and that wasn't really what I wanted to do.

DJ: What did you want to do?

AC: I wanted to get married and have a wonderful, happy life. That was all I wanted. But it took me a long time to find the right guy. And I didn't even find the right guy, but I got married when I was twenty eight. Then I later found the right guy. I knew that when people were singing in opera and all this, they had to travel and I'd be away from anybody I liked here.

DJ: Did you grow up here?

AC: Yeah. I was born in Bridgeport, Connecticut. At the age of seven I went to Italy with my mother who was an opera singer. She was singing in Rome and she put me in a convent there, because she couldn't keep the kid around with her. I was between the ages of seven and ten at that time. When I came back here I couldn't speak a word of English, so that was where I still have that Italian language and the fluid way of singing. Singing helps a lot when you speak the Italian language and all.

DJ: Where were you living when all of this took place, this *Snow White* stuff?

AC: I was staying at my father's house at the time, though my mother lived separately because my father now lived alone. They had divorced.

DJ: You were living with your father?

AC: Not really. I just happened to be at his place that day.

DJ: Where were you actually living?

AC: I was living up on Alta Loma Terrace. It's a little place right next door to the Hollywood Bowl; it is exactly next door to the Hollywood Bowl.

DJ: Was that where your mother was?

AC: That's where she lived.

DJ: And you were living with her?

AC: Yes, I was, but I happened to be seeing my father at 233 South Lafayette Parkway. He had a little studio there and it had a little apartment and downstairs he was teaching singing there. That's when they called there and I happened to pick up the telephone. It was only about two days later that we went down to Disney's and [Churchill] played for me and I sang this little bit of song and I think I did something else for Disney, but I don't remember what it was—I mean, that day. I'm sure I sang a lot of high notes for him and this is what really hit him.

DJ: *Le Rossignol* **you did?**

AC: Yeah, I did it, but also something more like high notes or something. I can't remember what it was, but apparently that hit him, because he saw that now he had a singer on his hands, but one [who] still had the little girl quality, which is unusual. Now with the lines I was not very good at first.

DJ: Is this still the first day we're talking about?

AC: No, this is the next time. They said, "We are not too pleased with the way you are reading your lines." I said "I don't know anything about reading lines, I'm a singer." So, he said, "You're very good in many [ways] and we feel that if we work with you you'll be able to do it." I knew that was exactly what I needed.

DJ: Who was this?

AC: Larry Morey.

I was a live model also. I would be photographed while I was singing and he copied my hair. He was going to have a blonde, originally.

DJ: Who was this? Disney?

AC: Disney, yes. And form what I understand, he said something like, "I'm going to go with Adriana's hair." I had black at that time. And I really looked like Snow White. So I was copied much more than Marge [Champion], but she was doing all the calisthenics.

DJ: Yeah, the dancing.

AC: I mean they needed her because I was not a dancer. So she was great for that purpose.

Then there was Ham Luske. The two of them [Luske and Morey] seemed to be with me a great deal, especially the first few days.

I remember Disney well, once I knew who he was. I had been working with him several days and I didn't know he was Disney.

DJ: Oh, you didn't know?

AC: No, because nobody introduced me. He was just sitting there. He was sort of like a punk kid, and he was sitting with this funny old T-shirt on a stoop somewhere. He wouldn't sit on a chair, so I think he's just one of the guys. What I remember was that he was watching and then once in a while he'd get up with all the other guys and he'd say, "Now if were you, I'd do such and such and such and such." And I'd say, "OK." I'm listening to Ham Luske and I'm listening to Larry Morey and I didn't know what to do, you know. So Larry or somebody said, "Hey, you just walked away from Walt Disney." I said "Oh, OK." So I walked back and I said, "Now what were you saying, Mr. Disney?" And he said something like, "Call me Walt. What I was trying to tell you was that you should do such and such…"

DJ: In an interview from 1938 you mentioned that you would spend sometimes a whole day on one word like "Hello." Just how to say it.

AC: Yep.

DJ: Can you go more into that?

AC: One of them was when Snow White arrives at the dwarfs' cottage. They had changed it, I don't know how many times, and they couldn't make up their minds. I remember one was [in Snow White's voice], "Oh, what a cute little house." There were two or three things in between and then they stopped referring to a house and they said, "Let's just say," [in Snow White's voice], "Oh, it's adorable!" So they changed, and then we would go over that about five times, ten times, until I just didn't know what adorable meant anymore. But I kept going through it, and then they'd call me back and I had to do adorable again.

DJ: Now when you say the whole day do you mean like two or three hours? Is that what the whole day was worth?

AC: The whole day was about twelve to fifteen hours, because there was no union. I was getting twenty dollars a day and didn't care if I worked overtime. There was no overtime.

DJ: Oh, you got paid by the day.

AC: Twenty dollars a day and that was it, kid!

DJ: How long did you work on the movie?

AC: The whole thing has to be only forty-five days, the way I come out to think of it, because I made nine hundred and seventy dollars.

DJ: It was over a period of about how long?

AC: Two years.

DJ: But the movie came out in 1937 and then if you started in…

AC: All right, it wasn't a full two years. You're right, but it's almost, though. They stopped for a long time because they ran out of money.

DJ: And then they called you back to do some scenes.

AC: I had to do some things over.

DJ: Do you recall what some of those were?

AC: Yeah, they decided they were going to hire a dramatic coach for me. So now she had me saying, instead of saying [in Snow White's voice], "Why Grumpy, you do care," now she had me going [in deep, supported voice], "Why Grumpy, you DO care." Because dramatic coaches want you to speak from here [indicating her diaphragm] and all. What she didn't realize [is that] this is a little girl. You don't do this.

DJ: Do you remember who this person was?

AC: Mosley. I think that's her last name. Or Moser. She used to have me lie down and do these lines.

DJ: Was this at the studio?

AC: Yeah. So I would lie down on the floor and she'd say, "Now try to do it while you're relaxed. I want to hear you say the line this way." I wasn't good at lines. I wasn't an actress, I'll admit it.

DJ: But the movie turned out fabulous. I mean it was fabulous.

AC: Because they worked with me. You can work with me from now until doomsday and I'll get that line finally. I'm not an actress. I'm a singer.

DJ: Now this Moser or Mosley: did this come like mid-point in your work?

AC: It was more mid-point. I worked with her about five days and [Larry Morey and Ham Luske] said, "We're going to let her go and you're going to go back to what you were doing, because you're losing everything. We're going to have to go back and you just do it your way. Let's see what you can do." I came out better than anybody telling me what to do. I think what really was happening was that I was so scared I didn't know what I was doing, because everybody was changing me. So they said, "Just do it the way you'd do it as yourself. What would you do?" And this is when it was perfect. After that I had no more trouble.

Now in the singing part, a couple of times they wanted me to put in what they called a little more schmaltz into "Some Day My Prince Will Come," so they called my father and they had him come back and he sat there with me and we talked it back and forth and we got it right away, in half a day.

DJ: Do you remember when your father came and you talked back and forth?

AC: Yes, yes.

DJ: What did you talk about?

AC: He would come over to me and say, "I think they want you to put a little more body into that, a little more expression, because they want [it to] sound a little more amorous. You're too little girlish, try to put a little more like a more grown woman," or something to this effect. I mean, something like that.

DJ: Now let's just talk about dialogue. Were you by yourself?

AC: I was always alone. I never had anyone with me. There was no momentum of any kind, whether it be in singing or in speaking.

DJ: Except when you worked with the witch, Lucille LaVerne.

AC: Only a couple of times I worked with her. And I also worked with the dwarfs a couple of times and that's it.

[...]

AC: The last time I saw Walt Disney was when I was on a tour for him on *Song of the South*, and I was so happy that he was there at that time, the way he acted with me, because in the beginning he really did not want me to appear as the voice of Snow White.

And this hit me very hard because I had no chance to ever do anything like *The Jack Benny Show* which I was invited to do and many other things which would have launched a career for me.

DJ: Because you had to be anonymous.

AC: Right, but now what I found was that he *did* want me to be with him and traveling for him. Because now I was on another tour, the third tour for him, actually, and I remember the last time I saw him. We were in Atlanta and his wife was there and the whole crew and the whole cast, everybody was there.

DJ: This was the *last* time you saw him?

AC: The last time I saw him. Disney, in 1947. It was on the balcony of the Summit Hotel in Atlanta. He put his arm around me and he said, "Now Adriana, we have a big, big parade going on down here today. So when they are there I want you to stand with me and we're going to wave to the people." This was for *Song of the South*. He would send me on tours that had nothing to do with *Snow White*.

DJ: You used to travel with Pinto [Colvig]. That was in the forties, wasn't it?

AC: Yes, it was 1944 with Pinto. We went all through Canada and we even met those kids...

DJ: You did some opera in the late thirties. Wasn't it in Baltimore?

AC: You're right, I sang *Gilda*. I did it in Baltimore, and in Binghamton and Albany, New York.

[...]

DJ: Did they have a soundtrack in the back of the dwarfs laughing?

AC: No, no, nothing, I got absolutely nothing coming back, *nothing*, nothing coming back. They would hand me a pretty long sheet like this with thirty, forty lines and I might even sing a song that day.

DJ: Typed?

AC: Yeah, they were typed. And I might sing a song that day besides.

DJ: Let's talk a little about the music now. You were given the manuscripts of these songs, obviously.

AC: Yes.

DJ: Did Frank Churchill give them to you, let's say at the end of a session, and say, "Please learn this by tomorrow or the next day?"

AC: No, no. He knew I would read it right off.

DJ: Oh, so you actually didn't take it home to study in the interim...

AC: There was no reason. There was no reason. Today you could hand me anything and I could sing that melody.

DJ: So "Whistle While You Work" posed no problems?

AC: It was absolutely nothing. I was there when there were going to write "Whistle While You Work." I was there that day and what happened was Disney was standing and Frank Churchill was at the piano, a little upright piano, a very old thing. He was at the side there and they were fooling around about something and Disney was acting like the lion, he said a line as a lion, he *looked* like the lion. I mean, Disney was this kind a guy, in everything he did. And all of a sudden he said, "Let's get back to that thing we're writing." It hadn't been written yet. It was only partly written then, if I remember correctly. They weren't satisfied. And that was called "Whistle While You Work." So here's what I'm hearing: I'm standing there... I just happened to overhear it. You know, a little kid doesn't know what they're doing. So I heard Walt saying to Frank [sings beginning of "Whistle While You Work], "Hey Frank, doesn't this sound a little like 'London Bridge's Falling Down?'" Frank said, "I don't know." And they were back and forth for a long time. Disney said, "Look, we're going to keep it." I was there when they decided.

I remember that Disney said "I'm taking you to lunch," so I went with him.

DJ: Where did you go?

AC: We went across the street. It was a sort of a nice little restaurant. So we went in to have lunch and it was a very nice lunch and it was fifty cents. He said, "See, Adriana, how inexpensive this is. You can eat here every time." But he didn't know I didn't have the fifty cents. When mother would give me a candy bar I didn't have... We had no money. If she could make a sandwich, she'd make a sandwich and I would eat the sandwich at Disney's, but they didn't know I had no money to go across the street. If I had the nickel to come home, it was great, but if I didn't have it, he took me home a couple of times.

DJ: Disney did himself?

AC: Yes, he took me himself.

DJ: And if he didn't you would walk?

AC: No, no, I would have the nickel. See, they didn't pay you the day you worked. You had to come back next Thursday. I think he knew that I was pretty broke, so he'd offer to take me home, and this was when he said to me one day, "You know, if you come up with any ideas that are good, I would certainly enjoy that, because we could use that and then I would give you five dollars."

And [one day] I was on the set and he happened to be there. So I walked over to him and I said, "If you could get a bird to imitate me, we would do something like..." And I had the exact melody and he used it exactly: [sings ahhhhhhh]. And he said, "Hey, guys, come over here! Look what the kid's got. She's got an idea!" This is the truth. That's used in the movie. And I still wanna know where's the five bucks! I never got paid.

[...]

DJ: Was it difficult to not sing like yourself? I mean was that treble...?

AC: No, it was very easy. I used to imitate Betty Boop. This is what helped me all the way. This is what made me do Snow White.

DJ: Now, you would go to a session and they would have these storyboards out there and...

AC: Yes, yes.

DJ: And they would go over the scenes with you.

AC: This is how they did this—each day, as a matter of fact, that I would go there. Now, this is the next sequence, and so forth. And I'm looking at all these guys and I didn't even listen to them.

DJ: Oh, you didn't?

AC: No. I was getting bored. I was just a kid.

DJ: You just wanted to do your own thing.

AC: Yeah.

[...]

AC: Paul Smith was the fellow who would play with one finger, instead of the orchestra. I had no orchestra, ever. How can you be sounding like you've got a whole orchestra under you when you've only got one finger? And it was so soft, because they wanted to orchestrate to me, the way I would do. I didn't have to sing with the orchestra. The orchestra played with me.

DJ: So he would just accompany with one finger.

AC: And it was so soft, so soft that I could hardly hear it, but it didn't matter, because all he had to do was give me the first note and I'd keep going. Frank Churchill stood there with a baton all through this.

The whole score of *Snow White* I did acapella. There was only one time I had an orchestra. It was when we did a retake on "Some Day My Prince Will Come."

DJ: Why was there a retake, do you know?

AC: Some little thing that I don't know what it was and I don't think it was me. I think it had to do with the technical [side of things].

DJ: And you remember an orchestra then?

AC: Yes, and it was so funny because I choked that day. What happened was I had just had my tonsils out and I was scared to death, because I thought, "What if I can't sing after having my tonsils out?" It was just about five weeks later. And I was called back. This was just before the premiere! So I was called back and now I was scared to death because my mother said, "I don't want you to have your tonsils out, because maybe you'll never be able to sing again." And I got scared to death and oh my god what if they call me back and I have to do a retake. Anyway, I sure had to go back and do the retake. So here I'm going and somewhere in the middle of the thing I choked.

DJ: So what happened after you choked?

AC: After I choked they said, "That's OK, we'll make another take. It was nothing." But to me that was terrible because I'd never done *that*. That's the only time I ever had any trouble at Disney's when I was singing.

DJ: Now I want to talk about Lucille LaVerne who was the Witch and she was also the Queen. What do you remember about her? The very first time you met her, what was it like?

AC: I only met her that one time, maybe twice. It was the day that we were doing the pie scene. And I remember her as she came to the thing and she said, "Baking pies, my pet?" I went through that with her and I don't remember anything else.

[...]

AC: I used to travel with Pinto Colvig. He would say, "I did the bubbles for Dopey!" What a nice guy! He was the fellow who was always very happy. This was the funny part about it. When we would travel together and I'd get tired... We would do seven shows a day because we didn't have television in those days. I had to go to schools, I had go to radio stations. Then we might go to the Elk Club, whatever we could do, get to see everybody we could. Because there's no television. It took a lot to catch a few thousand people. So, I would be so tired back and forth and here and he's *happy*. Oh, he's having a great time with all this stuff. One day I said, "Pinto, what in the devil are you doing? You're happy. You get up in the morning at six. I can't even open my eyes. You're up. You're singing, fooling around with the guy at the train, the Pullman porter. You're doing a 'boop,'" because he had a clarinet. And he's playing this thing and he's doing a whole show and he'd go "a heulk, heulk." He was Goofy, the whole thing.

So he's doing a whole show and here I am thinking, "Ah, gee, I don't even want to hear this." They'd take the piece of the train off and put it up for us, because we had to stay overnight. So Pinto's off doing a show for the porter. He'd do a whole show. The whole bit. And here I am trying to sleep and oh my God. So I said, "Pinto, how can you do this? How can you be so happy?" He said, "Adriana, when I get up in the morning, I say to myself, 'I'm not mad at anybody.'" And I thought to myself, "My God, we should all be like Grumpy. If we all thought I'm not mad at anybody, do you know what would happen? Everybody would be better off in the world, because nobody'd kill anybody because we'd never think anything terrible." And this is what I learned from Pinto. He had a wife going through a cancer thing and she was dying and all this. He had five boys that he had to raise. It was rough. But this man was the happiest man of the whole group of Disney. This was a happy guy. And that was Grumpy. This is what I learned.

[...]

AC: When Harry Stockwell went to audition for Disney he went ahead and he sang his song and they called him back and now Walt himself was there. He said, "Harry, this is very good, but I want you to hear a couple of others, because we have three or four others we're trying to consider. I want you to listen to all of them, and you tell me which you like best." This is what he asked *him*. You see, Walt's always asked everybody's advice. He would go into a restaurant and ask the waitress' advice about something, because he felt this was natural, this was a human way of doing things. He felt that everybody should tell his story. If you've got an idea, please tell it. He wanted Harry to give his opinion. This is very funny. So now, he's got four guys singing the same song. Harry listens to the first one and second one and Harry said, "Gee. This is a nice voice." [Walt] said, "Do you like it, really?" And he said, "Well, yes, I do, but I want the job." Walt said, "Well, that's your voice!"

DJ: Oh, that's hysterical.

AC: Harry told me.

Adrienne Tytla (1914–2006)

Interviewed on November 13, 1991.

Disney historian Jim Korkis wrote about Adrienne Tytla:

> For 30 years, she was the wife of Bill Tytla, often described as "Animation's Michelangelo." Among Tytla's most famous animation work was Stromboli, the evil puppeteer in *Pinocchio*; Chernabog, the winged devil featured in *Fantasia*; and baby Dumbo in *Dumbo*, for which Tytla used his son, Peter, as an inspirational model.
>
> Adrienne died at her farm in East Lyme, Connecticut—the same farm she and her husband had bought back in 1942 before he left the Disney studio. She was 92 years old. She is survived by her son, artist Peter Tytla, daughter Tamara Schacher-Tytla, and granddaughter Fantasia, who accepted the Disney Legend award for her grandfather in 1998.
>
> Adrienne le Clerc met her husband in 1936 when she was a 22-year-old actress and fashion model from Seattle, earning extra money by posing in art classes. She was paid 75 cents an hour (for a three-hour shift) to pose for life drawing classes at the Disney studio for one week. That first night, a dark, intense, good-looking young animator who was finishing his work on *Snow White and the Seven Dwarfs* asked to give her a lift home and lightning struck.
>
> In addition to being a model, Adrienne Tytla had quite an active career as a stage actress and even dated playwright William Saroyan before she met her husband. Bill and Adrienne's 30-year marriage began on April 21, 1938. Some accounts state that they were married in 1937, possibly because they lived together for a while before they married, but Adrienne herself confirmed the April 1938 date. Their son, Peter, was born approximately 10 months later.
>
> She was a great inspiration and support for her husband, although she complained that in order to get her husband's attention when he was intently working on his animation, she had to stand in the doorway naked.

After her husband's death in 1968, Adrienne resettled in East Lyme, Connecticut, opened an antique garden furniture shop in the barn on her property, and continued her lifelong hobby of taking photographs. In 1974 she became the food columnist for the local newspaper, the *Old Lyme Gazette*. In addition to sharing recipes, she included stories of her adventures in Hollywood. Her "Joy of Eating" column continued until the paper was sold in 1982. After leaving the paper, she began concentrating on photography in earnest, primarily still lifes and landscapes. She exhibited her work, sometimes in shows along with the work of her children.

Adrienne Tytla died from cancer on December 13, 2006.

ADRIENNE TYTLA: Everybody was making money, I thought, except those of us who were extras. I mean the principals were and the stars were and the management was and we weren't. So I got a petition. I got twenty-seven people to sign the petition and we wanted at least traveling money, just car fare and money for make-up, because we were just working for nothing. Twenty-seven people signed the petition. When it came time to go out on strike, one person came out there (me!). And that was the end of that job. It was in the *Los Angeles Record*, or whatever, and I never got a job in pictures again. I didn't know any better. With my background and all the radicals I heard mouthing off all my life, that just seemed to me to be a logical thing to do. They weren't about to fork over any money for car fare or make-up or food or anything else if they could just keep it among themselves. So I felt, well, screw them, we'll have a petition and they'll honor it and we'll get something for our work. We were hoping that our Playhouse was a showcase and we'd be immediately discovered by a producer and thrown right into a leading role somewhere. But because of my background and my sympathy for the underdog and realizing that the haves get it and the have-nots die, who cares? I'm afraid I encouraged Will [Bill Tytla], which was probably as instrumental as [Art] Babbitt was, and I regret it to this day. Because I know that from the day that Will left the studio he was a changed man. He was changed in the sense that he was broken-hearted. He loved that studio. He loved working there. We loved what he was able to do there, and he was never able to do [that] anywhere else. His talent had been recognized prior to that, but he certainly hadn't been able to develop it as fully.

We didn't socialize.

I knew about Will before I ever met him from a gal named Sandra Stock. She belonged to the same modeling agency that I belonged to. And we worked in films, we worked as dress extras. I worked for that furrier Willard George on Wilshire at the opening of the Santa Anita racetrack. I think it was Christmas week. I was freelancing all over the place.

DAVID JOHNSON: You're from Seattle, right?

AT: I was born there.

DJ: Are you French Canadian?

AT: Oh god no. Le Clare. My mother was from Rouen and my father was from Levere.

DJ: Oh, real French. What year did you come to southern California?

AT: I was 16. I stowed away on a lumber freighter.

DJ: By yourself?

AT: Yes. I had made a trip on her before and visited my sister in Hollywood.

DJ: This is fascinating. This was in the twenties, I guess.

AT: It was in 1930. Anyway, it was Depression times and those of us who were hoping to get into films did just about anything we could do in order to survive. Sandra Stark and I both belonged to the same modeling agency. Sandra was dating Art Babbitt and all the gals that worked for this agency were dying to go and model at Disney's. Many were called and few were chosen. Which is the story of my career in films. Which was practically non-existent. But anyway, Sandra told me about this mad Russian that lived with Art Babbitt. And he'd been in a polo accident and he was in the hospital and had his pelvis crushed and she'd been to visit him and she was telling me all about this character and I said, "Hmm, he sounds interesting." She said, "Oh, don't worry, Adrienne, you haven't got a chance." That was fine.

There was someone by the name of Eugene Fleury, and he was in charge of lining up the models for the art classes for those coming in. I stopped by my neighborhood drugstore (I was living down near Wilshire and Western at that time). Bullock's Wilshire was just a few blocks away. It was a relatively respectable neighborhood. From what I understand now it's terribly depressed.

I may have been twenty one, I think. I'm not sure if Will and I lived together for one year before we were married or for two years. Maybe it just seems longer. I don't know. But, anyway, I know that Peter was born when I was twenty-five and he was born about ten months and fifteen minutes after we were married. I made it a point that I got pregnant right away.

Anyway, I had dinner at this little drugstore counter, and dinner in those days was a hamburger patty about the size of a walnut and then mountains of rice or something. Probably cost 25 cents. And Eugene Fleury was there. I may have known [him] because I worked at Chouinard Art School and Otis Art School. And he said, "Are you available? Could you come and work at Disney's next week?" And I said, "Sure."

DJ: For the art class?

AT: For the art classes. So I arrived and...

DJ: Had you been to the studio before?

AT: No.

DJ: Do you remember the first day that you arrived?

AT: I probably had to take a streetcar and a bus to get there on time.

DJ: Was this during the day or during the evening?

AT: It was in the evenings. The art classes were evening classes, as I recall.

DJ: Did you have a good ambience? What was it like there at the Disney studio, this world-famous studio for you?

AT: For me, what was I getting: 25 cents an hour or something. That was a big deal! For one week, I was going to pay a few bills. I have no idea. I've been to other studios, I've been to MGM, I've been to Paramount, and at that time, I used to read Proust (*Swann's Way*) and I'd carry it under my arms and I'd read on the bus...

DJ: I can't believe that Art Babbitt didn't go for you because he liked all that intellectual stuff.

AT: Oh, well, that must have come a lot later, because when I knew him he didn't... Anyway, there's always been a thorn in his side and mine. We just don't dig each other!

Anyway, I was such a snob about theater and I would to a René Clair movie, I would go to any film at the Film Art Theater. I would maybe see American films or something, but I thought that cartoons were absolutely childish, except for Tex Avery, and I *howled* over it, but this was later...

DJ: You didn't even like the Disney stuff?

AT: Oh, no. I thought it so cute and so saccharine, it made me sick. Really, I heard about the animators and I heard about all kinds of things about the studio and that sounded fun.

DJ: What did you hear?

AT: Well, I heard mostly from Sandra, let's put it that way.

DJ: You mean all the wild carryings on, you mean?

AT: They weren't that wild. Hollywood, really, then wasn't any wilder than in the 1960s. I guess the '60s were supposed to have been wild. I don't know.

DJ: It was very tame by today's standards, but I guess in those days it was pretty racy. I mean the animators just loved practical jokes.

AT: Practical jokes, yes. But they were like a bunch of little kids. They were all children. I've never met an animator yet or a dancer, actually, or many artists, really, who aren't children. They never grow up. If they lose that child-thing in them, then they're burdened with all kinds of responsibility and detail and crap. I thought that they were very immature, but then I was dating Chuck Edward, a managing editor on a paper, and I had come from the wilds of Puget Sound and from an anarchist colony and there were no holds barred from where I came from. Now it is a national historical jandmark, just within the last couple of years. But at the time that I lived there as a kid and also in Seattle which was where I was born, it was... Oh my god, they were written about [being] free lovers and nudists and... So coming from that and then a stowaway on a lumber freighter to get to LA...

There were big Swedish fisherman and lumberjacks and people coming down from Alaska to be gold miners. Seattle was very much like San Francisco. It was raw, it was rigorous, it was healthy, but absolutely the opposite of, let's say, New England, or what's left of it. People from here who had any guts or balls at all, whatever it was that it took, went out there. And the people from all over went out there. And the people who were very dissatisfied politically: they started colonies, independent colonies, here in the latter part of the last century. But they kind of petered out. [That] was before communism, way before all that kind of stuff. But the ones that were formed on Puget Sound, it was quite different. Hollywood, after that, to me, was absolutely phony. I never felt at home, ever. I went around for years with a coat thrown over my arm, figuring it was going to rain, after Seattle. I figured it'd have to rain, and it didn't, because it was just an irrigated desert. Maybe in a slow flash I'd soon caught on. I mean, I finally caught on. That first week that I worked at Disney, the first night, some young inbetweener or somebody, I don't know, asked if he could take me home, and I said yep, so he took me home and I asked him all kinds of questions about the studio, all kinds of questions about the animators, about as much information as I could. And then the following night, I think, there were going to be some regular animators and that night Quakenbush asked if he could take me home. That was the second night. And I said yeah. I mean I saved ten cents bus fare. That was a lot: half an hour's work. Anyway, Quakenbush told me that the next night was going to be the key animators. I found that very interesting, because I thought that this Bill Tytla that Sandra had been talking about maybe was going to be there.

DJ: He had recently had his accident, when he was in the hospital.

AT: I can't remember how recently, because I had no idea how long a period it was between the time that Sandra and I discussed this and the time that I actually met him. It could have been quite a few months.

DJ: But it wouldn't have been more than a year?

AT: Oh no, I don't think so.

DJ: So it was during *Snow White* that he had his accident.

AT: That I can't remember.

DJ: Because they were doing Snow White in 1935 and '36 and you were married in '38, I think.

AT: That's right and Peter was born in '39. We were married on April 21, in 1938, and Peter was born on February 21, 1939.

DJ: *Snow White* had been out about six months prior to your marriage and before that they were heavily involved on it for years.

AT: No, it couldn't have been, because I thought he went back to the studio the next day to work on *Snow White*. Then he went back to the studio the next day to work on something else. Because we didn't have a honeymoon, that I know. Joe Grant and Jennie Grant were our witnesses and we went to Musso and we had a lovely dinner and we had a good time and drank a lot of wine, and then came home and the next day he went right back to work. We never had a honeymoon, ever. But then who believed in honeymoons in those days? Who had the money?

DJ: Well, you had a honeymoon the year before you got married. That was very daring in those days. Even Marge told me you didn't even have sex with anyone until after you were married.

AT: Well, Marge didn't. The first time I saw Marge was at the Babbitts. She was sitting on a stool at the bar in his house and she was wearing a white silk dress and a white silk belt with long silk fringes, and she looked absolutely like an angel sitting there, a seventeen-year-old angel. I'm five years older and I thought she was such a child and this innocent sweet child... what in the name of God was she doing with that old, ex-married lecher? I thought it was terrible. I wanted to help her.

DJ: Were you living with Will at this time?

AT: No, no. Will was still living there at Art's. The house was sort of attached to the side of the hill up around Tuxedo Terrace and there was a downstairs bedroom and that was Will's bedroom. We came home from riding or something, and Art introduced us and I thought, "My god what a lovely..." Here was this young creature. She was...

DJ: Back to the night that you met him.

AT: Anyway, that night I knew the animators were there. Of course women don't usually reveal these things. They always act as if they're so pursued and all that stuff which is a crock. But, according to Will's version of the story, he said he waited for fifteen minutes for me to turn around to see if my face matched my behind. That I don't know. That was his thing. And he did come over and muttered and mumbled something and anytime he ever had to mention his name to somebody he'd always spell it, Bill Tytla, T-Y-T-L-A. Peter does the same thing.

DJ: Did he have an accent at all?

AT: He was born in Yonkers.

DJ: Didn't he learn Ukrainian?

AT: Not much.

DJ: Didn't he speak Polish with his mother?

AT: He went to Catholic schools in Yonkers.

DJ: I just assumed he spoke more than one language.

AT: He may have when he was younger. Maybe he knew more of it than I realized. But there was a generation of American-born whose parents were European and this was also true among Jews, let's say, there was a period when they wanted to relinquish all of that, and I have a feeling that maybe Will and his sister and his brothers...maybe that's why they tried, not to unlearn, but not to perpetuate... They wanted to be American. He loved the smell of pipe. He never drank a lot.

DJ: When you were modeling, do you recall meeting Don Graham?

AT: He may have been there at the head of the art classes or something, but I can't remember that for sure. I remember knowing him, I remember meeting him, I don't remember what his function was.

DJ: I've heard wonderful things about him.

AT: That was probably from people who worked with him a lot or who knew him well. But when you have a job for one week...

DJ: Oh, you were only there for just one week?

AT: I was there for one week. But that week was enough.

DJ: You lived quite a bit away if you lived on Western. You had to come all the way up Hyperion.

AT: I used to take buses all over the place.

DJ: That must have taken close to an hour.

AT: I wouldn't be surprised. That's why when somebody offered to give me a ride home I always said yes. And I certainly learned... I didn't know karate, but I knew how to defend myself very early on.

[Changing the subject]

AT: When [my son] Peter was frightened by a hooting owl from a screening at the studio I took him out into the hall and Walt followed us out and offered to stay with him until after the owl bit was over. He said, "I don't need to see that part either," which was an awfully nice thing to do, I think.

We didn't have anything socially to do with any of the other people at the studio, except Joe and Jenny Grant. Freddy Moore came by to see us once.

DJ: What was your impression of him?

AT: Oh, he was a dear, beautiful guy. He was young and he was cute and...

DJ: He was married at the time.

AT: I don't know if he was married or not. I was married at the time, but it didn't stop him from being young and cute.

DJ: No, I mean there's very little about him that's known.

AT: He died a hopeless alcoholic, which is so sad. But when he arrived at the studio, according to Will, or whomever (and I'm sure it's absolute fact), he was carrying a rolled up thing of paper and he'd never had a job anywhere else and he just walked [in] and showed it to them and he was hired. Now Will on the other hand had started here on this coast when he was just a kid in school.

DJ: I understand he didn't even finish high school.

AT: I'm sure he didn't finish. I don't know how much he even went to high school. I didn't finish the first year of high school, and I don't think Will did either. Of course times were quite different then, but when Will was going to this Catholic, parochial school, one of the nuns took quite an interest in him and she was the one that got to his parents and told them that they should encourage this child and he had a gift. Because I don't think that they really realized...although he'd come from school and draw Civil War battles and battles between the cowboys and the Indians, with all these characters and all this stuff. He'd do this by the hour. I don't know if he had rheumatic fever or something... He had something awful. Kids used to swim in the Hudson River. They were told not to swim in there. Even then it was polluted and filthy, way back then, seventy years ago, or eighty years ago. Bill's birthday was October 25, same day as Picasso's. Anne [his sister] said it may have been rheumatic fever, and he lost about a year in school and Anne would help him with his homework. She was younger, but by that time she was in the grade that he would have been in. He spent most of that time at home, drawing. He never told me when he got his first job.

The fact is that he studied sculpture and that he was aware of form, of weight, and balance, and mass and all of these things that you get in sculpting, that he incorporated into his work. You feel, when you look at Doc, or you look at Stromboli, you see these masses of flesh and they're moving and there're these wonderful "s" curves and all that stuff... Much of this, with an artist, is instinctive, much of it is intuitive, some of it he had when he was drawing cowboys and Indians and even the nun realized what was there. Whatever it is, wherever he got it, he got it. Also he spent years studying, as I say, at the Art Students' League and in Paris and everything, and he was really an outsider at the studio in the sense that he was different, being central European. He wasn't a WASP, he wasn't a guy who came in right off the street. And they held him in great esteem as an artist, but actually nobody socialized with him.

DJ: Was that partly his choice? He just didn't like to socialize. Or do you think they avoided him because they felt he was above them?

AT: Oh, no. It might have been either or both. But it's just that he was really so very different. I mean he truly was.

They were not politically motivated, any of them. I can say this because I came from this anarchist colony and I was reared there. My father was murdered. And the reason he was murdered was because he was an activist. But this is an intellectual anarchist, and it has nothing to do with this idea the people have about anarchists throwing bombs and killing all these people. I mean, real Bolsheviks. These people were looking for a new kind of life and that sort of thing. I grew up listening to political discussions all my life. The anarchists hated the communists and the communists hated the socialists, the socialists hated the anarchists and they were always fighting among themselves. This was in Seattle, not out in the colony where I grew up. Anyway, we always discussed politics. That was our lives. I grew up on the stuff, and my father wrote a letter to a friend in Mexico. They knew he was active in Seattle with a group of anarchists...intellectual anarchists, I keep insisting. He wrote describing the intolerable working conditions in Seattle at that time in the shipyards. People were dying; they were falling off of scaffolding; they were expendable. It didn't matter: there was no protection; there was no insurance; there were no benefits; there was no union; there was nothing for these people. Their living conditions were absolutely horrible. They died, so what the hell. There was a big line-up waiting the next day for their job and other jobs. And his letter was confiscated, probably by the FBI or the equivalent at that time, because they were all rednecks. They were lynching black people in those days, even in the state of Washington. They were tarring and feathering them and they were selling the postcards. I remember seeing a postcard of a black man hanging from a... Oh, it was horrible, it was just horrible. Anyway, his letter was intercepted. And they arrested him. They came to the house, they got my father, they took him to the common jail in Seattle and the next day they found he was hanged. Now, he was a man thirty-nine years old with a very good position, a bright man, and a family, a wife and two children. There is no way in the world that Papa hanged himself. He was hanged. My mother had to try to rear me and my sister and during the Depression.

DJ: How old were you when?

AT: I was 4 years old when he died. My sister was nine. And Emma Goldman, the anarchist, used to come and kiss my feet when I was a baby. I was named Emma. I was never named Adrienne. That was just for later when I went to Hollywood.

DJ: Oh, that was a stage name.

AT: Oh, of course. You think I'd go through life as "Emma." Come on!

After having lived in that kind of a volatile political environment and gone to radical meetings and known IWW [International Workers of the World]... There was a great deal of political activity in Seattle. I can't even begin to *imagine* that Art Babbitt was involved with anything political. Maybe during the Young Communist League thing in Los Angeles. I was going with a violinist before I knew Will, and he was a member and he would go to those meetings, but that was kid's stuff.

DJ: [Art Babbitt] started the strike, you know.

AT: That I know.

DJ Because he believed in unions and he felt that the people were worked without being...

AT: He was right. He was right in that sense. I have always been pro-union and I totally agreed. [But] I regret to say this and I will regret it as long as I live: I'm afraid that I was as much of a motivator in getting Will to go out on strike as Art Babbitt was, because of my own political background.

DJ: In other words, he didn't want to do it, you're saying.

AT: I think that he emotionally felt that it was the right thing to do, but I'm sure that it's not something that he would have done on his own, either without Art's influence or my influence. Because I think that he was the kind of person who was cautious. He was a Catholic.

DJ: Was he religious?

AT: No. He had been, I guess as a child, and as an altar boy...and god knows he was an altar boy forever.

DJ: Do you think that he believed in a spiritual form other than people?

AT: That there is some greater force out there?

DJ: Yes.

AT: Oh, I think anybody with a brain in his head has to believe that.

His favorite music was Gregorian Chant, and those wonderful, wonderful chorale things. And he loved Russian music. He just absolutely wallowed in it. There again, the stuff is so tragic, it's so somber, it's so sad, it's so glorious. That was really his favorite and it is incredibly moving to hear. He was a spiritual man. His mother was a Roman Catholic and his father was a Greek Uniate Catholic although he was a Ukrainian; I guess that was the church in his village. Will's father's family had hoped that he [Will's father] would be a priest. What he really wanted to be was a dancer. And that was absolutely out of the question.

DJ: Do you mean a classical dancer, like ballet dancer, or do you mean a traditional dancer?

AT: I imagine a traditional dancer. I imagine [the Russian style of dancing]. But how do I know.

[Changing the subject]

AT: Will was the world's worst driver. His mind was always somewhere else.

He had trouble with his eyes because of the constant drawing over the light board.

He went through life sitting and staring and brooding. He was volatile, too, and emotional. We used to have outrageous fights. I mean, screaming and yelling! There was a door here and a door there, and I'd go through and I'd *bang* the doors. Then I decided what are we doing with all these doors? So I took all the doors off, and then we had a fight and I got mad and I went through the house and reached for the door and there was no door and he burst out laughing.

Berny Wolf (1911–2006)

Interviewed on July 2, 1992.

According to Shamus Culhane's book, *Talking Animals and Other People*, Walt made it hard for "old-timers" and ex-New Yorkers at his studio, chiding them for their "bad drawing habits" and training on "cheap productions." Berny Wolf was one of those New Yorkers who joined the studio during the quick expansion phase which preceded the creation of *Snow White and the Seven Dwarfs*. Having been on the "wrong side of the fence" during the 1941 strike, he had been mostly forgotten by animation historians."

When Wolf passed away in September 2006, animator Mark Kausler wrote the following about his all-encompassing career:

> Berny, or Bernie, Wolf started his animation career in New York City in 1924, inking on the silent Krazy Kat cartoons that Ben Harrison and Manny Gould released through Paramount. He got a job at Max Fleischer's Inkwell Studios soon after, inking and maybe animating on the KoKo Song Cartoons, such as *Mother Pin a Rose on Me* (1924), *Goodbye My Lady Love*(1924), and *East Side, West Side* (1926). He became friends with Shamus Culhane and Al Eugster at Fleischer's. In Shamus' book *Talking Animals and Other People*, Shamus relates the story of how the three amigos broke into animation on the Talkarartoon *Swing, You Sinners* in 1930, although it appears that Berny may have animated before that.

> Berny became a Betty Boop specialist in the early 30s, working on such cartoons as *Minding the Baby* (1931), *Betty Boop's Bizzy Bee* (1932), and *The Old Man of the Mountain* (1933). The trio then went west, winding up at Ub Iwerks' studio and worked on the Willie Whopper series and ComiColor cartoons. Berny animated and designed characters with Grim Natwick on such cartoons as *The Cave Man* (1934), *Viva Willie* (1934), *The Valiant Tailor* (1934), and *SUMMERTIME* (1935).

> Berny joined the Disney studio on May 20, 1935. He overcame the prejudice against New Yorkers and animated Jiminy Cricket in *Pinocchio* (1940). Some of his scenes are Jiminy meeting the Blue Fairy in Sq. 1.5, Sc. 46, where he says "No tricks, now!"; Sq. 1.7, Sc. 59.7, where Jiminy dances with a music-box doll and slyly says: "How

about sittin' out the next one babe, huh?"; and Sq. 4.9, Sc. 17, where he emerges from a birdseed container in a cage and shyly speaks to the Blue Fairy ("This *is* a pleasant surprise!"), tips his hat, and gets a shower of bird seed pouring from the hat. Berny was one of the key animators on Jiminy, doing many such personality scenes, no doubt working closely with Ward Kimball.

On *Fantasia*, Berny worked on the "Pastoral Symphony" sequence, animating fauns, unicorns, and the centaurs and centaurettes that Fred Moore designed. He animated a beautiful scene in a part where the centaurettes are dancing around Ward Kimball's Bacchus, and a tender scene of a centaur shielding a centaurette from the raindrops at the beginning of the storm sequence. Berny also animated the famous scene at the end of the "Romance of the Centaurs" sequence, in which the cupids close the curtains on the proceedings, leaving one cupid to peek through at the centaurs. His hovering buttocks form a heart. This scene, which infuriated critics such as James Agee, was animated by Berny Wolf.

By 1941, Berny seems to have fallen in estimation at Disney: he got one sequence in *Dumbo*, of the clowns bragging about their "coitain calls" in Sq. 14.1, all in silhouette. This is really an outstanding job of animation, as all the poses have to read solidly just in black, showing that Berny had good caricature and staging skills.

In 1941, Berny did not go out on the famous Disney strike. He left the studio on September 12, 1945, and landed at MGM Cartoons, doing layout and storyboard for Tex Avery. He was then drafted and wound up directing animation for the First Motion Picture Unit.

After the war, Berny worked for Rudy Ising independently and headed up a company called Animedia Productions. He probably got involved in the television-commercials boom of the 1950s. In the 1980s, he produced such shows as *The Flintstone Kids*, The Scooby-Doo movies for Hanna-Barbera, and worked as a film editor and Producer on a TV feature cartoon, *The Little Troll Prince*, in 1985. He would have been 74 then.

I suppose Berny must have retired after that, as he disappears from the credit sheets. Evidently he kept up his artwork in his last twenty years, making many drawings and doing some painting. My only memory of Berny is seeing him hanging out at the old Gus Jekel FilmFair studio, with his friend Rudy Zamora Sr. They probably worked at the Fleischer and Krazy Kat studios in New York together in the 1920s and 1930s.

Berny Wolf was a very talented animator who is largely forgotten today, due to the anti-New York, West Coast prejudice, the fact that he was on the "wrong side" of the Disney strike, and worked in limited TV animation. He had an amazingly long career, and by all accounts was a very nice man.

BERNY WOLF: Grim Natwick was in the same room as co-directors, co-partners. Sometimes I would do one scene by myself and he'd do another or we'd do them together. At that time a young kid started there, Chuck Jones. We're all about the same age, we're all quite young, except for Grim.

DAVID JOHNSON: What was Grim like? I understand he had a great sense of humor.

BW: Oh, yeah, Grim had a wry sense of humor. You see, I was very much a loner. By loner I mean... I love people, but I didn't hang out.

DJ: Did you live by yourself when you were here?

BW: Yeah. I came out by myself and brought my folks out later.

DJ: Oh, you did?

BW: Yeah. I brought in my dad. My dad was knocked silly in the crash, stock market.

DJ: California was beautiful then.

BW: The Iwerks studio was in Beverly Hills up near Santa Monica. I sat there and looked out at hills and palm trees. After looking out at streets at 5th and 66th in New York, nothing but buildings, it was a different world entirely. I was making $150 a week, too, see. And I'd send $75 a week home because I couldn't spend it, I didn't need it. And the folks did need it. Because they were flat. $75 a week bought what was then a top-of-the-line camera, a Leica camera.

Grim and I worked together on the shows and he could always draw much better than I could. I couldn't draw that well. It was just the two of us for a little over a year. Marvelous guy. There were a lot of wonderful people there who were more interested in making little powered planes. And we'd go out, noon hours, over Baldwin Hills and drive over there and fly these planes. A guy by the name of [Irv] Spence, who ran the unit, a hell of a good draftsman, a good, great animator, was with us. One or two guys.

DJ: Do you remember a man named Robert Stokes?

BW: Bob Stokes? Sure. I can see him now.

DJ: I haven't been able to get any information about him at all. He animated about fifty percent of the Queen in Snow White, and in

all the books on Disney, Art Babbitt is given sole credit. He also did a big sequence of Snow White when she's baking the pies. That's all Bob Stokes' work. But he vanished off the face of the earth.

BW: He was slender, very thin.

   We all left Iwerks about the same time within a period of a few months, because it was going under.

DJ: Now, tell me how you got your job at Disney's.

BW: I just applied for it.

DJ: Did you apply in writing or did you go in person?

BW: Grim was already there, [Shamus] Culhane was already there, and [Al] Eugster was already there. They all left Iwerks before I did. They came out before I did. And whether they paved the way, I don't know, but I just know that I got the job. I couldn't tell you who I talked to now. They had 125 people in the whole studio. [Note: there were approximately 450 people when Berny Wolf came.]

DJ: Did you bring your portfolio?

BW: No.

DJ: So the first day you walked in there you don't remember that, like your impression of the whole joint?

BW: No. See, a lot of these to me were a blur; they were happening very fast. And I wasn't even that interested. Otto Englander told me that when I came out here I was very cocky. I could see where I might have been: a young kid out making good money and sailing up in grade like that. At any rate, I started, and then they put me on to the Ducks. In those days there was a fellow there at Disney's named Herb Lamb. He was the accountant. You're talking about a small studio, OK? Herb had a habit of sending out pink notices all the time: "How about this? Where's the footage?" And, "What about that?" He became a laughing stock. No one really paid attention to it, but it was a pain in the ass. To make a long story short, I started at the same money I worked for Iwerks.

DJ: Did you meet Walt the first day?

BW: No. And then, oh, sporadically, casually in the hall or something like that. That's all.

DJ: Were you hired as an animator or director or what?

BW: Animator. I was in the business since I was 16.

DJ: Did you have your own office or were you working with someone at Disney's?

BW: No, at Disney's I had my own office. It was a small room, a small, narrow room, and I had an assistant with me. Later on I had two assistants in the same room. One of the assistants was David "Bud" Swift. He eventually left Disney's years later. He came up and originated [the TV series] *Mr. Peepers*.

DJ: And he was your assistant?

BW: Yeah, he started that. His father was a magician and had a house over there, on the corner of Los Feliz and Riverside.

Everything went along swimmingly, and I did a lot of Duck shows. I worked with Woolie [Reitherman] on one called *Goofy and Wilbur*.

I was there until 1941. The salary was good. And then *Snow White* started. And they started to pull guys off the shorts to work on *Snow White*.

DJ: Just to back up a moment. This accountant, Herb Lamb, why would he have the authority to send out pick slips asking about footage when I thought that would be a director's job?

BW: He was a watchdog. He might have sent out how many feet you did, and in general, watching what you did, because reports would come in to him. Maybe he was appointed by Roy to do this. We never knew Roy. Roy was over in another area.

DJ: I was always told and I was under the impression that they didn't have any quotas for footage at Disney's.

BW: No, I wouldn't say exact quotas, but you turned out what you were supposed to turn out. For example, when you got on to the feature, on Jiminy Cricket... Down the road a bit, I was doing twenty or twenty five feet a week, maybe thirty feet a week.

DJ: That's a lot.

BW: Yeah. For some reason, it just rolled out and it was good footage. Today you don't do that, and the footage may not even be as good. We were all maybe in some sort of swing or something for a time. When they started, then my ego demanded that I get onto the feature, too.

DJ: Do you remember talk of a feature without necessarily knowing that it was *Snow White*, getting wind that a feature was in the works?

BW: No. The only thing I ever heard of was *Snow White*.

DJ: The first memo I was able to find was dated 1934, August 9 or something, and it went out to everyone asking for gags and things.

BW: It was well under way at the time.

DJ: No, that was the first memo that Walt sent out.

BW: But mind you, writing starts way back.

DJ: Did you go to gag meetings?

BW: Maybe sporadically, very rarely.

DJ: On the shorts?

BW: On the shorts you'd get involved, but some other guys would be doing the storyboards and the write-up and you could be called in now and then. Or you'd drop in and sit there, like I would with Otto [Englander] at times, drop in and see what he's working on, sit there and start talking. Next thing you know, some of your thoughts are getting up there if they're any good.

DJ: So actually it wasn't really a story meeting with all the men.

BW: Not with me. I think in a way you're talking about a strange animal with me. Because when I hear what other guys remember, I wonder, did I miss all that or was that fiction? I don't know. Now, for example when *Snow White* started and the guys started to go off onto it, I wanted to as well. I wanted to be on the first feature. So I talked to Walt about it and I said, "Look, Walt, I want to work on it." And he said, "No, Bernie, you're needed on the Ducks. We got to keep the bread and butter going, the money coming in while we spend it on this thing." I got pissed off, went back to my desk and I sat there, disgruntled, and got back to the Duck show. Every six weeks there was another short. Finally I said, "I want to get on it, Walt." He said, "All right." So I got on for a very short period of time.

DJ: When you went to meet Walt did you have to make an appointment or could you just go into the office?

BW: I think I called up, and went up there to see him.

DJ: What was your impression of Walt?

BW: Arm's length. Arm's length, with me. I was one of the new kids there, see. And it grew a little bit, but not much. The first thing I started on was the Silly Symphony *Elmer Elephant*. And there's a funny story there. In the sweatbox and everyone was rushing to get this stuff in for a Friday showing, okay?

DJ: Now, could you describe the sweatbox when you first started there?

BW: Physically?

DJ: Yes.

BW: Physically it was a room with about a dozen theater chairs stepping up in the projection room back of you and the screen up there.

DJ: This is in the animation building itself?

BW: Oh yeah.

DJ: Was this on the first or second floor?

BW: It's a good question. Second floor, I think. The directors were on the second floor, the animators down below. The life class and all the classes were down below on the first floor. [Showing a photo] This is my room, a door here and you go out and there'd be the life class. That was the remarkable thing about Disney's: the life classes.

DJ: Don Graham.

BW: Don Graham, and he'd bring in people like Rico LeBrun, who would show you what would be the essence of line. Frank Lloyd Wright about structure and architecture and all, marvelous. Humorous man, Ted Cook was in the newspapers at the time.

[But in the sweatbox,] I was on *Elmer Elephant* and my stuff is on the reel and I rushed to get it in. It was a pelican on a branch of a tree and all he did was a simple thing: he looked down there and goes, "Ha, che, che, che, cha!" [Jimmy] Durante. Walt looks at it, "Who's that?" I want to die. Down in your chair and a little voice says [in baby voice], "Mine!" I wasn't sophisticated, I would cringe. And he looked around with one eyebrow [raised], which you've heard about that, "You should know better than that, Bernie!" "OK Walt, I'll fix it." I didn't know what the hell was wrong with it. It was a thing we were doing for either [director Wilfred] Jackson or [Bill] Roberts. I go over to Will [Wilfred Jackson] and say, "Hey, Jax, what's wrong with it?" "I don't know." So I took the reel down to look at it again and couldn't think of what it was. I called one, two of the other animators in, to look at it. "Looks all right to me." So I tried to do something else with it. Tickle it. Put it in for the following week Walt looks at it, says, "Bernie, when you gonna fix that?" "Sorry, Walt, I didn't have a chance to get to it." I don't know, something like that.

DJ: And you didn't dare just say, "I don't know what's wrong"?

BW: Oh no! No one.

DJ: No one would do that?

BW: No one would.

DJ: Why? If you didn't know what it was, then why wouldn't you go back to the source?

BW: Because you just wouldn't. At least I wouldn't. And most of the guys I knew wouldn't. Walt had you in awe and it was the idea that he—to me, anyway—he represented something else. And Jaxon didn't tell me. Jaxon could've asked him. But Jaxon wouldn't have either. At least on this one thing.

DJ: I wonder why not.

BW: The point is: "What the hell am I going to do?" So we had what we call trace-overs. If you have a character here and suppose another's here and here and doing the same thing, in unison, little x marks...the inkers and painters would trace them up over like this. So I put it in by myself, in pencil and then put it back in the reel. I did it several times. I told someone I did it thirteen times, but it couldn't have been that much, but a lot of times.

DJ: This went on week after week, the same scene?

BW: Walt would ignore it many times, figured I hadn't gotten to it.

DJ: Wouldn't this hold up production of that short, though? I thought they had to get out like every other month or every month.

BW: Every six weeks.

DJ: So this would be holding things up.

BW: They'd bypass you or they'd go around it. They'd go to ink and paint on some other thing, I don't know. Anyway, it took a long time. Finally, I was exasperated. So I quit... What should I do? Jaxon didn't know, no one knew. I looked at it, and said, "Let me have the whole reel, not just my stuff." And I took the whole reel down. Each animator had a moviola then, which was wonderful. It's unheard of today.

DJ: Unheard of then, except at Disney's.

BW: I didn't realize that. But at any rate, I put it on there, sat there, back and forth, back and forth. I looked at the scenes before, the scenes after. "Holy cow, maybe this is it!" The action was flowing, let's say, this way. And I was going "Ha, che, che, che, cha!" this way, see. Maybe that's it. So I had them reshoot the test with them flopping the other way. I put it in the reel. Walt looks at it. Finally he approves it!

DJ: Why didn't he just say, "Bernie, it's the wrong direction."?

BW: Maybe he didn't know himself. There are two guys I know today, wonderful artists: they don't know what they want until they see it. When they see it, then they know it's there.

The other thing I can tell you about Disney's, is about the Penthouse Club [on the roof of the Burbank studio]. I had access—entry, I should say—to the penthouse. You'd go up there if you were tired or bored of your work, whatever. If you wanted something, you'd go up to the penthouse. And they had a little guy there [Carl Johnson, a wrestling champion from the 1928 Olympics] throw the medicine ball back and forth to you. He was built like an ox and just gave you a work-out, see. You'd be passing it back and forth, or passing it to the guy next to you, things like that. And I got it one day and without looking or anything like that, went *whopf,* and it was Walt. I wanted to die, you know. I wanted to die! Jesus, what am I doing, killing the boss.

And one time I was out there lying on a mat—more like a mattress in those days. And about fifteen minutes later I thought, "That's enough, I want to get out of here." So I get up to get out of there and Walt's lying there next to me on another mat. And I am so uncomfortable. He was half dozing. I got up and left quick. That's me. Now, [Ward] Kimball, no.

DJ: I guess you felt he intimidated.

BW: Oh, he definitely intimidated me. We were not on what I would call anything close, sort of, on a par. Kimball was different . Ward would tell him to go fuck himself, you know.

DJ: And he's younger than you, I mean.

BW: Age had nothing to do with it. It's ego.

DJ: Well, he was known as the *enfant terrible*.

BW: After I left the studio, they had the big strike. I didn't go out on strike, but I got the shaft anyhow. I came back to see Ward. I'd walked down that hallway and asked the girl there, "Where's Ward?" "Oh, he's in the room there, the director's room." I opened the door. The room was dark, but there was a light coming in back of the door. I look around and there's Ward with a floor lamp and he's reading. "What the hell are you doing?" And he says, "Well, he won't give me a picture to work on until I agree to do what he wants me to do, and I'm not going to do it!" Walt wanted him to work on a certain picture and he refused to do it. Walt says, "OK, don't work on anything till you do this show." It was like today's actors who walk off the set. The last I heard, he finally acquiesced and everything and the breach was healed. But he has a stronger ego, courage of his convictions, call it what you will. He was that kind of a guy and I love him for it. I admire him for it. I never could do that.

[About *Snow White*]

BW: I worked on the dwarfs. I had a little piece of the eating sequence and the sleeping sequence. I was on it for such a short period of time.

[Regarding Roy Williams]

BW: [Milt] Neil was a good little athlete and a good little artist, too, on one of the teams with us. We were playing volleyball there. And he used to tangle with Roy. And Roy had this car. You heard about his car with the bumper? Roy started chasing him one day, in the car, on the volleyball court. He lifted the net and Neil takes off and there's a hill going up and Roy goes after him with his car. Chasing him up around like that and then down again, to the street. If he had slipped once, he would have killed him, because he'd have run right over him. Roy was a wild man.

Don Brodie (1904–2001)

Interviewed on September 10, 1989.

Actor and director Donald Lee "Don" Brodie was born on May 29, 1904, in Cincinnati, Ohio. He performed live-action reference for the Witch in *Snow White and the Seven Dwarfs*. He also provided one of the voices advertising Pleasure Island's attractions in *Pinocchio*, and played a gasoline station attendant in *Escape to Witch Mountain*. He died on January 8, 2001, in Los Angeles, California.

DAVID JOHNSON: How did you get selected to do the Witch in the first place?

DON BRODIE: Walt tested about twenty people.

DJ: Had you done any work for him before?

DB: Yes. I did a lot of voices for him on the Mickey Mouse and the Duck pictures: not the principal characters, but all the other characters that worked with the Duck. See, I have a very extensive background in this business. I'm a director and a writer and I've done everything there is to do in this business. I'm the only man living today that's got that background.

DJ: When you came to do the live action, was the voice track already finished?

DB: Yes.

DJ: So what you would do was the sync to the soundtrack?

DB: Yes. But I had to do very little of that, because most of my stuff was the action, see. Then, after I did the action, a lot of the voice was put in, in the certain scenes that I did. Because the animators kept revising the action. So, the voice had to come in and fit my action.

DJ: So actually the voice was done after, sometimes.

DB: Yes, it was sort of a combination of things.

DJ: Do you remember who the director was that worked with you?

DB: Dave Hand. [Note: Ben Sharpsteen was the director for this sequence.]

DJ: What was he like?

DB: He was a hell of a nice guy. About six two, big fellow. See, Disney offered me a job directing live action. [This was after *Snow White*.] I did the live action on *Pinocchio*. I did Gepetto. And we went up to Walt's pool and we shot all that stuff of me going in the whale's mouth. The reason I didn't accept the offer was he offered me $175 a week and I made that much in one day in a picture and I couldn't afford to do it, because I had the responsibility of contributing to my mother's welfare. I turned him down only for that reason. He's a very peculiar man. I'll tell you an incident. I had a contract with him for about ten or eleven weeks. I was on the picture about ten weeks.

DJ: What movie are we talking about now?

DB: *Snow White*.

DJ: In other words, you weren't paid by the day like Marge Champion was?

DB: No, I was paid by the week.

DJ: Because she was paid $10 a day for all the time she was in on it.

DB: I had a very nice contract. However, I told him I was going to New York. I was going back there to dialogue-direct a big picture called *Carnegie Hall*, with Stokowsi and all the big performers in it. [Note: He's confusing this with *101 Men and a Girl*.] I had a contract to start that picture on a certain day. And I was going to drive back, because I like to drive and I wanted to have my car while I was in New York because I wanted to stay in New York when I finished the job. That's where I met my wife, in New York, during that. So I told Walt, "I am leaving Los Angeles on a Friday." I had a house on Highland Avenue. He said, "That's fine. We'll make that arrangement. You'll be done on Friday." I said, "Now, I want that in the contract." So what I did, I closed the house. I shut off the electricity. Shut off the telephone. Shut off the gas. Shut off everything, because I didn't know how long I was going to be gone. And came the Thursday that I was getting ready to leave I drove to the studio in my car and I had the car all loaded with my bags and everything. Everything was shut off. My house was locked up. I put my dog in a kennel. Thursday night Walt came on the set. And he said, "Don, I'd like to talk to you." I said, "All right." So we went over in the corner. He said, "I got to have you Monday." I said, "I've got this Thursday contract." He said, "I know, I know. But I've got to have you on Monday."

DJ: Why?

DB: Because they had some additional stuff they wanted me to do. A couple of scenes they wanted to do over. My action, that crazy stuff. So I said, "I'm sorry Walt. I just can't do it." He said, "I want you to think this over now, because this is very important. I've got to have you." And I said "I can't. I'll tell you why: I'm allowing myself four days to drive back to New York. And I start the picture in New York in four or five days. I have to be there and get settled, get a place and I have to be ready to go to work." He said, "Now you think this over. I'll give you an hour to think it over. I'll pay you for the extra, the Saturday." He wanted me Saturday, too. Saturday and Monday.

When he went out, he was a little bit disturbed and I went to Dave Hand and I said, "You know what he wanted?" He said, "What did he want?" I said, "He wanted me Monday." "Yeah," he said, "I know. We've got some stuff they have to shoot with you, Don." I said, "I'm not going to do it. I can't do it. My house is locked up. What am I going to do?" He said, "Come here." So we walked over to a corner of the set so nobody could hear us and he said to me, "I'll tell you what you do. We really do need you, Don." I said, "I'm sorry, I can't do it." So he said, "I'll tell you what I'll do." I was married at the time. Now my car is on the lot with all my bags and everything in it, because when I got through Friday night I was going to get in the car and head for New York, take Route 66. He said, "I'll tell you what you do. But don't tell them your director recommended this. But if you can work it out so you can stay Monday, I think we can get through with you by about 2 or 3 o'clock in the afternoon." We start in the morning. He said, "You tell Walt that you want him to put you up at the Roosevelt Hotel and triple your salary for those three days."

Now I was getting $75 a day. So sure enough, in about an hour, Walt came back on the set. "What are you going to do?" "I'll tell you what I'll do. You put my wife and I up at the Roosevelt Hotel and I want triple my salary." He said, "Oh God, almighty." I said, "Walt, just a minute. I can't go back into my house. That's the only way I'll do it. Now if you don't want to meet my arrangements, I'll..." He screamed his head off. I said, "I'll walk out of here at 5 o'clock and I'm done." He said, "All right. It's a deal. My God, you got me over a barrel." I said, "You got me over a barrel, too. Put yourself in my place. My car is out there ready to drive out of here, full of bags and everything else." He said, "Well, OK. It's a deal." I checked in at the Roosevelt Hotel and they had to pay all the bills, had to pay the food, the breakfast, Saturday, Sunday, Monday, two dinners and everything else. He had money, but he was an awful chiseler. He's a wonderful man, but an awful chiseler. My niece was an animator for him. She was very good.

DJ: What was her name?

DB: Bonnie Bawn.

So I finished at noon that Monday and I said goodbye and I got in the thing and I left. It was a very interesting experience and everybody was so wonderful. Now this is a kind of interesting twist. In the later years, up to a month or two before he died, I was at the studio having lunch and I was playing a character part in another picture. I just came out of the animation building and he had two men with him from New York, some executives, and he had just come out of the cafeteria. Now I hadn't seen him since we made *Snow White*.

DJ: Is that right?

DB: Yeah. Oh, I saw him on the lot, but I never stopped to talk to him. I had nothing to say to him anyway.

So just as I came out of the building, he and his two men were passing. And I said, "Hello, Walt." He looked at me and he said, "Hello." He walked up and he said, "By God, your face looks familiar." I said, "You don't remember me." Two men were standing right next to him. "I did your Witch for you." "MY GOD," he said and came up and he took me in his arms and he said to these two men, he said, "This is the guy that played the Witch." And we shook hands and everything. And he said, "How are you? What are you doing? Do you have any children," and so forth. We had a very congenial two minutes together. Then he walked off and in a very short period, he was dead. So that was my experience with him.

DJ: Do you remember if Norm Ferguson was involved in directing you in front of the camera?

DB: No. Dave Hand.

DJ: Only Dave Hand?

DB: Only Dave Hand.

DJ: Several times in the movie the Witch looks directly at the audience and one time she says, "Wait, there may be an antidote." Was it your own idea to do that or did they tell you that they wanted to have that effect?

DB: They wanted that effect. It was not my idea.

DJ: Your work on the Witch was all at one time?

DB: Yes.

DJ: You said it was ten weeks?

DB: Yes.

DJ: Can you describe a little bit anything that you can remember?

DB: I became exhausted a couple of times because when I had to climb that mountain, I must have climbed that mountain at least... You see, they had this scaffolding built like a mountain. It went clear up, in one corner of the stage. Now it's a big stage, probably 35–40 feet up. And I had to climb that thing twenty times, at least twenty times. It was very exhausting. I didn't do it all in one day. But there were times when I would climb it two or three times and a couple of days three or four times again and maybe four or five more times, to get the action exactly the way they wanted it.

My action was crawling up this scaffolding which was boards, from one board to another, like a ladder. There were places for me to put my feet and things that I grabbed a hold of that looked like a rock. And I pulled myself up and then I looked back at the dwarfs, you see. Then some of the fake rocks that they had, I'd push 'em down and the dwarfs would duck and the rocks would go bouncing over their heads.

I had one cute experience. I went into the men's toilet with this outfit on and at the urinal Walt Disney's brother Roy came in and said, "Hey, you belong next door," in the ladies room. It was a very funny thing.

Roy had a funny habit: there was a little store across the street and he'd go out and come back and he had a cigar box open with no lid on it and he'd put chewing gum and peanuts and stuff in there that he wanted in his office. He came on the set one day and he had this box. I didn't know who the hell he was, so I took a package of gum and dropped a nickel in the box. [Laughs] Dave started to laugh and the whole crew started to laugh. They saw me do it, see? Roy laughed like hell. [Laughs] He gave me the nickel back and he said, "I'm Mr. Disney," and I said, "Oh, I'm sorry, Mr. Disney." I didn't know him, I didn't ever see him at all. Little things like that that weren't important, but it was a very, very pleasant experience. When the thing was all over and I got back from New York, why, I went down to see everybody. Ben Sharpsteen was one of the staff members of the crew and Ben said, "Don, everything came out fine." I was very well treated.

Oh, when I got through at noon, I still had to make New York, but I'm now two days behind, see. So my wife and I drove between four and five hundred miles a day. I'd drive and then she would drive while I rested and that's how we could just make it, see. Fortunately, I got back there and there was two days delay in starting the picture, so I was all right. But I was tired when I got there.

DJ: When you did the Witch, how many hours a day did they actually do the filming?

DB: I'd start at 8, 8:30 in the morning and I left the studio every night about 6 o'clock.

DJ: But you weren't working the whole time, were you?

DB: No, there's times when I would sit on a set.

DJ: And what would be going on then?

DB: Making changes in the set and angles with the cameras and stuff like that. Just like making any other picture.

DJ: Did they use more than one camera to film it at the same time?

DB: Yes.

DJ: How many?

DB: I never saw more than two.

DJ: Did you ever do any work with Marge Champion herself, the girl who did Snow White?

DB: I saw nobody else in the cast, at any time.

DJ: Nobody.

DB: I never had any days off. Sometimes they'd get through with me at noon, like that, two or three times. But most of the time, I was there. Why they stayed with me I don't know, but I think it was because of continuity. There was so much action on the Witch's part. I think they wanted to definitely get me on film. I would say that I probably worked as consistently as anybody did on the picture.

DJ: Do you recall the first scene that they actually worked with you?

DB: Yes. I'll tell you what it was. The first scene was when I had the crow on my shoulder and I was... You remember the big pot. I was stirring and saying, "Round and round..." And the crow's on my shoulder. That was the first thing that I did.

DJ: Funny, I don't remember the crow. This is when she says, "Dip the apple in the brew." Do you remember that?"

DB: Yes.

DJ: Now what did they have for a vat, do you remember?

DB: Just a big tub, kind of a wooden tub. I don't know if they had it built or not. It was made of wood. There was no liquid in it at all. I just had the stick. It was the action that they wanted to see anyway.

DJ: Now in this part when the Witch is rowing her boat out, do you remember any of that?

DB: Yes. I was on a platform with a long paddle about six feet long. And I went through the ocean, I was looking... And then I went on the side. It was just the action, my body action.

DJ: It's hard to believe it would take ten weeks of filming, because it's not more than fifteen or twenty minutes in the finished movie.

DB: I was there a long time.

DJ: So they kept doing it over, and over, and over, I guess.

DB: That's right.

DJ: Every single section.

DB: Yes, because Dave Hand would stop me and say, "Don, slow down your action a little bit here." Or, "Let's do it again and slow it down." Then sometimes he'd say, "Now we have to do this two or three times, each scene. And when you do that, watch your left arm so that your left arm comes up like this and we can see the action of your left arm." Or the action of your right arm or whatever it was, see? Of course, I'm hunched over a lot of times. I had this thing on my back and I'm hunched over a lot of times. A lot of times he'd say, "Now, look back slowly over your right shoulder. Now let's do it again and this time I'll cue you and you'll do it a little later. Do it three seconds later," which is eight frames or whatever it is. I did every scene over and over again. And then they picked out the best that they wanted.

DJ: Did you actually have a hump on your back?

DB: No, no.

DJ: Oh, you just bent over.

DB: Yes, I bent over like this, see.

DJ: Did they talk much about that they wanted it very broad. Do you remember anything about that? The acting, they wanted it almost like the old-fashioned melodramas. Do you remember them discussing that with you?

DB: Yes, of course.

DJ: They did?

DB: Dave and I talked it over from the beginning, before I even started it.

DJ: Can you talk some about that?

DB: No, except that he told me what he wanted. And then, of course, Walt would come on the set sometimes and he'd say to Dave, "I want you to do so and so and so and so and so." Dave would say, "You have to change that, Donny, so and so and so and so." He never talked to me. He talked to Dave. Disney never came to me and said anything to me at all, except "Good morning," and "How are you?"

DJ: But you said you talked to Dave before you ever even started doing it.

DB: Yes, we discussed the action. He said, "This is broad, this is very broad, Don." See, they made a test of me before I ever did this. They made a test of me, without the makeup for my action. They wanted my facial expressions too, see... I have a very good face, a very mobile face. I can do anything with it. Have you seen my commercial on television, the beer commercial? Where the lady in the light yells at me and says, "I wanted a Bud Lite not a bed light." I made it a year ago, this coming October. I made it a year ago in Chicago and they tested 45 men and picked me because of my facial expression. So, I've been known to portray almost any kind of a character that they wanted. And he liked my body movements.

DJ: When you did the Witch, were you influenced by any performance?

DB: No, never! I've never been influenced by anybody in this business.

DJ: But when you did the eyes moving, nothing influenced that personification?

DB: None WHATSOEVER! Once I had an understanding with Dave Hand of what Walt wanted, I did what they wanted.

DJ: Do you remember what they wanted from this Witch. How did they want her to be?

DB: I always said I was the only male actor in the history of Hollywood that played the greatest female heavy. That's a distinction that I have. I can tell you this much: I enjoyed doing her. I enjoyed it. It's a challenge to an actor. The charm of the whole thing is that I felt that I was performing physically for a motion picture, for a theatrical picture and not a cartoon. So I enjoyed acting, in other words, which I have done all my life.

DJ: Did you happen to catch any of the recording sessions of the musicians?

DB: Oh, yes. Leigh Harline was the musical director. And I used to wander around the stage, whenever I had time. I had time off when I could go get a cup of coffee. I couldn't go off the studio because I was in all this stuff.

DJ: You didn't use a mask?

DB: No.

DJ: What about for the nose?

DB: I made up the eyes and then I put the nose on with spirit gum and they fitted right in here like this, just like the picture. And with two big nostrils and it was quite large. And my hair was inside my cap, inside the hood. Long straggly grey hair was inside the hood and I could take it out just by peeling the hood off.

DJ: Now they must have had some wind machines for the drapery blowing?

DB: You mean with my cape?

DJ: Yes.

DB: They didn't have any big, powerful ones. They had these fans, about this big. That one stage was confined to just the mountain stuff and all the other stuff, like close-ups, was shot on other stages.

DJ: So it wasn't all done on the same stage?

DB: No. As I recall there was only two stages, and one stage we didn't do very much on. Like with the pot, that was on the stage and the raft was done on the same stage and this shot of me coming out of this thing that was done on the same stage, but all the mountain stuff took up the whole stage.

Several times climbing the mountains, my cape would get stuck and I'd trip and I'd have to grab hold of something and it got in the way several times, especially when they blew the wind on me. That cape came clear down to here.

DJ: What kind of material [was it]? Was it your own cape?

DB: No, they had it made. It was black cotton.

It was Dave Hand who suggested me to Walt.

When Max Rheinhardt was going to do *Faust* at the Hollywood Bowl, Conrad Nagel was going to do the lead. And when he saw *Snow White* he asked Walt who did the action of the Witch. And they told him who it was. "I would like to have his phone number because I'd like to have him do the Witch in *Faust*." Sure enough, my phone rang one day and in his slight German accent, he says, "My Brodie, I would like very much to talk to you. My name is Max Rheinhardt and my office is on Sunset Boulevard. Would you come in please and see me? We are going to do a big extravaganza at the Hollywood Bowl and I would like to talk to you." So I went in to see him. And when I came in, he got up and he came around from his desk and he shook my hands. He said, "Oh, Mr. Brodie. You were so great as the Witch! You were so wonderful! Sit down, sit down!" He said, "You know, I'm going to do *Faust*. Do you know *Faust*?" I said, "I know very little about opera, but I happen to know there's a witch and I know basically what it's about. It's very heavy." And he said, "I would like very much to have you play the Witch for us."

[Changing the subject.]

DB: I was born in Cincinnati, Ohio, of Scottish parents.

DJ: What got you into the acting profession?

DB: I was in the theater at night in Cincinnati. I was an actor in the civic theater.

DJ: Was this while you were in high school?

DB: No, I never went to high school. I never graduated from the eighth grade of intermediate school even. I had to go to work, help support my mother. Then I became a director of the Civic Theater. And when I was in the Jewish Theater in Cincinnati, I was the only Protestant member of the [garbled] Center which was founded by one of the greatest Jewish rabbis, who has written many books. And I was taken in there.

DJ: What was his name?

DB: Rabbi Weiss. I was taken in from the Civic Theater by them and I was the stage manager there for about two years. Then I became the director. I directed there and then I decided to give up everything that I had there. I sold automobiles. I worked in a bank. I did everything to save up enough money to come to California. I came to Californina and I had $180 when I got off the train. I came here to get into the motion-picture business. I knew that my only chance was to get into some plays.

DJ: What year did you come out?

DB: 1929. September 16, 1929. I got in as an actor and then I finally became a theater director and I directed about twenty-five plays. During that time I started Tyrone Power, Alan Ladd, and Tony Quinn. They all came from my theaters. Because they came to see me. They were going make a big picture at Fox called *Tales of Manhattan* with twenty-one stars in it, and the producer came to see the play and it was such a smash hit, this partic-ular play that I did, that he hired me as a dialogue director to work with Julien Duvivier the French director who was hired to make this picture at Fox. I was with him for five big pictures. He and Charles Boyer were partners. And from that then I went into directing and dialogue directing and playing parts and I got myself an agent like everybody else. And from then on I advanced as the years went by.

DJ: Now, how did you get your own theater? How did you finance that?

DB: We didn't finance it. We found places we could rent for $50 a month and a group of us would get together and everybody'd put in 10 or 12 bucks and we'd pay the rent and then we'd build our own scenery and everything. We took over a church in Hollywood and we kept the pews but we rebuilt the podium and we did a play in there called *Gentleman for Sale*. Tony Quinn got his break in that play.

DJ: Now, the theater that had *The Drunkard* in it...

DB: That was the Press Club. It was called the Theater Mart.

DJ: That was your theater, you said.

DB: It wasn't my theater. It was owned by a woman by the name of Alice Pike Barney. Her father owned the Pullman Company, the Pullman cars for the railroad. She was very wealthy and she was quite elderly. She saw a play that I directed and she came and said, "I want you to direct in my theater." So I went there and I directed six or seven plays. And she passed away and left me the theater.

DJ: And *The Drunkard* ran for years and years.

DB: Twenty years.

DJ: I think it was still running in the 1950s when I was a child. I remember reading about it. … Did you do any socializing with the Disney people when you were doing *Snow White*?

DB: None whatsoever. The only touch of socializing I had was when we were working on *Pinocchio*, out at [Walt's] pool and he had lunch on the veranda…

DJ: Who would do the cooking?

DB: He had a housekeeper.

DJ: His wife didn't do any cooking?

DB: No Very lovely woman. We were up there about five or six days.

[Changing the subject]

DB: They made a picture called *Escape to Witch Mountain*. The producer, Jerry Corban, hired me as the dialogue director for that picture. Also I dialogue-directed lots of pictures and played parts in them.

Joe Grant (1908–2005)

Interviewed in Winter 1988; transcription by Joost Blox.

One of the most spectacular projects to come out of the Disney studio in the recent years is a beautiful short that blends 3-D and 2-D animation in the most skilful way ever achieved. What makes this short, *Lorenzo*, even more special is that the idea behind its creation came from one of Disney's "old-timers," Joe Grant, one of the artists who, like John Hench and Mel Shaw, worked at Disney in both the first and second golden ages of the company, in the 1930s and the late 1980s.

Like Molière, Joe Grant died while performing his art. At the time he experienced his heart attack, he was at home at his desk and had just completed a new drawing. His life is discussed in detail in John Canemaker's book *Before the Animation Begins*, but is best summarized by quoting extensively from the official press release that was issued by the Walt Disney Studio at the time of his death:

> Born in New York on May 15, 1908, Grant moved to Los Angeles with his family when he was two years old. The son of a successful newspaper art editor, he received his art training through frequent visits to the newsroom with his father. His first big professional break came when he was hired to create cartoons and caricatures of famous personalities on a weekly basis for the *Los Angeles Record*. Those whimsical, stylized drawings brought him to the attention of Walt Disney, who personally hired him to caricature major stars of the day for the short, *Mickey's Gala Premiere*. A few years later, Grant joined the studio on a full-time basis and quickly found his calling in the areas of character design and story. His first assignments included a stint on the short *Who Killed Cock Robin?* and the task of designing the Queen/Witch for the studio's first full-length animated feature, *Snow White*.
>
> Following the success of that film, Walt tapped Grant to head up the newly created character model department. There, he oversaw a talented team that experimented with character design, sculpted three-dimensional models and did early story development. They provided inspiration for such films as *Pinocchio*, *Fantasia*, *The Reluctant Dragon*, and *Saludos Amigos*. Grant became a close associate of Walt's

and an important figure around the studio. It was often said that no model sheet was official until it bore the seal, "O.K., J.G."

Outside of his role in the model department, Grant made his mark as one of the studio's top writers and gagmen. Along with Dick Huemer, he accompanied Disney and Leopold Stokowski on a retreat to select the music for *Fantasia* and subsequently lead the story development for that film. Grant and Huemer reteamed to write *Dumbo*, which was inspired by a children's book in the form of a tiny scroll. In 1939, Grant and his wife, Jenny, came up with a story about a springer spaniel named Lady, which later became the genesis of *Lady and the Tramp*.

During the war years, Grant and Huemer contributed story, gags, and designs for many of the studio's patriotic-themed shorts including *Reason and Emotion*, *Education for Death*, and the Academy Award-winning *Der Fuehrer's Face*.

When the character model department disbanded in 1949, Grant left the studio to pursue his own artistic ventures. He started several successful businesses including a ceramics studio (Opechee Designs) and a greeting card company (Castle Ltd.).

In 1989, after being away from the studio for forty years, Grant received a call from a Feature Animation development executive asking if he would be interested in consulting on a project. The film turned out to be *Beauty and the Beast* and Grant's talent, enthusiasm, and humor proved to be just as vital in his eighties as it was in his twenties. He contributed gags for the objects in that film and enjoyed working with a new generation of filmmakers.

This led to a full-time return and Grant began coming to the studio on a daily basis and working on nearly all of the films that followed. Taking the title of creative director, he contributed concepts, character designs, story ideas, and gags for *Aladdin*, *The Lion King*, *Pocahontas*, *The Hunchback of Notre Dame*, and *Hercules*. For Disney's 1998 animated release, *Mulan*, Grant is credited with conceptualizing the cricket character, Cri-Kee, as well as some of the humorous moments with Mushu the dragon. For *Fantasia 2000*, Grant came up with the idea of flamingos with yo-yos for the "Carnival of the Animals" sequence. For the Pixar film, *Monsters, Inc.*, Grant came up with the film's title, and provided inspiration to director Pete Docter, a longtime admirer and protégé.

At the time of his death, he was developing several feature-length and short animation projects, in collaboration with his friend and Disney colleague, Burny Mattinson.

JOE GRANT: [Regarding Walt's enthusiasm for *Snow White*.] You had no idea of the power of this thing. He headed a thing in art that was unique. Painting, drawing, motion, music, all locked up in one thing, one film, something artists of the past have always wished for. I mean, the attempt in art has always been to make it move and to show dimension. And the accompaniment of music... It was a total picture, for an artist, I mean.

Walt had a way of taking what someone had to say about the dwarfs or the animals, or whatever happened to be there, and to incorporate it into his storyline and in his thinking. In other words, nothing derailed him. All he did was add more passengers to his train.

DAVID JOHNSON: I find a resemblance to Katharine Hepburn in the Queen, with the mouth drooping like this and the high cheekbones, and I'm just wondering if that was a conscious thing on your part.

JG: It might have been unconscious, because having made many caricatures of Katharine Hepburn it might have seeped in somehow. But it was not deliberate, no. As a matter of fact, it was more or less inspired by a woman whose name I do not remember, who we did the rotoscoping of.

DJ: I don't know who did that. It wasn't the same woman who did the voice.

JG: She was a very beautiful woman, made up with the arched eyebrows and all to give the impression that the Queen gave. I would say that she inspired the final drawings.

DJ: And you don't remember her name?

JG: No, I don't. She was a rather well-known feature player in films.

DJ: Lucille La Verne?

JG: No, La Verne only did the Witch voice.

DJ: Did they use Lucille La Verne to do some of the live action for the Witch?

JG: Yes.

DJ: Did you actually use La Verne as a model for the Witch?

JG: No, the Witch was conceived before we saw her. But I would say that she inspired the final model sheet. We picked up her expressions, which were very broad and caricatured.

DJ: What inspired the Witch for you?

JG: The closest thing that inspired me was John Barrymore in *Jekyll and Hyde*.

DJ: You were pretty young when that came out—that was 1922.

JG: Yes, but I remembered it along with other Barrymore films, *Beau Brummel* and *The Sea Beast*. He inspired me unconsciously, even consciously. He had all of the exaggerated gestures and the caricature that was necessary for that.

DJ: Can you talk about some of the early stages of *Snow White*, some of the early story conferences? You were in on it from the beginning?

JG: On and off, yeah.

DJ: How did you find out that they were doing the feature?

JG: I was told when I first came to the studio. They were just finishing *Three Little Pigs* when I came there and Walt mentioned among the projects... well, as a matter of fact it was an open secret then. Everybody knew that he was planning it. But before we got on it, I had gone through a series of short films that I had worked on. When the time came I started making inspirational sketches.

DJ: What did you think about a feature? Did you think it was a great idea or were you kind of skeptical, the way most people were?

JG: I think I would be in that category, skeptical. But as I told you, we were carried along by his great enthusiasm and, once he got through telling you the story, you were totally convinced that this thing had to exist. Because it already existed in his mind.

DJ: I've read in several books about this marathon story that he gave one night at the studio. He went through the whole film and he acted out all the characters. Do you remember that?

JG: I remember him doing it a number of times. Every day. Not only that, it became up to a point of boredom that he would repeat each sequence. If he was involved with your sequence, he would tell you everything that preceded it and everything that followed it and recite the entire picture.

DJ: So even before the dialog was recorded...

JG: It was all in his mind.

DJ: ...he already had a lot of the dialog in his mind, you'd say.

JG: Roughly. In other words, the essence of it was always there. We were there to polish up his ideas. You might think we're giving undue credit to him and belittling our own efforts, but you have to have lived then and been with him to understand the power of this thing. Remember, we had no experience, we the outsiders, with the idea of a full feature. The charm of it was the novelty.

The only thing I can say about that is that our skepticism was over-powered by his enthusiasm. It swallowed us up. He was a prophet, you know; he knew this thing could go. We did the finishing touches and we all contributed something. But we were completely enchanted and mystified by everything he did.

DJ: So he was really magnetic.

JG: Yes. Some people, I think if you talk to Babbitt...

DJ: They hated each other.

JG: Yes. But we had nothing but great admiration for him. Remember, he had a thing in art that was unique. Painting, drawing, motion, music, all locked up in one thing, on film. Something artists of the past have always wished for. The attempt in art has always been to make it move, and to show dimension. The accompaniment of music...it was the total picture for an artist. Particularly me, being young and having had considerable background in art from my father and his father and so on.

DJ: What would be a typical early story meeting? Who'd be there?

JG: I don't know, I'd have to think about that.

DJ: Would Walt be there?

JG: Oh yeah, there were no story meetings without him.

DJ: Frank Churchill and Wilfred Jackson would probably be there?

JG: Yes. Larry Morey would be there. The directors, the storymen. Everybody concerned, background men and so on. But it depended on what stage it was in. The early stages, it might be a meeting between Walt, Bill [Cottrell], and myself. Just early discussions and ideas, maybe based on an inspirational sketch that might be up on the wall, or an idea that Bill had. The story meetings were, again, a recitation of the whole story. Everybody that would contribute something... Walt had a way of taking what someone had to say about the dwarfs, or the animals, or whatever happened to be there, and incorporate it into his story line. In other words, nothing derailed him. All he did was add more passengers to his train.

DJ: Can you recall any funny anecdotes from these meetings?

JG: No, nothing really. I don't think there was anything funny at the time. The business of humor is seriousness It was all instructed for a purpose. No, I don't recall any.

DJ: Did any meeting particularly impress you?

JG: The word "hovering" over something. Just little things that Bill and I would gag about. [Walt] would refer to things as "hoovering," instead of "hovering." Mispronunciations, idiot things like that. Nothing to detract from his character, but he would get locked into things like that and it would somewhat grate on you.

DJ: Do you remember anything specific that Walt did in one of these meetings, any piece of acting that you particularly were impressed by?

JG: No, because with his very mobile eyebrow he could enact any one of the characters and pantomime beautifully. All of his physical motions were related to the characters. I can't think of anything else.

DJ: You mentioned that Albert Hurter was inspired by this German artist...

JG: Vogel was his name.

DJ: Were you working with Hurter? In the screen credits you're both given as character designers.

JG: No. At the very beginning we did a little bit, but I moved over with Bill.

DJ: [Looking at pieces of artwork] These are early witches...

JG: But see, they are different. We changed over to the one that I started.

DJ: Do you have any idea where he got this idea, for the Snow White costume? It's neo-medieval, I guess. Did he ever mention it to you?

JG: No. I would say [Albert Hurter] got it from a costume book. Not the drawing, but the costume itself. If you look at it carefully, you see that there's only a suggestion, not a complete costume. You can't make a model sheet from that.

DJ: What amazes me is that these sleeves, the dress, the length of the dress, the cape, the collar here, the bow in the hair, it's basically the same costume...that early on. I was just curious to know if he got it from somewhere particular or if it just came out of his head.

JG: I would say out of his head, because this wouldn't be researched. Although he did do some research, but he was remarkable. I mean, all this stuff was in his head. He had an amazing graphic sense.

DJ: You would say that it's safe to say that he designed the actual costume of the girl himself from a very early stage?

JG: Yes, but I don't know who refined it afterwards. It probably wound up in the director's room or...

DJ: Who would have been responsible for the character design work? Would this have been other story men?

JG: Well, I think in some of these drawings, this may have been somebody like Perce Pearce, because this is very comic-y, you know.

DJ: Did he draw?

JG: Yeah, he could draw. He played a very important role in the development of these dwarfs, I thought.

DJ: Can you elaborate on that? In what way did he do that?

JG: Just in his gestures and his feeling for it. Some of a middle-western quality, he got some of a country music background to these guys. He had a certain cartoon element, his gestures and his physical appearance. Whatever he did, he had a good deal of it. He pantomimed a lot of it. I don't know how much the animators used of it, but it's obviously something of him.

DJ: When you saw the film recently, could you recall anything of the dwarfs that you think came from him?

JG: Business like "show your hands" and all that, that's his kind of stuff. That's the closest type of thing; I can't think of anything else right now.

DJ: I didn't know that he was involved in any kind of story.

JG: Oh yeah.

DJ: Shamus Culhane doesn't believe that he had anything to contribute, that he stole everything from everybody else.

JG: That accusation's been made, but the guy physically was a character, you know what I mean? Particularly Grumpy, he did a very good job on that, and I think if Tytla were alive he would confirm having been inspired by some of the things he did. As far as stealing from anybody, I would say there wasn't really much to steal.

[Looking at picture] This is the girl, I knew her very well, Dorothy Ann Blank, who wrote the dialog for the Queen. The "mirror, mirror on the wall," all of that. She was very important in that. She was an old newspaper woman. She's responsible for all of that and she wrote and rewrote that stuff. When you read it now, it's very simple, but she really suffered through this stuff.

DJ: Why was that? Because Walt didn't like it?

JG: It didn't quite hit him. And when she finally got what is now the final version... but he contributed to that. In fact, everybody did. But she laid it out and she lived and breathed it for a long time.

DJ: This was early 1935, I guess, when they were doing some of this stuff?

JG: Yeah.

DJ: She did the dialogue for all the scenes of the Queen?

JG: Most of them, yeah.

DJ: Just the Queen?

JG: No, she did some for the Witch, too. The apple bit, the dipping of the apple and all that stuff.

DJ: An old newspaper woman. From what newspaper?

JG: I think she was somewhere in the East, I'm not sure.

DJ: What about the mask in the Magic Mirror; did you help design the mask?

JG: Yes. This isn't my drawing, but I have one very much like it.

DJ: When the mask was originally conceived...

JG: The voice was Moroni Olsen, wasn't it?

DJ: Yes. So what inspired you for the mask, a theater mask, obviously?

JG: Yeah, you know...comedy and drama.

DJ: And the idea of using the different colors...was that suggested by you?

JG: You mean the bottom lighting? Yeah. As a matter of fact, I think it was Bill's idea.

DJ: The effect of the bottom lighting?

JG: Yeah.

DJ: You remember anything about who designed the *Snow White* title logo?

JG: I don't know the guy's name. I think it came from the same title department that did the shorts.

DJ: And this kaleidoscope...what do you call this background?

JG: That's a material you buy, that's a made...

DJ: It's a material?

JG: It's a paper. I don't have a sheet of it here, but it's not very colored. It has sort of a metallic quality to it and you can see how it shows up...

DJ: So that's actually a paper then? They just photographed the title over that?

JG: Yes.

DJ: I always wanted to know that.

JG: Yes, that's an existing stock. This kind of thing would have taken months to make.

DJ: Would it, really?

JG: Oh yeah. But whoever did this stuff was an excellent man. I can't remember his name; he was an airbrush artist who did most of the titles. He cut them all out of celluloid, all the letters. Sometimes it would be seven different layers of cels and he would airbrush each one, for each corresponding color.

DJ: Your work would be character design of the Queen and the Witch, basically.

JG: And the vultures, and the raven.

DJ: What was Lucille La Verne like as a person? Funny? Eccentric?

JG: Oh, full of fun. She was already famous for pictures she was in with Lillian Gish. In *Intolerance* and all those pictures, way back. She was a famous stage actress as well. But she was a delightful person, very willing and very obliging. The only thing I remember about her is what I told you, her trying out the voice. Somehow we felt that it didn't sound witchy enough and then she came up with the idea of taking her teeth out.

DJ: She came up with the idea?

JG: Oh yeah. As a result of it, it gave that wet sort of...when she did that, then she became the Witch, her jaws collapsed and she was...

DJ: When she recorded the soundtrack, was that done first, before the live action was filmed? Do you have any recollection of what came first?

JG: In most cases it was the soundtrack. I mean, you worked to that.

DJ: Ward Kimball said that Walt would often be present at the soundtrack sessions.

JG: Sometimes. He would prefer to hear it after the session. It gave him a better view, because you began to look at the individual and it sounded right for her, but then when you tried to think of the character it didn't jive, you know what I mean? So he would like to hear it away from the stage.

DJ: On occasion he may have been there...

JG: Oh yeah, sure. He was everywhere, he was omnipresent.

DJ: When he would drop in, would he actually stop it and say: "No, I want it done this way?"

JG: He'd make suggestions, sure. "Next take you try something else." He might think we were a little too conservative with it; he would always come up with the exaggerated and the more...in other words, he always came up with the thing we didn't think about.

DJ: When you were recording things with La Verne, did they have to be done over many, many times? Or was she really pretty good?

JG: She was such a pro, I don't think we did too many takes on her, no. We'd try everything, because naturally we were going to present it to Walt, so he'd get the right version. Then we'd make our choice, or Bill would make it usually, and present it to him. And then of course the animators had to hear it. Fergy [Norman Ferguson] was present at many of the takes. They were all in on it; there was really no one-man show anywhere. When you think about it, the director was brought in while the takes were taped, and very often the animator, naturally.

DJ: Was La Verne dressed? Did she have a fake nose and all that?

JG: With a cape on. I don't think we put a nose on her. I forgot what we had her in over the cauldron, but her gestures and everything were...

DJ: You actually used a cauldron?

JG: We had some kind of a substitute thing. I forget what it was.

DJ: And it actually had liquid in it?

JG: No, it was all pantomime.

DJ: The look of the Witch preceded her coming into it?

JG: Oh yeah, sure. She would be helpful for the animator. You can see that in Fergy's animation. He's following a human there.

DJ: Did your design for the Witch evolve or was it like this from the beginning?

JG: Pretty close to that, but it got better as time went on.

DJ: The eyes were pretty close to...

JG: Oh yeah, the bug eyes.

DJ: That you got from John Barrymore, from *Jekyll and Hyde*?

JG: I'd say it was unconsciously, not a direct copy of him. Bill and I would get a kick out of a thing like that: it was the dramatic scene. This thing lifting and that head coming forward. Just the location of it and the drama that that would suggest. The surprise.

DJ: Did you do any of the sketches that show the dungeon with the Prince and the flooding and they had originally thought of?

JG: No. That again is all pretty much background designers.

DJ: [Looking at model of the Witch] This was from your drawings?

JG: As a matter of fact, that was modeled even before I made drawings. It was a direct piece of papier maché and Jenny [Grant's wife] dressed it up, all of that stuff, the hands and everything. Walt got a big kick out of that. We had it around the studio for quite awhile. I don't know where it is now.

DJ: This was really early on in the production then?

JG: Oh yeah, this is what probably got me into that particular sequence.

DJ: If you weren't assigned to the sequence, then how did this model come about?

JG: I don't really know. In those days, if you knew something was coming up and you wanted to get on that particular picture, you'd do something that would inspire Walt and it would be up to him to say, "You seem to have a penchant for this sort of thing, let's use that for it." I would say offhand that both Bill and myself liked the macabre and that more or less tricked us into doing this situation.

DJ: Your wife did this model?

JG: No, I did the model, she just dressed it.

DJ: In other words, it was your idea to have the...

JG: Yes, but that's all traditional stuff. We can't say it's invented, because there have been thousands of illustrations of witches in the past. It's what we did with it that counts.

DJ: The hands of the Witch...

JG: Gnarled fingers.

DJ: Was that your idea?

JG: It might have been my drawing, but as far as the idea is concerned, it would be part and parcel of the equipment of a witch to have rheumatic hands and long fingernails, you know.

DJ: Did you actually draw the model sheets of the Witch?

JG: I did one of them. I made it originally for Fergy and then it was passed around. I think it has an "OK" on it and my name. Everything you got here might be something I worked on at home, not necessarily at the studio.

DJ: Did you do a model sheet of the Queen? Art Babbitt, who did the Queen, says that he doesn't recall a model sheet.

JG: No, I don't think so either. You see, in those days model sheets didn't proliferate. There weren't models of everything.

DJ: But you did the original inspirational sketches.

JG: Yes, that's what he worked from. That's about all there is to it, because from that point on he put that thing down in mechanical form so that it could be translated.

DJ: But they had model sheets for the Witch. And since Norman Ferguson drew the Witch, why would they bother with model sheets for that?

JG: As I say, that was drawn for Fergy and put together for him as a reference.

DJ: You mean he asked for it?

JG: Yes. I think it was Bill's insistence that he take that model sheet so that he didn't lose the character. Because Fergy was not the number-one draftsman. But he followed it very closely. His assistant did, anyway.

DJ: His assistant was John Lounsbery.

JG: Yes, he was very good. Top animator.

DJ: Do you recall when you were given this assignment to do the Queen? Walt just said, "I want you to design the character of the Queen and the Witch?" How did that come about?

JG: I think that came about when he decided to let us... He saw the model first. I don't know how he teamed us up with Bill, we were working on something... When did *Who Killed Cock Robin?* come out?

DJ: 1934, I think.

JG: We had done *Cock Robin* before, together, so we were working as a team, Bill Cottrell and I. So we did that picture together and he saw us as a team. Bill probably chose the sequence. I'm sure he did.

DJ: He's not listed as a character designer, he's listed as a sequence director.

JG: That's right. And in a sense he was, yes.

DJ: Whereas you're listed along with Albert Hurter, so I thought you were designing things along with him.

JG: No. That's what I told you; there's all kinds of misapplications here. We worked together on both story and design and the whole thing. The idea was where to put who, you know what I mean? I wasn't the story director here, although I worked on the story. But I also worked on the design, so you could have put me in the design and the director category, or in the background category. We really invented the model department, the character models really were invented in this *Snow White*.

Ken Anderson
(1909–1993)

Interviewed in 1988.

The "jack-of-all-trades," good at animation, great at scene layout, character design, and art direction for movies and theme parks, Ken Anderson is considered by many as Disney's "tenth old man." He was one of the most influential artists at the Disney studio from the mid 1930s to the late 1970s.

Born near Seattle in 1909, he studied architecture at the University of Washington in Seattle, then won a scholarship which allowed him to study at the École des Beaux-Arts in Fontainebleau, France, and at the American Academy of Rome, in Italy. When he returned from these studies in Europe in 1934, he worked for six weeks at MGM sketching sets for *The Painted Veil* and *What Every Woman Knows* before joining the Disney studio that same year.

His first special assignment: animating a moving background on the short *Three Orphan Kittens* (1935). After that project he left animation to join the layout department, headed by Charles Philippi and Hugh Hennesy.

On *Snow White and the Seven Dwarfs*, all his skills were put to good use: he storyboarded scenes from the party-in-the-dwarfs'-cottage sequence, created layouts and sketches for the proposed dream sequence, experimented with the multiplane camera, and built a model of the dwarfs' house to guide animators.

Anderson served again as one of the art directors on both *Pinocchio* and *Fantasia* (on the first part of the "Pastoral Symphony" sequence), as well as on the short *Ferdinand the Bull* (1938).

For *The Three Caballeros* and *Song of the South*, he teamed with Mary Blair, devising ways to adapt her unique style to the screen. Around the same time, he was credited as contributing to the stories on *Melody Time*, *So Dear to My Heart*, and *Cinderella*, and doing color styling on *Alice in Wonderland*.

In the early 1950s he joined WED (now Walt Disney Imagineering). As an Imagineer, he was the principal designer on the Fantasyland "dark rides" and his many memorable projects included designing Storybook Land and the interior of the Sleeping Beauty castle. He was also one of the first artists to tackle the project that would later become the Haunted Mansion.

Returning to animation, he worked again as production designer on *Sleeping Beauty*, then introduced the Xerography technique on *101 Dalmatians*, for which he served as solo production designer.

Virtually all the animated features that came out of the Disney studio from that point on were marked by his style. Anderson served as art director on *Sword in the Stone* and tackled both art direction and character design on *The Jungle Book*, *The Aristocats*, *Robin Hood*, *The Rescuers*, and *Pete's Dragon*, for which he created Elliott.

One of the last projects he worked on was *Catfish Bend*, a proposed animated feature for which he did preliminary sketches.

Ken Anderson retired in 1978 and died from a heart attack on December 13, 1993.

DAVID JOHNSON: What are your earliest memories of *Snow White*?

KEN ANDERSON: The first I heard of it was kind of unusual. It was during Depression time—and that's said very lightly, but it's not a light subject, it's a very heavy subject. I was a young animator. Everybody started there, either as traffic boys or you were animators.

DJ: Was it $15 a week?

KA: Yes. And the only thing that exceeded the $15 was my wife. I got her a job there which was illegal. You couldn't have man and wife work at Disney's. I made fashion drawings for her with my left hand so people wouldn't catch me, so that it would not be my technique.

DJ: So you draw with your right hand, too?

KA: I have never drawn with anything but. And they weren't too much, because they got her a job at $18 a week. So she exceeded me at $3 a week from what I got. But anyway, Walt gave each of us—there were about 15 of us—a dollar, I think, and told us to go have a good dinner and plan to come back and be there at 8 o'clock. He had something to tell us. He told us to come to the soundstage, which was a big old barn-like place and had a ramp running up at one end and there was a projection booth.

DJ: It had recently been built, the soundstage?

KA: Yeah. About seventy-five feet long and about thirty-feet wide and about fifty-feet high inside. It cost a lot to light it, so you didn't have it lit, just the end where he would be. There were six rows and we filled that up pretty well and were happy because we had had a very good dinner for a dollar...or 50 cents.

DJ: Did he give you the 50 cents?

KA: Yeah.

DJ: So this was a treat?

KA: A treat. Besides the good dinner we got for 35 cents, we had a magnif-
icent dessert for 15 cents. And some of those guys even saved the money,
the 15 cents. We were feeling pretty affluent, came back to the studio and
got those seats, and Walt came in and stood alone, all by himself on this
dark floor. It was all dark behind him. I wish I could impart to you...because
the whole thing of *Snow White* was right there. He had lived this story
so deeply and so fondly, and had visualized doing it. Of course we didn't
know that. There may have been some of them in the group who did, but
I didn't know. And we sat there from 8 o'clock till midnight. Didn't even
know the time had passed. Usually my butt gets sore and I have to move,
but I didn't in this case. I sat there just listening to this man. He chose to
be each of the characters. And he was a superlative actor when he didn't
know he was acting: he just acted. He took the parts, and it's amazing how
much he was into this picture.

**DJ: Did he describe also like trucking in, like with the castle in the
beginning? Did he actually begin it like: "Now we see Snow White's
castle and the camera moves in..." Do you recall anything like that?**

KA: I don't think so. I don't think he told it with the camera directions.
I think he told it so you felt that there were a dozen ways you could do
what he was talking about.

DJ: He probably started with "Once upon a time..."

KA: No, it wasn't that prosaic. It was pretty unusual. And he didn't hesi-
tate about going through part of the story and going back and taking up
the thing, going through it again as a different character. He brought to
life all the characters. He visualized the stepmother and the Huntsman
and all these people, and he knew how they felt. He told the thing so well
that if we could have pursued it that well... We had a fire in under us and
we just were fascinated with the idea of doing this fantastic thing. It had
never been done. No animated feature had ever been done. And nobody
had ever taken the cartoons seriously. They were just throwaways at the
beginning of things. Here was a feature and the way Walt told it, it was
a beautiful feature. He hadn't broken it down into regular sequences for
us. He did that during later developments. But he did see it all.

DJ: Did he use any props or costumes in this performance?

KA: Not a one.

DJ: Nothing.

KA: But he had on the Witch's costume, and he had it off and he had on...

DJ: Oh, he did use some of the costumes.

KA: Didn't use a costume. But he had them on.

DJ: Oh, I see what you mean. In his head he had them on.

KA: He made you feel he had them on. And he transported us into this strange world. These dwarfs came alive: everybody knew how they looked and everything about them. It was a fantastic evening. It was probably the one greatest evening in all my life.

DJ: Is that right? The one greatest evening.

KA: The one greatest evening. Because it meant more, not just to me, but I think to all of us. We worked as if that was the only thing we were ever going to do. We didn't even think beyond the end of this picture. We were so engrossed in this picture, we worked Saturdays and Sundays and nights.

DJ: And at the time when this took place, I believe it was early 1935, were you at that time still an animator or had you already gone into art direction and layout by that time?

KA: Let's see. The reason I went into art direction and layout is because... It's a personal thing. I had worked as an inbetweener and then as assistant animator and worked so hard and so many hours that I got sick.

DJ: Who were you assistant to?

KA: I was assistant to all of the animators. I wasn't assigned to any one animator.

DJ: Oh, you weren't.

KA: Neither were Milt Kahl, Frank Thomas, Ollie Johnston, Jack Hannah, or Jim Algar. We were all in a room. We were animators without a cause. We weren't given anybody yet. But then I got sick. It was a very bad deal. I was sent to a man who was a friend of this George Drake's. He was on Van Ness Avenue, in this old house. He had an operating table and had a big leather pad on it. He was an orthopedic surgeon. He said I had galloping European tuberculosis and it's a good thing I had come to him because in ninety days I'd be dead. I wish I knew all the things he had said, because they were so improbable that almost anybody would catch on. But I didn't and they took my full salary. They didn't know that I had my wife working there. They took my full salary every week to give to him and he in turn split it with George Drake.

DJ: I can't believe this was going on.

KA: So then Walt came to me and said, "Ken, you know perspective and all that. I'm going to set it up where you can sleep in the day whenever you're weak and you can have this cot." It was in this room where we developed the multiplane camera. "I want you to do a little model of the house [of the dwarfs] and paint it." So I kind of got off on this other track.

DJ: How long were you sick?

KA: Five weeks.

DJ: And then you had a miraculous recovery?

KA: My wife's father was an MD. He came out from the state of Washington and we went to see this guy and all hell broke loose! If it had been a better atmosphere, they would have sued. But they just decided the best thing to do with the political scene there was not to sue, and was to get out of it. So I got out of it. Anyway, now I'm back in animation.

DJ: So, you went back into animation?

KA: Yeah.

DJ: But briefly, I suppose?

KA: Briefly, because I liked this idea of being in story more than layout. There weren't the divisions that've grown up since. I could still animate. I liked to be with Walt, I liked to know the story, I liked to push the thing. And I could draw the things that hadn't been drawn yet, the characters, and get some ideas. So I did that and thought that worked out pretty well.

DJ: Now, when you designed the dwarfs' house, was that when you were sick?

KA: Yes.

DJ: So he gave you that project to do so that you could sort of keep yourself occupied. And you designed it from some of Albert Hurter's sketches and things like that.

KA: Later we were told that our drawings had to look alike, but you can't really do it. Charlie Philippi loved to do cobwebs and stuff like that.

DJ: Tell me more about this little house you designed.

KA: It was one inch to the foot. And I had been trained as an architect. In fact, I have my architectural license. I had never intended to get into cartooning. I didn't know I could. I worked at MGM as a set designer. Anyway, when I came to Disney's I got this one-inch-to-the-foot thing, and it was Walt really who said that we're going to shoot the real girl. Opening the door, your little dickey door, looking around in the room, she comes across the room, she'll pivot around—she knows it's the dwarfs' household—pulls up her skirt and sit in a little chair. This is from the exact distance…that little chair. And she sits in it. The idea is that he wanted a new style. We would take this and photograph this thing, and we would then use wash-off cels.

We'd photograph the thing with the camera and every frame would be on film and we would wash it off and all that would be left would be the lines, the outlines. Then we would back that up with cel paints. So anyway, that was going on while they were doing other experiments.

DJ: What did you build this house with?

KA: Plywood.

DJ: Was it all made of wood, or did you use cardboard or plaster?

KA: All made of wood.

DJ: Even the chimney?

KA: Everything.

DJ: Did you paint it?

KA: This was the whole trick. I painted the house white, basic white, all over. And I outlined every place there would be a line drawing. I very carefully took a pen and made black lines, which weren't as fine as they should have been, because it kept spreading on the panes and so forth. But I got this black-and-white thing all done. Then we photographed Marge Belcher opening the imaginary door—two sticks—pivoting around, running across the room, sitting in the chair. Then we got her to open the door, run across the room, and sit in the chair. But the effect wasn't smooth because of the fact that these wash-off cels shrank differently at different rates. Some of them would shrink an awful lot. Some of them would never shrink at all, so the whole thing jittered.

DJ: How did this house open up to the inside? Did it open on hinges?

KA: It all came apart. We'd lift the wall off, lift the ceiling off, lift all these things out. You could have any part you wanted.

DJ: How long did it take you to make that?

KA: Geez, I don't know. Probably six months, but I've forgotten.

DJ: Oh, a long time, then.

KA: Oh yeah.

DJ: You were working on it off and on?

KA: All the time. And I was also working on what they call those multiplane cranes. That time we were doing a horizontal multiplane crane, I was modeling trees and on how many levels...and so on and so forth. And Bill Garity was doing the overall imagining how it was going to be.

DJ: Now the horizontal eventually became the vertical multiplane.

KA: That's right.

DJ: How long did they experiment with this horizontal before Bill Garity decided that he would switch to the vertical, can you recall?

KA: He didn't decide, Walt did.

DJ: So did this go on for a year or two before they finally switched over? Because I know the vertical didn't come in until spring of 1937.

KA: That's right. It was a big decision Walt had to make. I think, probably about that, about a year.

DJ: So Walt made the decision?

KA: Oh, sure. He made every decision.

DJ: What was wrong with the horizontal?

KA: It wiggled. It wasn't stable. You had to have something absolutely solid. So, Walt had the ground tested against earthquakes and rumbles and rattles and all that sort of thing and we set a *huge* block of concrete...

DJ: Now did you work on any of the design for the multiplane or was that strictly Garity with McFadden?

KA: Your last people. And we had a man named Firth Perce. He was a young engineering genius who came from CalTech. And we opened up the multiplane... We were going to have a big show for Walt. He had a $20,000 Cooper lens. There's an inset there where you turn the screw and so Firth got up there with this lens and he was setting this whole thing up to show how it was working. And he turned the thing and it wasn't set. *Phew*, it came bo, bo, bo, bo, bo, bo through all the planes of glass.

DJ: It broke all the planes of glass?

KA: And it broke the lens. Firth wasn't there the next day.

DJ: Or ever after.

KA: Yeah, never after. I don't know if he quit or Walt fired him or what, but poor guy, it was just an accident and he was gone.

DJ: $20,000 for a lens. Were you there when this happened?

KA: Yes.

DJ: Good grief. You designed the house, then you were also working on the horizontal multiplane. When did you actually start work on sketches and things for *Snow White*?

KA: My most memorable thought was in the entertainment sequence. [Wilfred] Jackson was a very meticulous director, very musical. He was the one who invented the way of transposing drawings to sheets of music, to relating the sensual thing. Anyway, I had no idea how you made layouts, what you did. Jackson and I considered ourselves a team. Walt gave us the entertainment sequence to do. So we figured how is the best way to do an entertainment sequence. We had to figure out what it was, get the music, and had to get everything together. Walt kind of left us alone for some reason. We decided the best way to do it was for me to go through as a story sketch, layout man, and design all the scenes and all the dances.

DJ: Did you design this [the organ pipes]?

KA: Yes, I did. So I was going to make a video with the music. We were going to have a miniature sequence all done and photographed and show it to Walt.

DJ: Was this live action or just cartoon?

KA: All cartoon. We didn't have live action. Because we were still working on the story idea. We had to come up with the songs and know they were right and we presented the songs to Walt. "Yeah, yeah, yeah, go ahead and do it"

DJ: And [Frank] Churchill wrote the music. Did he do it quite quickly, do you recall? I understand he was a prolific writer.

KA: I've seen him play the piano with his toes. I don't remember if it took him a long time, whether that was one of those things that he just burst on and had it all in one day. I forgot just how it came up.

DJ: Did he write more than one tune before you finally got it okayed? In other words, did it go through a lot of metamorphoses?

KA: No, I don't think so. I think it was right off the bat.

DJ: And Larry Morey would be writing the lyrics then and you all would be working together?

KA: In a way. So I didn't know what the hell a layout man did. Nobody ever told me. So if you're going to make a set-up, a stage for an actor to act on and to do certain acts and go here and pick up something to do, you have to design the actor. You had to know what the actor did, you had to move him from this place to that in key poses. So I did far more work than was wanted or was necessary or was even good. I did all the animation, I did all the layout, and everything that you would never do. But I did it all thinking I was helping the picture and thinking it was what was wanted.

DJ: Did you design these [musical instruments]?

KA: I worked on them. I don't remember if I designed them.

DJ: Could you maybe have worked on them with Albert Hurter?

KA: Well, Albert didn't work on these, Jack Miller did. I worked on them. Anyway, what I did is in the manner of confession because I would never have... I probably could have confessed it to Walt at a later date. Because it was an honest mistake. I just thought that a layout man should prepare everything and put the characters where they're supposed to be and having them doing what they're supposed to be doing and all these things that was going to be done. So I did the whole sequence that way and timing it. And we shot it. Jackson was happy as a tick, got this whole sequence all done, showed it to Walt, and Walt said, "Goddamn, you guys! Now we can't animate it this way: everything's all tied down."

DJ: When you say you shot it...what did you shoot?

KA: A Leica reel, in time with the music, poses. But the number of poses was astronomical. I even have another sequence and I didn't know any better yet, nobody had gotten to me. I still thought I was doing the greatest job that could be done. This Grumpy sneaking up to the bench and going up to the window sill... Anyway, we were all learning. What we were strong in, we all pushed, we all tried to do our best.

DJ: So what happened to the entertainment section when Walt said that there're too many drawings?

KA: We started over. We kept all the good stuff and made it much more open.

DJ: Now was the dialogue and everything recorded by this time with a piano track in the background?

KA: Yeah. When we shot *Snow White*, the thing grew rather naturally with that. That was the only sequence I know of that was done that way. And if I had stayed in animation, I would have got one of the scenes or two of the scenes or maybe ten of the scenes at the most in that whole sequence. But I got the whole sequence. I felt very good, because I loved the whole sequence. And everything in it was a feeling of mine, and there it was. So, I'm still confused. I don't know how a layout man makes a layout for an animator without animating it. You gotta put these things where... It's easy to make a set, but what the hell is a set? I was never a layout man for long. They had a hard time pegging me, because they didn't know what I was: a story man, a layout man, or just what the hell I was. They tried to make me an art director and we went to the art director's union and one guy there, the president, said they can't do it. The idea of a cartoonist being an art director! "We're big shots!" something like that, thinking cartoonists couldn't do that. So they kept spreading my name around those different things. Sometimes they'd put me in one side and then another. And I never did settle down. Walt used to call me the jack of all trades.

DJ: You said you were at MGM prior to coming to Disney.

KA: Yeah.

DJ: Why did you quit MGM to go to Disney?

KA: Well, the unit I was working in quit.

DJ: So you were without a job then.

KA: Yes, three beautiful pictures, one was Helen Hayes' *What Every Woman Knows*, the other was Greta Garbo in *The Painted Veil*, and I have forgotten the third one. Our unit was a separate unit from the rest of the studio. Then, when we didn't have any more pictures coming, they just folded the unit, and said, "We don't have any work, kids, stick around the phone." Never mind if we had a phone. I couldn't stick around a phone. But anyway, that's what happened there.

DJ: How did you find about the job at Disney's?

KA: I had sent up to Washington for my girl, Polly, and said, "Honey..." This was when I was still working at MGM. Gee, I was making 165 bucks a week. I had no idea... I was a millionaire, and doing work I loved, and I thought it was going to go on. I figured that if you were satisfactory, it was for good, it was forever. And it struck me terribly hard when it turned out to be otherwise. Anyway, I was working at this and I wrote to her and she was niece of Hormel [who owned Hormel ham]. The Hormels had a huge place in Bel Air, and they liked us. I had a suit and I wore the suit and went to their house and, gee, he was very particular. He said, "If you're going to get anywhere, wear a bow tie." This big, raw-boned German. Anyway, they married us. We were married at their property and I remember I had already lost my job.

DJ: What year is this? 1934 or 1933?

KA: 1934. And she had a car, she came down with her car. We didn't have a place to stay, because the little apartments that I was in were in the hands of litigation and they were padlocked. Akim Tamiroff and his wife were the bosses, and they liked Polly and me. They let us climb through the bathroom and we could sleep on the floor with an afghan rug. So we stayed in this place and rode around in her car and we lived on the beach two or three times. We ate canned beans. At least I was happy. It was about a month and I just went around and we stopped at MGM and got in and I asked if they started anything yet with the unit. No, they hadn't. So we were driving around West Hollywood one day we went by this Walt Disney place and Polly said, "Go in there and get a job!" I said, "Job? Me? You want me to go get a job, there? I don't know how you draw that stuff." She said, "Well, you go back to the big billboard with the [Disney ad] Post Toasties sign and figure out how."

So I went back, I studied the sign, and said, "Ah, three fingers! That'll do. They're going to pop a funny question at me, 'How many fingers does Mickey have?' and I'll know." So I went back and went in to see Ducky Nash at Disney and he said, "You got any of your work?" and I had a few. I did nothing but serious stuff and I had a whole bunch of those things. I took them in the next time, because he encouraged me to come back. So I came back, I brought in a big armoire of that stuff, and left it in his office. Then I must've created quite a havoc, because in that time Walt was looking for guys who did more than draw just those stick figures. I didn't know that. Here are these paintings and he evidently went to some trouble to find out who had done them and so on. And so they got me and they put me in a class. They didn't tell me anything, they just put me in a class.

DJ: With Don Graham?

KA: No, the class was a trial class under George Drake. John La Gatta was in it and John Falter, people who were top magazine illustrators. Boy, my heroes! They were sitting alongside of me. We were all trying for the same thing, to get admitted to this thing. And they were taking quarters and tracing around the quarters. And they were doing everything that they could to make a perfect thing. Well, they were all so imbued in their own styles, in their own work, that they couldn't do this other thing. We couldn't talk to any of the animators or anybody. It was quiet; you had to keep quiet. You could hear them walking all the way up to Drake's room and they never came back. He had a glass cage. He sit up through this thing as if...[cracks the whip].

Anyway, two weeks went by and I was the last one. "Anderson!" Oh Jesus, I went up and I could see all these guys all cringing on the way up and whispering. "Anderson!" he said, "I think you'll do! I think you'll do!" Just then the other door to his cubicle opened up and in came Freddie Spencer with a bottle of booze and a little paper cup and he said, "Have a drink, George, and happy vacation!" So George said, "Oh, thank ye!" and they had a back and forth, they passed it off. Freddie left this cup on the counter with the whiskey in it and went on out. George said, "Anderson, you must feel pretty good. Your drink!" "No, oh no, thank you, George; I couldn't do that, it's yours; I saw you get it from him. What's this about vacation?" "Well," he said, "the whole studio's going to close. We're going to be all through for two weeks. We're all going to be gone."

DJ: Is this during the summer?

KA: Yeah, August. So I could feel the guys looking and listening in from the outside. He said, "Go and have it," and I said, "OK." So I drank this thing down. And it was bitter. He gave me a chaser out of his Sparklet's bottle and I looked at him, and Jesus, his ears were red. They were waving in the breeze; he was real mad. Then he raged up and down like the mad gnome king. He said, "Goddammit, get off of the property. Don't you ever show your dirty, stinking face in here. Dammit, it's against the law to drink on duty. Get out of the studio, get going!" And he chased me clear out the gate, yelling at me the whole time. I would slow down and he kept coming up and he pushed me. So I went over and got in Polly's car and went all the way back to Culver City. Polly said, "Did you get the job?" I said, "I got it and I lost it inside of a minute!" I told her how, the whole thing. She said, "You're going back there in two weeks." I said, "Oh, no! I'm never going back to that dump! Not so long as I live!" She said, "You're going back." "No, I'm not!" "Yes, you are!" Anyway, she won the argument. In two weeks' time I went back.

DJ: He probably forgot all about it.

KA: "Anderson, how are you! Come on in! I'll see you." He had forgotten the whole damn thing.

DJ: How come Disney hired somebody who was so crazy?

KA: Disney never, ever saw him, I don't think. He was Ben Sharpsteen's brother-in-law. A bricklayer.

DJ: Because I understand he's a real neurotic and absolutely crazy.

KA: Anyway, there're a lot of ramifications about this George. He had a good pair of eyes for guys that knew how to use him, like Perce Pearce came in. Perce was an old *Captain and the Kids* drawer. He worked in a bank first and then when the Depression came they closed up his job and he went into doing drawings for this *Captain and the Kids* and make what he could on that. And Perce came out to the studio and he was a pure... He wore thick wool suits in the summertime with celluloid collars. Ah, geez, he was a little old man. Perce got on to George Drake. George was going to can him. In fact, George did can him. And you weren't anybody if you hadn't been canned by George Drake first. Perce was a very smooth operator and he found out that George loved to play bridge and he *had* to win. Perce knew how to make it work so that it looked like he was giving him a hell of a time and he could still let George win. George became absolutely fascinated with Perce Pearce. Because Perce and his wife would come over and they would work with Betty and George and let them win. So they told Walt about this marvelous guy: he had real funny ideas, real funny ideas. He was a great character developer.

DJ: Shamus Culhane told me that he stole most of his ideas from some of the other animators.

KA: He did, oh sure. That didn't have anything to do with anything. His way of doing it...he had a battery of pipes. He'd take a pipe out and [imitates Perce Pearce], "Well, I think, you know..." He needed to get this tobacco out. He'd take a stalling situation so that the words that he needed were supplied to him. He was always doing that with Walt. He never, ever came out with a blank idea: he waited until he could get it drawn out of Walt.

DJ: And Walt never caught on to him?

KA: Never caught on to him. Anyway, he was a real manipulator.

DJ: But didn't he draw some of the...

KA: Lousy drawer. Oh God, he was awful.

One of the stories is told about Dopey. Dopey was the only dwarf with blue eyes and the only dwarf who could wiggle his ears. And Walt had seen me wiggle my ears. And he said, "Hey, that's an idea! We'll do Dopey that way. You'll be Dopey. Dopey can really wiggle 'em. Here he can really make 'em go and he'll have blue eyes." [Ken Anderson has blue eyes.] So Dopey went from this to Fred Moore picking up on that.

DJ: Ward Kimball told me that Dopey was also inspired by *The Yellow Kid*, that old comic strip.

KA: I think he was, originally.

DJ: Do you know who might have thought of that?

KA: Well, I imagine it would be Walt.

DJ: Oh, Walt would have known about that?

KA: Oh, sure. Dopey was not drawn after the Yellow Kid. That was after the fact. The Yellow Kid was a character that probably Walt would say, "Hell, yeah, that's a good idea," or something like that and then they did it. But nobody drew it like this guy until at the end, after it was all done, came back and he acts like the Yellow Kid.

DJ: You don't think it was a conscious imitation of the Yellow Kid?

KA: No, I don't.

DJ: Do you recall who was the designer of the Huntsman?

KA: I can't tell you much about that because I didn't have anything to do with the Huntsman. I don't even know who did it, except Albert [Hurter]. I think he was a non-entity from the very beginning.

DJ: The Huntsman was originally called Humbert; he had a name. Then a man named Horvath drew one sketch of the Huntsman. I'm just curious if anyone seems to know where he came from.

KA: I always thought the Huntsman was one character who was poorly conceived. He just was a big nothing.

DJ: Do you recall when experimental animation on the dwarfs was begun? Was it right at the beginning?

KA: The way I remember it, they were always going to do it. There were never any indecisions about how's the best way to do it. Freddie [Moore] was one of the animators that they put on it early, because he had a natural fun way of drawing. He drew feet and things without knowing why and in positions that you'd never find in a life class and everybody would go ask Freddie, "How do you do this?" Then there was a great draftsman: Bill Tytla. And Bill kind of approached things differently than Freddie. He thought very deeply into things and came up with the thinking, but his drawings didn't have the same pleasure in them that Freddie's had. It didn't take very long after a dozen animators were on the picture for strong things to come forth. Freddie Moore wasn't necessarily a better draftsman than some of the others. He drew cute girls: everything was cute, everything was fun. And Walt took personal pleasure, so that it got that we were all kind of leaning on Freddie without meaning to. If we ever ran into a bug, why we'd go talk to Freddie and it'd be fixed.

DJ: Was there any period of, like months, before any animation was attempted?

KA: No, they were trying to animate from the beginning.

DJ: So they didn't spend two or three months on the story, they actually started experimental animation right off.

KA: The only way you can tell about a character is animating it. So they were animating scenes which were thrown away, or they were changed and used. They were working over and over and over again on this.

DJ: Do you remember seeing any of the early animation, like in sweatbox.

KA: Oh yeah.

DJ: What were they like or what scenes were they?

KA: I believe the bedroom was the first scenes that I saw. There were scenes of the dwarfs discovering the little girl.

DJ: That's what Wilfred Jackson said. He remembered that as being like the pilot scene.

KA: Right.

DJ: How did that differ from the final version? Was it a lot different or was it pretty much the same? Because the dwarfs hadn't really been developed by that time, had they?

KA: They grew through stages, all the way through. Then you'd find one that Freddie Moore had done and, "Gee, that's a good Doc!" And there'd been other Docs, but we were going to change them in cleanups and they'd be like Freddie's, and so on and so forth.

DJ: Do you remember any other early scenes other than that one?

KA: In the mine, sorting out diamonds and things. Those were scenes that the guys could have a lot of fun with drawing without ruining the picture.

DJ: Now, I know that early on in the story and in the story sketches, they made a lot of slapstick. For instance, in the early scene the Prince is shown...

KA: I remember why they were done. We were at a loss. The girl wasn't too bad to animate. The boy, the young prince, if you were going to believe him, really stumped you. He had to have flesh and bones; he had to move like he wasn't walking on broken eggs, and he had to be a good-looking guy without... He was just a terrible problem. So we figured the way to have him do things is to have fun with this guy. Fall in the water, and treat him like a cartoon character. Keep one character, the girl, and the Queen more believable. We don't need to make the Prince sort of a real guy.

DJ: So you think the comedy was a way to overcome the difficulties of drawing?

KA: Oh, absolutely.

DJ: So the whole movie wasn't conceived as just a bunch of slapstick scenes?

KA: Never. It was the only way we knew how to handle a human man. We didn't have anybody... We had Milt Kahl there, but we didn't know he could draw so well at the time.

DJ: And then Grim Natwick, of course, came in and did Snow White. Do you recall who Ham Luske had as his assistant?

KA: Ward Kimball. Ward was the only one who could thumb his nose at George Drake. He could say anything he wanted to about George Drake and they couldn't get him. Geez, he loved that.

DJ: Yeah, he told me about that.

KA: Ham had a hell of a time trying to figure out what you would do when you tipped her head back on the drawings and what kind of line would you use. He never did get it really settled. Walt figured the girl was supposed to look like our girls. Really his big problem was turning the head back. You're going to get it underneath the line even here. And once the line gets past that, if you don't carry that difference in this plane, the plane under the chin, with the drawing you're up against it.

DJ: Did Ham ever say anything to you about the conflict between the two approaches to drawing Snow White?

KA: Yeah, he did. Ham was interested in animating. He'd made the drawing of the girl very cartoony, much younger. He was always too humble. He didn't think he was the guy that should do this. Walt had picked him. He said, "Here I am in this god-awful spot. I have to do this girl and don't know how to do it."

DJ: He was that insecure?

KA: Very. He didn't jump in there saying to himself, "Hell, I know all about this, I'll do it." He was feeling his way all the way. I never heard Ham say anything against anybody. Ham was probably the nicest guy that ever lived.

Lucy and Isabelle Wheaton

Interviewed on February 1, 1990.

Isabelle Wheaton joined Disney's ink and paint department on June 22, 1934, and left the studio on September 17, 1943. Her sister joined the same department in 1935.

LUCY WHEATON: She's [Isabelle] the one that started there first. And we were very, very poor.

DAVID JOHNSON: From where?

LW: Arkansas. It was during the Depression. And everybody, all over the United States, was poor. My sister had the ability of air-brushing, which they needed at the studio. And they hired her in June.

DJ: Of what year?

LY: Of 1934.

DJ: Were you both living in southern California at that time?

LW: Yes.

DJ: And how did you come out to California from Arkansas?

LW: We came out in a Model T Ford. It took us three months. I worked along the way. I was a teenager. I had a sick mother and a sick cat. And I drove this car out. I burned my brakes out on Superior Highway in Arizona.

DJ: You were just looking for a job?

LW: I was coming to California to do art work because there was no work available in Arkansas. You either had to come to the coast or go to New York. My sister had gone to Buffalo as a secretary to a blind inventor. You took any job you could think of. It was just horrible. She was there and had a very good job, but that played out. And then she then worked with the Albright Art Gallery there in Buffalo. My mother was an artist. All of us had made money by working with photographic art. I was an art painter. Before Technicolor came in, you did painting of the sepia pictures.

DJ: Yes, you would color them in.

LW: That's a dying art. But that's how I came to California and started working at Austin Studios doing the artwork there at five cents a print.

DJ: What year was this?

LW: That was in 1932.

DJ: And your sister was in Buffalo at this time.

LW: Yeah, she was in Buffalo. She went east because she couldn't find anything for work and I didn't have any job so we just left, lock, stock, and barrel. With our security deposit we got enough money and for twenty dollars we bought a car, a Model T Ford. We started out with $30. Mother had just gotten her pension check.

DJ: What happened to your father?

LW: My father drowned when I was two, so there was only the three of us all our lives. Mother did retouching of photographs. That's how she raised us. Then she did painting of photographs, and always taught watercolor painting. We all made little art and painted Christmas cards. We did everything we could to make money, just to put food on the table. We started out, Mother and the cat and myself, with as much canned goods as we had, and we'd had a real bumper strawberry crop that summer. So we had canned strawberries, and we had some cans of tuna in the back of the car. That's how we managed. And whenever we needed a little money... The first stop was El Paso, Texas, and I started to work with a photographer there, and mother did retouching, and that is when Roosevelt was elected. All of a sudden beer was the most important thing. I had never had any beer. We just didn't drink. I never was so astonished by people wanting beer. Roosevelt was in and there was beer!

DJ: How old were you at this time?

LW: I was seventeen. I just graduated from high school.

DJ: You were in Texas.

LW: In El Paso. So we stayed there till Mother's pension came again. We only had $30 a month to live on. She had a $30 pension from my father, because he had been a Spanish-American war veteran. I was of older parents. Both my parents were up in their forties and fifties when I was born, so that's all we had. By the time we got to El Paso where we had money again, we had to wait till the next pension came. And so we just started to work. We were there, having started in September, until the pension came the first of November. Then we started out again. We got as far from El Paso to Lordsburg, New Mexico, and that happened. And then we wired for money from the east and my sister said she didn't have a penny. And the people in Arkansas didn't have any money to send. So we slept in the car. We were homeless. Finally we got a little bit from more work and we came up over the Roosevelt Highway and got as far as Globe, Arizona. We could get a place for a dollar and a quarter a week. We spent a little bit of money on a dollar and a quarter a week, with this old lady in her house, in a housekeeping room. And immediately we started out for the first photographer and we found a woman photographer, Mrs. Reeves, that was a widow raising two children. All of our friends were always widows raising two children, or one child. It never exceeded that. There are two times that are good for re-touchers: June for the brides, and November and December for Christmas. So if it's May and June you live pretty good and November and December there's lots of work. The rest of the time you sort of squeak by. And Mother did very fine hem stitching for the Jewish people in Little Rock. That's how we managed, and she did beautiful embroidery. She never finished the garments, she only did the beautiful artwork, the embroidery on them. Anyway, we went and stayed till after Thanksgiving, and the first check came in December. And then, we just felt real good. Coming down Superior Highway… You don't notice that now with the roads the way they are, but the road down from Globe, the canals are very high and go down this winding road like this into Phoenix. Anyway, my brakes burned out, coming down this road in this Model T Ford. It's a two-lane road with gullies on both sides, like Louisiana which were gullies on either side. If you got out, you'd go in the swamps in Louisiana, and in Arizona you were into real deep cliffs where the water goes when they have the storms. Drainage ditches is what it is. So I saw this one little road going off to the side and I quick-wheeled into it. It was a gypsy camp. I went as far as the car would take me till it stopped, and I stopped in the middle of a gypsy camp.

DJ: You must have been terrified.

LW: I was, and I was praying all the way and the Lord opened that place. They finally turned me around and got me back. Then I coasted down the rest of the way till the next auto court.

DJ: Was your mother talking during all of this?

LW: Mother was not well. The cat was quiet. It was a little coupe that we had, with just a little back, where you could put your provisions in. That was it. It was a 1926… But anyway, we got into this motor court and that night it snowed. It was the coldest night that you could imagine. That next morning we had to be pushed around the auto court three times before the engine would start. Fortunately, there was somebody to push us around till I got started. But every one of those sand dunes were like lemon meringue pies with the snow cap on every one of those. So you never tell me the desert was hot, it was so cold. [Laughs]. And we got into Los Angeles under difficult circumstances, because I still didn't have brakes. I was still very, very cautious in my driving.

DJ: How did you stop for a stop sign?

LW: You didn't. You'd go around a car. We didn't stop at signs back in those days. Way, way off you'll see a stop sign and it'd be hanging down the middle of the road.

DJ: So you would just gear down.

LW: Oh, yeah. I learned how to tighten those brakes. They have these things that are like that and you can turn the screws. I found out where the box was and I did that. And I changed tires. I did everything.

DJ: Where was this studio, the Austin...?

LW: It was up on Seventh Street and you would climb steps: it was either second or third floor.

DJ: So it was actually downtown.

LW: Seventh and Hope, between Hope and Spring.

DJ: Where were you staying then?

LW: In an auto court out on Florence Avenue. I went down there and got a job. I left my mother and went on the streetcar down to Los Angeles, got this job, and worked hard. I got to the point where I could make sixty cents an hour if I worked real fast. And I've always been a very fast artist. But it wasn't right at the beginning. Anyway, I think I made $3 that day and that was just wonderful.

DJ: This was in 1932?

LW: That was December of 1932.

DJ: How did you get to the studio?

ISABELLE WHEATON: There was a Depression on, you know. I had friend from Camden, Arkansas, who was moving from Seattle to Buffalo, New York. The young man was blind, and he needed a driver for his car. And the family followed in their car and had wrenches and one thing and another out of a baseboard box all the way out. Mr. and Mrs. Vickers had to follow with the lunches and stuff. I drove the car. It was Memorial Day and I remember looking out and it was very beautiful along this road when we went through St. Louis. This had all happened very quickly. Friends who knew the Vickers in Little Rock had recommended my driving. At any rate I didn't wreck the car. And we got to Buffalo, New York. The young man was an inventor and he did his work through modeling clay parts and he and his father were going to go into business with somebody in Buffalo. Buffalo was a very interesting place at that time, because every other building was a small business trying to get on its feet. There was lots more activity going on there than any of the other big cities. I had done negative re-touching, but what they needed at that time was positive re-touching. They would invent some kind of a machine and test it out and crack it up. They knew what the bugs were in it, but they had to have nice cut for a catalogue months in advance and the time it would take them to make the finished article. There were just hundreds of small businesses there. I went from one to another with my samples and got an airbrush. And the young man's sister drove him part of the time, I drove him part of the time. And I taught her to do the work. We had a studio in the basement in the house they rented in Kinderhook, New York, and we had pretty good business that way. However, it wasn't entirely wonderful. I managed to get on the WPA [Works Progress Administration]. Anyhow, I went to work at Albright Art Gallery, which was a salvation, and two advanced classes in painting and art, creative work. And I ran lantern slides for Rockwell Kent. I put the lantern slides on for his lectures, and altogether found the art gallery a very interesting place with lots of interesting people around. And the warmest set of boilers in the boiler room anywhere in Buffalo. It got to 27 below while I was there and driving on solid ice was no joke. Even Niagara froze over. But the two of us did fairly well, sharing the responsibility and the work. I would get off the bus, plow through the snow, and go in the boiler room door. It was wonderful, that warmth! [Laughs] I don't know whether I was more interested in Buffalo's industry or the warmth of those boilers. It was a large thing in my life. In 1933 I got word that Long Beach had gone all to pieces and where my family was had fallen apart. It was terrible. I didn't hear from them and I guess I wrote because we couldn't get through on the phones. I wrote the police department to please check on my family and see if they were all right.

DJ: Just your sister and your mother.

LW: She sent the sheriff after us.

DJ: But you were in Los Angeles, though.

LW: In Huntington Park, where it was the worst part of it, next to Long Beach. It was terrible.

IW: They had to sleep out in the yard for three weeks and it was a terrible time. The police went right over and I got a scorching letter from Mother. She said, "Oh me! To have the police..." [Laughs] He said, "Madam, have you written to your daughter?" And she said, "No, I haven't, I really couldn't get things together!" [Laughs] Anyhow, that was terrible, but in 1934 I got together enough money to come out to join them and live in Los Angeles. We were kind of a close-knit family and I very much wanted to get together. So I took the bus in March, I think it was, in 1934, from Buffalo, New York, to Hollywood.

LW: Across from Charlie Chaplin's studio [United Artists].

IW: So I got there and I read the want ads. I had my samples with me, and it was really funny because the bus was stopped at the border, and I said, "What are you looking for?" I had a large, flat portfolio of my work and the officer said, "Well, I was looking for boll weevils." I said, "I just came from New York and they don't have them there. I don't think you're going to find any and you might ruin my samples. I don't want my artwork ruined." There was a light-hearted girl that I happened to sit with on the bus and we sat and giggled while he went through the boxes and got his arm caught in the boxes and couldn't get it out. He let mine alone. I arrived right on the corner of Hollywood and Vine. And a little elephant came down the sidewalk.

DJ: Elephant?

IW: Yeah.

LW: They used to put on these shows at the Chinese Theater with live elephants.

IW: Anyhow, I caught a bus and went up to La Brea where they had an apartment in a cluster of little bungalows, like they used to have a court. I looked in the newspapers and I saw an ad for artists at Disney's. So I took my samples and bounced over and Hazel Sewell, the sister-in-law of Walt...

LY: Married to Walt's sister.

IW: ...looked at the samples and she said, "What can you do?" I said I thought maybe special effects or something like that, with the airbrush. That was fine. She got me into a seat in the inking department and there weren't very many girls. I don't think there were more than twelve or fourteen girls there at that time. That was just after *Three Little Pigs* made a big hit. They were doing *The Band Concert*, the first color Mickey picture, and they needed somebody to do the tornado airbrush. So she sat me down and got everything together. They had punctured needle-heads, punctured the roughed outlines... Instead of inking it on the cel to be done, they had punctured the holes in the drawings and then you blew that in and you knew where to do it. I said, "Is there an air outlet?" She didn't know. She said I just wanted to go over to the background department. So she took me over to the kind mercies of [background artist] Mique Nelson. He set me up for the airbrush. And I did the brush. That was 1934.

DJ: Was this your first day at work?

IW: Yeah, that was my first day. I started to work and there were visitors, as usual, because everyone, his cat and dog, wanted to see what on earth Walt was doing with this and that.

DJ: Had you met him yet?

IW: No. I hadn't met him yet. So I looked up and who was looking over my shoulder but Amelia Earhart. She smiled and watched me while I just went on working. I mean we were all exhibits. When we finished that picture there was some debate about the inking.

DJ: You were hired right away then, the first day?

IW: As I remember, I think so.

DJ: And were you hired for $16 or more?

IW: I have some of those figures.

LW: Ken Anderson's wife, Polly, and Isabelle and I all started at $18 a week.

IW: Then I went in to talk with Hazel and I said, "I want to get into the inking department." Actually, my inking was not that good. So she said, "It takes a great deal of skill. Why do you want to do that?" I said, "Because they make better money." She said, "I'll put you in charge of the painting, but not in the inking department. We're going to build that department up. We have to have a lot more workers and so I need somebody to be a supervisor of painting."

DJ: How long after you had started did she offer you this position?

IW: I think it was around a year or two.

LW: It was 1935, after I came in.

IW: 1935. It was when the inking...

LW: The push came on for *The Band Concert*, because when I started to work there it was black and white. In 1935 the Silly Symphonies were in color, but Mickey was not. We didn't start on *The Band Concert* till after I'd been there a month or so. At that time they wanted somebody to do airbrushing that wasn't black shadows, because up to that time it had been solid shadows and they wanted that you could see through it. This is why they were interested in her airbrush work.

IW: At least you could put a light spray and then you could see through it. It had a certain transparency.

DJ: Right about this time of *The Band Concert*, *Snow White* was starting in the early stages. Did you know they were planning a feature? Did the word filter down through the grapevine that Walt had decided to do this cartoon?

IW: There were rumors of it.

LW: But we didn't know what it was going to be. It was on the shelf and it was off the shelf and on the shelf and off the shelf. It was that way for ten years on *Pinocchio*. We knew about *Pinocchio* a long time before it actually came out. [Note: Not quite.]

IW: It was worked on for a while and then laid aside and then worked on again, all through a whole series of Silly Symphonies and shorts.

LW: We were doing *Water Babies* at that time. I did voices for *Water Babies* and that was fun.

DJ: Did you go to any story meetings on *Snow White* where the gag men would talk about different scenes?

LW: You want to know about the studio in those days? The studio in those days was definitely divided between men and women. I don't know if anybody's brought that up to you.

DJ: I know they called the ink-and-paint department the nunnery.

LY: It was the nunnery. We were not allowed over in the animation building and the animators were not allowed over in our building.

DJ: I didn't know that.

LW: There was no mixing.

IW: I was quite horrified.

LW: The only one was Walt's secretary and Roy's secretary were up there. And little Mary [Flanigan] that would deliver Cokes and candies and things like that. They were the only ones that were up there. And Hazel Sewell was our boss. Of course, being Walt's sister-in-law, she had the right to go up there and back, but her office was down in the nunnery with the gals. The only man that came through to us was the traffic boy. We only had one traffic boy in those days. And he went so fast that all our papers would flutter like this as he went past. [Laughs]. But that was how I met my husband [Al Taliaferro]. He was one of those people who didn't pay any attention to rules and regulations. He was a cartoonist. He worked on the newspapers. And his work paid for the salaries of all the animators and everybody else. At one time the whole studio was paid from the comic strip department. Because that was the only cash coming in.

IW: And all of sudden I was really bothered by it because it *was* against regulation. And after all I *was* responsible for getting her there.

LW: She was very embarrassed that anybody would smile at me and especially my clothes. She was very embarrassed if I wore anything revealing.

DJ: Did you go in as an inker?

LW. I went in as a painter. Not as an inker. Inkers were the inner sanctum.

IW: Special.

LW: They were so above the painters. Polly Anderson and I were both painters and we were looked down upon. They all were. They *felt* their position.
I sat by the window. Here was the animation building and a beautiful entry
way. Two stories. And the one they moved over to the studio there [the
cartoon bungalow]. The guys all came by and I just looked up and I smiled
at all the guys as I was turning my work over. Woolie Reitherman and Roy
Williams were right across from there. They used to flash their mirrors
[from their animation desks] at me to get my attention. And Woolie and
I got to be very good friends. Roy Williams was something else. We got one
of those ashtrays of Roy's. Everybody's got one of those, if you see them.

DJ: Is he still living?

LW: He drank himself to death. Most of them drank themselves to death.

DJ: I wonder why.

LW: Oh, it was awful, it was awful, really. But anyway, I don't really remember ever smiling at Al Taliaferro particularly. I just smiled at all the guys.
And then he went over to this little bungalow where he worked. And the
little bungalow was over there, out of my sight. That little bungalow is the
only thing that's intact at the studio today where he worked.

DJ: You mean at Burbank?

LW: They moved the bungalow intact. There were three buildings moved. But
that little bungalow is the only one intact, and it's right at the entrance as
you come into the studio right now. It used to be where the post office was.

IW: And Mary Flanigan had her little cubby-hole there, and then they added
some buildings to the back of her and from the top floor, the second floor
of those buildings, we looked down on the little new car that Roy Williams
had bought. And there was just one gag after another going on all through
the studio. Anyhow, the fellows filled the car *completely* with water. I mean
not with water, but a wheelbarrow balanced just with the handles here...

LW: Full of water!

IW: ...and the wheel here. And they filled that wheelbarrow so that you had
to start with a spoon not to get it [the water] in the car. We watched from
the second floor while that poor Roy sweated out getting that water out.

[...]

I can tell you some interesting things that happened about the music [for
Snow White]. We were living too far from the studio for commuting and
we moved into the apartments on Griffith Park Boulevard that Walt took

in as part of the expanding studio. There were four apartments, two lower, two upper. And he put the music work down in the apartment downstairs next to the studio and rented the other three. I rented one of those to be close to the work because it got pretty heavy there. One night we heard the most *awful* noise you have ever heard in your life. The screaming was going on and everything and we thought that somebody was being killed downstairs. We rushed down and so did the other apartment dwellers and it was the music group using that apartment and practicing for *Snow White*, practicing the witch's scream and so forth. [Laughs] We stood around and just leaned on each other and laughed. It was terrible.

[...]

I was looking frantically for a transparent paint for shadows and we followed up a number of different concoctions and I heard about somebody in the commercial district of Los Angeles that had gum tragacanth, I think it was. I went down to get some and ran through a red light and I was so tired... We worked so hard on the thing [*Snow White*] that I was just on edge. When I ran through the light I had picked up the gum tragacanth and the policeman caught me at it and was going to fine me for going through the red light. And I burst into tears and I sat there and I must have cried for, oh, I don't know, maybe fifteen or twenty minutes. And he said, "It isn't that serious. You're really going to live through this." I said, "It's just important that I get back to the studio. I've already been gone too long, trying to pick up this thing where we're doing this experimental work." He laughed and finally let me go. He said, "Now, I think maybe if you'll calm down a little more, you can drive on back to the studio."

LW: But that's how the tension was.

IW: We were *so* dedicated. It was just the most important thing that we were on. Mary Weiser was in the paint department and when I was looking for the transparent paint she wanted to know if I...

LW: See, we had a Guatemalan that was the one that mixed the paints, and they were such a special, special kind of paint. Mary Weiser worked with him, Emilio Bianchi. He's dead, but he was the scientist who mixed that paint just right. And he was from Guatemala. He was someone real special.

IW: The terrific devotion we had, the dedication to the purpose of everything would be rewarded by a bonus. And Roy [Disney] put a squelch on that.

DJ: You had a night crew on *Snow White*.

IW: Yes, and that was when I lived in the building back of the studio. I volunteered for the night crew. I was always volunteering for something. So I volunteered to take a night crew. I was looking everywhere, but I can't find the dates on it. We worked very, very hard, and I couldn't sleep days.

We were working on scenes from *Snow White*, trying to get it through. And I had a lot of inexperienced girls that wanted a job there and it was really quite rough. I would be so tired, I couldn't even climb the stairs to my apartment. I'd get down and crawl up. We had the girls, like the one that came from somewhere—I believe it was Boston—and got the job and she was so hungry. Walt served cookies and tea as a pick-up about mid-morning and afternoon and at night, like that. He would serve the cookies and hot tea. And she ate all the cookies on the whole thing. And the girls were just horrified and she couldn't do the work. It was really very sad. Finally we had to get transportation for her back to Boston through the Traveler's Bureau or Traveler's Aid. But the girls would come around and look at me and say, "That's just terrible! Look what she's done." So we had quite a time at night. I was so tired one night I came up and there was a wrinkle in my sheet and I sat down on the floor by my bed and cried. Mother, in the meantime—we had a fairly active little mother—got tired of my working so hard, so a friend came by going on the way to Yellowstone and asked if she'd like to go along. She left a note on the table, "Have gone to Yellowstone, will be back later." She didn't appear for, I guess another year or something. [...]

Evelyn Parsons, I believe, was the checker for the night crew.

When the picture was finished Walt came in with a painting cart, in which they delivered the paints to the girls to put on the cels, piled high with these great big compacts.

LW: Mirror with a powder.

IW: Enameled back and beautiful things from, I suppose, Robinson's, or someplace. And he gave each girl one, and the howl went up all the way down the thing. "Oh!" they looked in the mirror, "Oh, how *awful*!" They were so tired that when they opened the compact, with the mirror, and looked at themselves, they looked perfectly horrible! You could get pretty beat up at the end of a session of work at the pace at which we went.

LW: No written thanks, no note, just a compact.

IW: No, but he just came and walked down the aisle himself and handed that compact to the girls. Each girl had one and they all opened them up and looked at the mirror and they were all disheveled and face-smudged and everything and worn to a knob. They just howled. [Laughs] I don't know how conscious he was at what happened, but the girls were just *horrified* at what such awful hard work had done to them.

I did not get one thing extra for my work and I fell short of getting a vested interest by a few months because I took a leave of absence and did not go back. I went into the war.

LW: She joined the Army.

IW: Our grandfather was a mathematician of quite outstanding accomplishments and he had worked out wireless at the same time Marconi did. About fourteen of them came out with the idea at that time. He was not one of them. But every book in his library was on calculus and decimal calculus and all kinds of arithmetic which I didn't care for. I liked fairy tales and I had to go to the library for that. And *Snow White* was one of my fairy tales. So when I came out and joined the group out here, the way I did, I just felt like it was just a wonderful fulfillment and I thoroughly enjoyed the years that I worked there.

Marc Davis (1913–2000)

Interviewed in Winter 1988.

It's very difficult to imagine how drastically different Disney animation would have been without Marc Davis. As one of Walt Disney's "Nine Old Men" responsible for carrying the artistic brunt of the animated feature films, Davis was shrouded by the studio's policy of near (or total) anonymity for employees. But once Davis' accomplishments are revealed, his contributions seem ubiquitous in both the films and the theme parks. As a trusted Disney lieutenant, Davis' 34-year career provided the studio with three different sets of talents embodied in one man: his gifts as an animator and director, an expert story man, and his sense of character design.

Davis signed on at Disney in 1935 and was chosen to assist Myron "Grim" Natwick (creator of Betty Boop) to animate the character of Snow White—a plum assignment for the novice Davis. Realistically drawn human characters were far from routine studio fare and were light-years beyond the capabilities of most of the era's animators. "Marc was an expert animator even at that young age," Natwick said to John Province during his last formal interview, conducted shortly before his death in 1992. "I think they had him pegged as an up-and-coming talent even then." After the success of *Snow White*, Davis was given story and character-development work for *Bambi* and quickly become one of a very small group of exceptionally talented artists whom Disney trusted with the studio's crown jewels: the feature films.

Though the Disney studio was rife with budding talent, Walt was impressed with Davis' character work for *Bambi*, and he handed down the edict that Davis was to receive intensive animation training under the tutelage of future fellow "Old Man" Frank Thomas—a rare case of an animator's grooming coming at the boss' direct order. As a result, the Davis magic graced most of the feature films then (and now) hailed as classics, and Davis himself is personally responsible for some of the studio's most recognizable characters and finest moments, including some that Walt Disney himself cited as personal favorites. Davis' versatility in characterization seemed absent of limitations. Everything he did, he did well, from the cuddly Flower and the coolly patrician Maleficent, to the wild and angular Cruella De Vil and the shapely sprite Tinker Bell. These characters came to Davis' animation table as flat sketches and left as fully realized characters with distinct personalities that are today globally recognized. Indeed, Davis' realization of Tinker Bell is Mickey Mouse's rival as a virtual symbol of the Disney empire.

Davis left Disney's animation department after completing work on *101 Dalmatians*, transferring to WED (known today as Walt Disney Imagineering), where his talents were used to further Disney's interest in audio-animatronic attractions for the 1964 World's Fair, and later for the theme parks in Anaheim and Orlando. Once again, Davis' mastery of characterization, staging, and movement was harnessed to design and supervise the development of Great Moments with Mr. Lincoln, the Haunted Mansion, Pirates of the Caribbean, It's a Small World, America Sings, and the Country Bear Jamboree.

Marc Davis retired in 1978, but continued well into his 80s to be the soft-spoken yet intensely driven artisan that made him such a valuable asset to the Disney organization for decades. His influence was still felt as he advised a new class of Disney artists, and his retirement has been far from idle. His studio in Los Angeles was awash with projects in development, including a fully illustrated instructional volume on animal anatomy and movement and an illustrated treatise on the tribal inhabitants and folklore of Papua-New Guinea, a long-standing interest of his.

DAVID JOHNSON: You said that you came to the studio in 1935. When in 1935?

MARC DAVIS: December 2, 1935.

DJ: Do you recall how long were you there before you were made the assistant to Grim Natwick?

MD: I would guess maybe four months. It couldn't have been more than that. The studio was divided into two parts. Across the street, the spot where now there's a little corner market complex, the building that is now to your right, on the edge of the studio, we used to call it the annex and that was the inbetween department, but also it was where anybody new applied for work, and all the try-outs and everything that you went through was in that particular building. So the first two weeks you were there you were in a life class with Don Graham. Then, if you passed that, you went in and began to learn how to do inbetweens, which was how you paid for your keep. At that time you still would be going to the life class, but also there would be lectures by various people, animators, like Dave Hand and Ham Luske. They would come over and give a little talk and so forth. Then, as I say, as you began to do studio work, you were more and more employed on that, then you were kind of expected in the evenings to go into the drawing classes which they had. And also all the tried-and-true animators were supposed to go. Some of them would go, but by and large most of them didn't and there were some that showed up very, very seldom. The man who taught this was Don Graham, a great guy and a marvelous person, and really a true scholar on the art of drawing. I think the man knew as much about art as anybody I've ever come in contact with.

DJ: He had an engineering degree from Stanford, not an art degree.

MD: Right. But he was just curious about art. And he taught at Chouinard Art Institute and that's where he was located. Then later, when he left and went up north, I took over his course at Chouinard and...

DJ: When was that?

MD: This was like in 1947. And I taught at Chouinard's one night a week. I was over at the studio for 17 years. Finally, when we got so involved with the New York World's Fair, that was enough. I just couldn't... It was a matter of having to get somebody to take my class, because I was going back and forth to New York or staying in New York. Anyway, that was the reason I quit. And Don really gave so much, and not too many people really realize that. A curious thing: a man by the name of Jack Cutting saw Phil Dike and he said that one thing that Phil Dike said of me was, "Marc's the only one that really ever understood what Don Graham was talking about." I did, and what I got from him was tremendous. He offered so much. What was happening was really marvelous here. I've said this to other people before, but if you take *Steamboat Willie* that started in 1928 and look at the time I came to the studio in 1935, I guess they must have been working on *Snow White* fully a year ahead of that. So you're talking about six years from this very primitive thing to putting a film like *Snow White* on the screen that had emotion, believability, a heart, everything. Here people were crying at the same drawings, the same technique that was this little simple-minded thing in *Steamboat Willie*. So it was really an *enormous* accomplishment in a short space of time. It you take other businesses and artistic things and whatever, compare something that can jump that far ahead. How long it took modern art to discover African art or...

DJ: I know that Don Graham had a lot to do with that.

MD: He brought in many people, too. He was more than just Don Graham. He had a couple of guys that assisted him in teaching drawing: Eugene Fleury and Palmer Shoppe. Palmer ended up teaching art at UCLA. I think the other one taught at Chiounard's and then also was active in the business, designing.

DJ: Can you recall any specific things that Don Graham helped you on when you were doing *Snow White*?

MD: Nothing directly that you would say, okay, this is the way to draw.

DJ: Any comment he made that you recall sort of stuck?

MD: Not directly. He admired tremendously the work of, say, Bill Tytla, who was a very powerful draftsman. And Bill at the same time learned a tremendous amount from Don. He was one that really went over and really did take advantage of Don Graham's classes. We were encouraged by Ham to take advantage of what we got from Don.

DJ: What were some of the things you learned from him?

MD: It's the process of learning to draw. I had gone to three different art schools before I ever got there. So you say, "What did you learn from Don?" You can't say that. Can you say a particular teacher taught you how to play a certain key on the piano? I don't think you could do that.

DJ: I learned certain things from one teacher.

MC: Yeah, but I couldn't say out of a hat that I learned exactly this from Don. He was a very inspirational man. He taught a sense of graphics, how to put things down. He taught you to see things like what was flat on a piece of paper and what had dimension on a piece of paper, and how to do that. And how to stage things, in regard to living creatures. I think these were the things that I'd have to say are things that I can point directly to him.

DJ: In the class, didn't they have films of some of the animator's drawing so that they analyzed them?

MD: Well, yeah. Not in the regular life classes, no. But they would have what they called an action-analysis class and then you'd go in and draw and maybe learn from some of the cartoons, and he'd run something by a particular animator that he thought was especially good, and he pointed out what he thought was good about that. Then he sometimes would bring animators in, but, generally speaking, he'd mention, "Fred Moore does this or that," you know, like the staging of a pair of feet when a character's standing. He also brought in many experts. He brought in Jean Charlot.

DJ: What schools did you go to and for how long?

MD: The first summer I took a course at the Kansas City Art Institute.

DJ: Is that where you're from?

MD: No, I'm from everywhere. I went to 22 different schools before I got through high school, so we won't get into that. I went to Otis Art Institute here for little over a year, and then I went up to San Francisco to the California School of Fine Arts up there, and then eventually I did go to some classes at Chouinard's, like evenings and that sort of thing. So I really went to four art schools.

DJ: I suppose that you took the job at Disney's simply as a way of paying the rent.

MD: Sure.

DJ: I mean, you didn't aspire to be an animator when you were a child.

MD: Not particularly, no. I enjoyed the Disney cartoons and... No, at that time there was a problem: how do you eat? You see, you don't need to buy paintings, you don't need to buy diamonds, and you don't need to buy fur coats or Rolls Royce automobiles when things are that bad. You need something to eat, clothes on your back, a place to sleep. This was the period where that was a reality to all young artists. You couldn't sell a painting for hell, and even if you could do one good enough to be worthy of being sold... So I worked in sign shops; I worked in a painting shop; I did a lot of things of that sort, too, to survive on. Then I worked for a theater owner, and he called me over one day and said, "You ought to consider this Walt Disney fellow. I have a film I want you to see." It was *Who Killed Cock Robin?* and I had previously seen *Three Little Pigs*. So, anyway, when I saw that I thought, "Hey, this is something." But I thought in terms of like being a background artist. You're thinking of being an artist. So anyway, to make a long story short, eventually I came down here.

DJ: Where were you at the time?

MD: I was up in Marysville, California. We'd been up there and my father died. It's north of Sacramento, fifty miles north of Sacramento. Twin cities: Uba City and Marysville, separated by the Uba River. The man that I worked for up there owned a theater in Uba City.

DJ: It was nice of him to think...

MD: A lot of people were very nice to me up there. And I have a lot of Chinese friends still and there were some Chinese up there. A Chinese herb doctor was wonderful. And they'd give me work painting signs for them, and I learned how to do gold leaf. I did gold leaf signs in Chinese and all that sort of thing. And I could go in to the herb doctor's place and sit down, a little tiny place, and he'd give me a drink. It was some of the hottest liquor I've ever tasted in my life. Or if I had a cold he'd give me some kind of nose drops or something that he had. I must say, they always worked. His name was EM Tom. Anyway, I eventually did come down. I sent a letter in, because Disney was advertising all around the country. So I sent a letter on printed stationery. And there was an idiot man by the name of George Drake.

DJ: I've heard about him. He was head of the inbetween department.

MD: He was head of hiring. I wrote this letter that I was interested. And I received a letter back. "Dear Miss Davis: At the present time we are not hiring any women artists. At which time we do, we'll be happy to let you know."

DJ: Did you save that letter?

MD: No, I was sore. I wadded it up and threw it in the trash and forgot about the whole thing. And that was that. Then I decided to come down to Los Angeles. I had some connections through people that I knew up there. So I came down and they said, "I can get you an introduction to Leon Schlesinger" if I wanted it. "Gee, why don't you go out to Disney's? They're hiring people. Probably the best place around to work." Anyway, I went out and I was accepted.

DJ: You just went in.

MD: Cold.

DJ: Did you ring up for an interview?

MD: No.

DJ: You just walked in off the street?

MD: Went in and sat down.

DJ: Who did you see?

MD: George Drake.

DJ: Oh, you actually saw him. Because some of the people actually went to Walt that came in.

MD: It had to be a long time ahead of when I was there. Nobody saw Walt at that time. I'm trying to think of the name of the fellow that was sitting there next to me. Mexican. Marvelous guy. Eventually he did a great cartoon strip here in town. *Little Pedro*. [Probably William de la Torre.] But anyway, we're sitting there and he was so nervous and he'd drawn all these Mickey Mouse things and I didn't have anything like that. I had some samples of things I'd done. I'd done a lot of animal drawings, and I'd spent quite a bit of time at the zoo in San Francisco and, as a matter of fact, when the art school had their exhibition I had damn near half a room at [the] museum of my animal drawings that I had done. I didn't get the scholarship, which upset me no end. Then I found out if you didn't have a certain teacher there, you never got a scholarship. So that was about the time I cut out of that whole operation. Anyway, I was accepted at Disney, and, like, in the art schools, I was probably accepted on a Friday and came to try out on a Monday, which I suppose was December 2. I was there ever after, practically.

DJ: What was your reaction when you found out that they were working on a feature cartoon?

MD: I didn't think much about it one way or the other, except that when I sat there, waiting for the interview, I saw one guy, George Goepper, and he had these drawings, and they were effects drawings and they were pie tins, a whole bunch of them. They were drawn in a single line. I saw this and I thought, "My God, I couldn't draw those in a hundred years!" Of course, you didn't realize how may roughs went into doing a thing like that. I almost thought, "God, I don't know whether I ought to stay here for this or not." Finally, as I say, I went in and Drake was charming and thought my stuff was great and so forth and that was it.

DJ: Were you curious about this new feature?

MD: I think we all were. I think curious is the word. But as I say, there wasn't that kind of communication particularly. And it wasn't until I moved across the street that I had much contact with really seeing drawings on that, because they weren't bringing dwarf drawings across the street particularly. They were working on shorts and we inbetweened on *Three Little Wolves*. This was the one that had the wolf pacifier. But that's about all that we did over there, which was just kind of a test. In the meantime they were building up the units across the street [in the main studio]. So the inbetweens on *Snow White* were done right in that one unit. Eventually, when I became Grim's assistant, I worked more with the extremes, and then handed them off to a third person who would do the inbetweens on these things. Then I would do the clean-up.

DJ: Do you recall the first scene that you did on *Snow White*?

MD: No. I can remember they were things in the dwarfs' cottage, if I recollect the first ones that I worked on with Grim. And some of the cleaning of the house.

DJ: That was the "Whistle While You Work" scene. I thought that was one of the earliest scenes done. I noticed that there are three main versions of Snow White on the screen.

MD: Oh, there's at least that, sure.

DJ: Three distinct ones, but the one that I dislike the most is the very cartoony one that is what I thought may have been the very earliest scene done before she became more refined and mature looking. And that is the scene right before "Whistle While You Work." It was after the forest scene, when Snow runs to the dwarfs' cottage and she looks in. She has these very big eyes, she looks like Betty Boop a little bit. Now after that scene she isn't like that except...

MD: Oh, I think that was Ham Luske and Jack Campbell.

DJ: Is it?

MD: I think so. I'm pretty sure. I didn't work on that.

DJ: I thought that may have been one of the earliest scenes, because then she looked like... Much of the movie she looked like your model sheet. And that looks like Marge Champion.

MD: Could be. Grim had very strong feelings of how he felt the character should look and was in conflict with what Ham thought. But Ham was the key animator on this.

DJ: Tell me about this conflict between Ham Luske and Grim Natwick, maybe apropos these drawings. [Looking at various Snow White drawings.] I notice a difference already. This one is very cartoony and Betty Boop-like and this one isn't as much.

MD: Yes, but what you're not understanding is that Grim Natwick is the man that invented Betty Boop.

DJ: Yes, I know that.

MD: But he was not drawing that way at all and these have to be drawings by Ham Luske or by Jack Campbell.

DJ: He did some nice work on Snow White, I thought.

MD: As I say, this depended on where you sat. There was conflict between the two units.

DJ: Tell me about this conflict.

MD: They didn't like what the other one was doing. That's conflict.

DJ: Yes, but in what way didn't he like it?

MD: Grim thought that what Ham was doing was a pile of shit and, in turn, Ham thought the same thing of Grim's stuff. So that's a conflict.

[Break in recording]

DJ: Things like "Heigh Ho," you wouldn't have heard that.

MD: Oh yeah, oh sure.

DJ: How would you come to hear that since you were in...?

MD: The rooms were like made out of paper there. Somebody's running a moviola and running some of their animation, you'd hear this, you heard it all day long. You heard all these things.

DJ: So you'd be working in one office and they'd be doing another scene and then you'd hear what was going on.

MD: Oh sure, sure. Then you'd hear this thing going backwards which was great fun when you hadn't heard this before. Listening to sound, dialogue, backwards, makes an awfully funny sound as you probably know. As I say, those were things that were new, and you listened, and this was exciting. This was what was new in this new business that you're in. We had great faith in this thing. We weren't close enough to the business end of it to realize the worries that Walt had at that time. In my position I certainly didn't. They were doing this, period, but we didn't know that he was sweating blood for money and everything else. And, you know, at that time, meeting Walt... I was just one of a number of guys that would be in the projection room. I'd be in when Grim had his stuff and there'd be three or four of us and Walt. But Walt would be talking to them and making suggestions. To get to know Walt at that time... You didn't. It wasn't till after I worked on *Bambi* that I got to know Walt. The reason I got to know Walt on *Bambi* was that he liked the drawings that I had done and he decided that he wanted to see those on the screen. I worked on story for about three years on *Bambi*. And then he decided... Anyway, he saw the drawings that I had done on story sketches and the model sheets also, and he wanted to see this guy's drawings on the screen. [He told] Milt Kahl and Frank Thomas, "Teach him how to animate." That's how I became an animator.

DJ: He probably wasn't even aware that you did all...

MD: No, he wasn't aware of anything. He had too much going on to be concerned about that. The interesting thing to me... I've done a hell of a lot of model sheets, but I've got lots of them in there, like Tinker Bell and Sleeping Beauty, and you name it. Some of them I worked on characters like Cruella De Vil and I never did a model sheet on her, because I did all of her. I never had any reason to.

DJ: Do you remember anything particular about Grim Natwick discussing some of the problems of Snow White with you?

MD: Oh yeah. He would sit down and give a drawing lesson, and he was a very interesting artist. He had a tremendous facility that I don't see in any of these drawings that would indicate that they were Grim's. [Marc shows his *Snow White* book of discarded drawings] Grim would work on both sides and true things up. He worked like hell! To say that anybody knew what the hell they were doing at that was a gross [exaggeration].

DJ: [Looking at Snow White drawings of "Some Day My Prince Will Come".] So he's the one that did make Snow White into the very believable character.

MD: Yeah, I thought so and I always felt I worked for Grim and my allegiance was to him.

DJ: You're a superb draftsman. Can you tell me why there is red and black?

MD: Oh, I don't know. It was a really stupid way that people had of drawing at that time. They'd rough it in with one color and then clean it up with another, which is quite unnecessary, and actually kind of dumb. It's not necessary.

DJ: They'd rough it in with red and then clean it up with...

MD: Yeah, you see the red drawings there would eventually be penciled in with black. It would just give a drawing two shots. It was just a dumb way of drawing, that's all I can say. Later we would never do that. These were kind of throw-away roughs.

[Regarding Grim's drawing on the reverse side of a sheet]: He didn't trace them on the back. He tried to true-up his drawing, because it was hard to see these things. So if you took and reversed the thing, the light board there, he'd try to... Then he'd erase the front and re-draw. Try to true-up the drawing.

[Regarding the "Soup Eating" sequence]: It certainly didn't belong in the picture.

DJ: Do you recall what scenes gave Grim the most problems or did he have trouble with all of them?

MD: I think everybody had trouble with all of them. I don't think you can isolate these. As I say, people were doing things they'd never done before and had never been asked to do before. This certainly wasn't Betty Boop and you were asked to make something believable. And with all that, even with the mistakes, it turned out that way: people believed in *Snow White*. This was the first time that anybody had ever done action where it was line to line to line. Even now, you wouldn't plan things to do that way. In other words, animating one line going right into the next line on each paper, close. A lot of the stuff on *Snow White* was inked and painted. And these cels were subject to humidity change and temperature change and waiting to be shot in color. And they warped. When you take line-to-line animation that's warped they'll jitter. A lot of the Prince, a lot of Snow White was that way.

DJ: So it had nothing to do with the drawings.

MD: No, it wasn't in the drawings. I was not in the original animation on the screen. It was in a completely technical situation. I was one that complained, because at this time the animation paper had just two holes in it. And I complained. Anyway, they got a guy from CalTech to come over and look at this thing. The result was the old pegs were two pegs up here, they were in between. You're flipping and flipping and flipping these things. It was awfully hard to keep these things from being uneven. So you could even ink and paint these things and have that jitter in them. Anyway, I knew there were jitters in stuff that I worked on that was not in it originally. And in the new studio out there they established humidity control, dust removal. So the new studio was built to accommodate a lot of things that were wrong with *Snow White*, besides the fact that they needed more space and they ran out of room down here. They couldn't build anything more. And it was a wise move, actually. They got property in the days when it was pennies out there. So anyway, somewhere along this time came in the six-and-a-half field plus the new peg hole.

DJ: Did you have any interaction, even though you were Grim's assistant, with Jack Campbell or Ham Luske?

MD: Oh yeah. But, as I say, I worked with Grim and whatever Grim did or said I felt obligated to do what he wanted. I couldn't be dishonest with this guy I was sharing a room with.

DJ: As the assistant animator, did you do any rotoscope tracings?

MD: No.

Interviewed again on February 5, 1990:

MARC DAVIS: They needed some guys who could draw. The majority of them could not draw very well. That included guys like Ham. Ham was a hell of a fine animator, but as an artist, as a draftsman, I don't think he was too great. But again he's the guy who did Jenny Wren. And that's a beautiful caricature done in the movement of Mae West. That was some great thing. Ham did that. He may not have done it all, but I thought that was so great before I came to the studio. It was one of the reasons I came to the studio.

DAVID JOHNSON: How interesting.

MD: Then when I was put in with Grim there was a conflict between the two units. Jack Campbell had worked with Grim and they were in complete disagreement.

DJ: This was just over the character of Snow White, or on other things as well?

MD: Oh well, no. This was the point. Anyway, Jack saw it was probably smarter to hang on to Ham Luske than it was with Grim. So he ceased to be Grim's assistant and I became Grim's assistant. A guy that followed me up on this was Les Novros.

DJ: Did you ever have a discussion with Campbell, did he ever sit over lunch and say, "Why are you doing this? Why do you feel this way? I feel it's this way and these are my reasons."

MD: I wasn't in that position really to do that. I felt that since I was work-ing with Grim that my loyalty was to go on with what he sought, so I did. That was it.

DJ: You must have been curious why there was a conflict and especially since you were thrown right in the middle. You don't remember ever talking to the other party?

MD: I had a lot more experience worldwide than a lot of these other people. I went to twenty-two different schools before I was out of high school. I'd seen a hell of a lot more life than a lot of these other guys who just came out of grammar school and high school and "here I am."

DJ: Twenty two schools? Was your father an Army person?

MD: No, he was a rainbow chaser. I lived in oil fields and all kinds of boom towns and you name it, I've lived there. As I say, I found going from one place to another or the different bunch of people, no problem. No, it didn't concern me at all that they weren't getting along.

DJ: I don't mean just the fact that they weren't getting along. But why there was such a disagreement. What was the core issue?

MD: As I say, I bought them because I was put with him and I felt obligated to do what Grim wanted. So I did. Naturally these things are disturbing. You can't help but be bothered by it. But as I say, I could take Grim's expla-nations quite well, and Grim was a man who had studied drawing in Europe and so on. He had great admiration for other people's talent. I don't think I've ever known anybody who had more than Grim. Something that was done, good god, he wanted you to see it. It was something that Tytla had done or something that Fred Moore had done. And it didn't matter who had done it, but he was that way. I think this was great.

DJ: What was it about Ham Luske's approach to Snow White that he disagreed with, other than the fact that she was a little bit too cartoony looking?

MD: Kind of a little doll, you know, that didn't have character and person-ality that Grim saw. And as I say, I think Grim was basically right.

DJ: Did he sit down and discuss what his feelings were? He must have talked about it.

MD: Nah, he yelled "Shit!" and a few things like that, too, like any human being does.

DJ: Then he didn't go into the concept of how he felt Snow White should be.

MD: Oh yeah, of course, because he drew it. It was on paper. It wasn't the same as the other. The other was kind of a little balloon-headed doll.

[Break in recording.]

MD: I dislike animation that doesn't have bones in it. To this day I feel a lot of things that are done...Including the Little Mermaid who has no bones in her arm, no spine in her back.

DJ: What you're saying is that Grim was really into anatomy.

MC: No, it's not anatomy. It's bringing a thing to life that you can accept, and it looks good, feels good. It's not anatomy.

You see, primarily you had something begin done for the first time by a bunch of people who had never done anything like this before. And since they're human beings, they disagree with one another, that's all. None of them knew what the hell they were doing, really, except trying to do a good job on this thing.

DJ: You mentioned how you went to ballets and films.

MD: Oh sure, because this was exciting. We were in a new business. Hell, we didn't know anything about it. We had to learn. So we went to things of that sort. I remember Nijinska, who was Nijinski's sister, had a ballet school out on La Cienaga, and another fellow and I used to go out there occasionally and ask if it would bother her if we came in and sat there and draw. She was delighted and she said, "Oh, this is just like Paris!" In other words, artists didn't do that.

DJ: But you took that on yourself, though.

MD: Of course. Anybody who didn't do that on their own was a dumb asshole, that's all I could say. I just don't see how you can take a stupid head and figure how you're going to get something that's going to be unique and marvelous unless you learn everything you can about it.

You have to again look at the times that this was. Now you can go out there and a guy can get a job, he can make more money than we were making by putting groceries in a bag in a checkout counter. We were struggling to survive. So you needed a pair of shoes, you needed a pair of pants that didn't have a hole in the seat. You needed a place to sleep, and you needed some food. Anything over that was a bonus. So this was the time the studio was going. You didn't have money enough to date a girl or anything like that. On Friday nights there were fights at the Hollywood Legion Stadium, and we'd go up there and for fifty cents get a seat around the outer perimeter, which were great seats. And see a great deal of fighting by guys, many of them who later became world champions. Then after that we'd go over to Vine Street, go to a bar. We'd have something like a Cuba Libre.

It's Coca Cola and rum and they squeeze a lime in it. We had a couple of those and that was for one dollar and that was your entertainment. This all had a hell of a lot to do with the studio in what we did. We would get the cheapest seats at the Philharmonic Auditorium when the ballet performed. We went to all the theaters and some of these great films you're going to see and so on. Then a lot of these things you'd go several times to understand why did they pan this camera and all of a sudden cut in to something.

DJ: Can you remember anything specific that might have related to *Snow White*?

MD: No, not really. A little later after that there was a theater on Vine Street and Walt would take over this theater and they would run an evening of unusual films. This would be Chaplin films, the comic things. Your travel films would be... I remember seeing one of the times of Krakatoa erupting, a film of that. Extraordinary things, some travelogue things that Walt... Oh, Mount St. Michel, I remember that.

DJ: Was this required?

MD: Probably. Yeah, I guess they suggested we see it. Kind of required.

DJ: But there wasn't any attendance or anything like that taken?

MD: Oh no.

DJ: Attendance was taken with the Graham art classes, wasn't it?

MD: I guess so, I don't know. But, you know, you wanted to do these things.

DJ: *You* did. But I think a lot of people resented it.

MD: I think the ones that resented it were the older guys that had a position and thought, "Why the hell should I do this?" I can't give you examples. But then again, along with the Don Graham art classes, they would have those guys from the studio proper come over and give talks. For example, the guy who was a director of *Snow White*, Dave Hand, came over and gave a talk.

DJ: What would he give a talk on?

MD: On being a director and so on, what his position was, what his relationship was to Walt. And Ham Luske gave talks. Don Graham also would run film. He'd run the Disney pictures. He would analyze what was done. He also would take film of action analysis, sixteen millimeter film, like a man driving a stake, something like that, to show how the anticipation would be and various things of that sort and analyze them for you. It helped, it gave a unity to a character which you could not probably have gotten with the talent of that time or even, for that matter, now. Why do it the hard way? A good animator... You rough in your conception of the action and then you would have it shot. Then we'd analyze this thing and we'd make changes on it and so on. We'd kind of call that your first rough. The live action also served as first rough. If you trace this thing you got something that was the deadest thing you ever saw. This was something I think a lot of people still don't understand. An awful lot of so-called Saturday morning animation is just practically live action traced, and it's dead. It's about as dead as anything can be. To use live action right, you've got to look at this thing and say, "This doesn't work for a lot of reasons for animation," and then make those changes. At least that was the way I was working at it. It isn't that you couldn't animate a lot of those things, but you're doing it the hard way if you didn't have the advantage of some live action.

DJ: Especially for drapery.

MD: A dance, for instance, or a personality walk or something like that. It'd be a great aid for those things. Also it's a unifying thing, because generally it's rare that one animator would ever animate a character from beginning to end. The only time I ever did was Cruella De Vil in *One Hundred and One Dalmatians*. That's a rarity on a picture. Margie Belcher was a great talent and she had this background in dance and I think they were very lucky to get her. She was a very good choice for the live action for Snow White.

DJ: Were you ever involved with any of the live-action filming?

MD: Not on *Snow White*. I was on other things.

DJ: But Grim would have been involved, wouldn't he, in some of the live action?

MD: I don't know how much. I don't recall.

DJ: I know Ham was.

MD: Well, Ham was the head. But I don't know how much Grim was involved with that if at all. I don't really recall that he ever was. See, there were two groups of people in the studio: there was one that had been there for a long time that was from the west, and then there was the group that came in from the east. Of course Grim was one of those, and Shamus Culhane and Norman Ferguson for that matter. But Norm had been here longer. He started in 1929. But he never, ever, became a westerner. He always dressed like he could walk down Fifth Avenue in New York. He was that kind of a guy.

Anyway, there was this feeling between Don Graham and George Drake... to build up the studio. And they took a trip to New York, and they were in Radio City Music Hall. They had advertised, and they were enrolling people there. Then they brought out a whole bunch of people. There was a big gang, and these were the ones that were coming in to be in the animation end of the business. But they were guys that if they'd had their druthers they'd have been doing all the cartoon strips. But animation gave a hell of a lot of employment. That was in the New York area as well as out here. There were the Fleischers and all the various studios. So this was the way, in hard times, to make a living. Starting a cartoon strip wasn't an easy proposition. If I remember correctly, two guys, Tom Codrick and Hugh Hennesy, came from Washington, D.C. Women weren't given much of a chance. There were some women that were damn talented people.

The younger people didn't have that much contact with the story department. We were not invited in the meetings at that time. The meetings that I would be in would be in the director's office, what they called the music room, or in the sweatboxes where you would review the film. And at least occasionally you'd be in there, sitting rather quietly if you were an assistant, but listening to what went on. And this would include Walt and whoever the director was of the sequence. In that case probably Dave Hand or Wilfred Jackson. So you began to see how these people worked.

DJ: When you were working as Grim's assistant, did Walt ever come in and comment directly to Grim?

MD: No, and this was a rule. Walt made a rule. He used to come in into animator's room and wonder what the hell this was. Finally, he realized you couldn't tell anything from that. It was costing a lot of money and everything else, so he made a rule that no director, including himself, could go into an animator's room and make comments about what the animator's doing. And that was the rule as long as I was ever there, and it was absolutely marvelous.

DJ: Did he ever come in to compliment Grim on one of his scenes?

MD: No, he didn't do that either.

DJ: Since you were such an admirer of Grim and later you became fairly close to Walt, did you ever ask Walt about Grim?

MD: No, I had no reason to.

DJ: The reason why I'm mentioning this is because I don't think they got along. I don't think Walt appreciated him very much because for most of the stuff discussed on *Snow White*, Walt always mentions Ham Luske as the animator of Snow White.

MD: Well, Ham was put in charge of the character.

DJ: But Grim did so much of it and so much great stuff.

MD: Still, Ham was the guy that Walt put in charge of the character. And this is what made the conflict very difficult, because of that. As I say, here's the guy that's the head guy and you're working presumably with him and you're not giving him what he saw in the character, you're going off on your own. I don't think Ham ever agreed with what Grim did. This thing was starting something from scratch, which hadn't been done before. I think that the two approaches could have been blended together better than they were. I look at it now and there's a lot of things I don't like. But I don't think that's important. I think that this thing pays off. I think it's damn good. It's a wonderful film.

Ham was a guy who had an awful lot to do with what was good at that time.

DJ: When you said he didn't understand or try to figure out what Grim wanted to do, what did Grim want to do that you feel he wasn't interested in?

MD: Grim was a more highly trained draftsman by a long ways, and he was trying to bring these things in that he felt… As I say, the two of them went in two different directions. Ham was for doing the kind little round-faced cutesy kind of thing, and Grim was trying to get a little more vitality than Ham was. I don't think that Ham realized that he wasn't… There was another man who was in the middle of this, Jack Campbell. Jack saw which way the winds were blowing and it was worth more to him to cooperate with Ham than to to cooperate with Grim. So Campbell and Ham had one approach and Grim had another. I tried to do what Grim wanted, because I was working for Grim. It was that simple. And I didn't do myself any good either by doing that, because, as I say, they wanted me to draw the thing their way. Well, I didn't have that right to draw it their way.

DJ: The thing that's interesting in watching the movie many times and looking at these model sheets is that ultimately the character in most of the scenes looked more like this than she did like this, which is the original way that Ham drew her, with those big eyes and very cartoony. Because eventually Ham got her to look much more like the way Grim did. Now that must have been Walt who must have seen the rushes.

MD: I don't know how much animation Ham really did after a while on this, but…

DJ: According to the production book, he did a fair amount.

MD: Never mind the book. What I'm saying is that Jack Campbell was working with him and I figure that Jack worked on most of the stuff that Ham did and Ham kind of set the character.

DJ: Grim remembers that you were his assistant and that also Campbell early on was his assistant.

MD: Campbell was his assistant before me and was kind of in between there, and then finally he was over with Ham and then he pretty much stayed with what Ham wanted. Ham was a very important man at the studio. This is like in the White House here, you're not going to do very well unless Reagan likes you, you know.

DJ: When you were first Grim's assistant, was Campbell still there? Did the three of you work briefly?

MD: Oh yeah, I think we did a little bit. I don't remember. I knew Jack pretty well, or got to know him very well. But as I say, he was kind of a loner as far as Grim's unit was concerned. There was Grim, myself, and there was Lester Novros and another fellow who came in there later and worked doing a lot of inbetweens and so forth.

DJ: I found out that Bob Stokes did a big scene on *Snow White*. He did the whole pie-making sequence. ... When you were working with Grim did he ever say that he was disappointed? The reason I'm asking you this is because... I didn't really discuss it with him, but I had a feeling that he was kind of upset about the whole Snow White bit, because if you read a book that was authorized by the studio all you'll read about is that he drew some of Snow White, but that Ham Luske really was the big guy on Snow White. Now if you read other books on Disney animation other than the studio-authorized books, you read that Grim Natwick was the most important animator on Snow White.

MD: To say most important, it's hard to say on that. I think that Grim's approach was a search for a little more vitality in drawing, and I see a lot of these things here that I know that weren't his, and there's absolutely no vitality in it. Every one of these pictures, I don't care which picture, there's always somebody that has a different feeling about something than somebody else. That's the hardest thing. When finally it's set and Walt says, "Yeah, that's the way I want it!" then how do you control this and say, "OK, but this is what was bought?" You cannot get down and keep changing the character, changing the character, and changing the character. I remember Frank Thomas saying one time, "When you get down to the last two scenes of the character on a film, then you know how you should have done the whole thing." I absolutely agree with that. I know many things I've done, God, in the last few scenes when you hit something, you know, geez, that's the way it should have been. But now three reels are already in the can, all set to go. So, a lot of this stuff that you're talking about here, disagreements and that, these are simply the discomfort of putting a lot of creative people together and they have to work together. See, I say the greatest thing that Walt Disney ever did was getting all these artists to work together and not kill one another. He did it very well, and the greatest thing he did was everybody was called by their first name. If everybody was Mr. Luske, Mr. Natwick, Mr. Davis, and so on, you might get a gun and shoot the guys that came out the door. There's always these things, but this was a family, and members of a family don't necessarily like one another either, you know. It's that kind of a set up. This is what a lot of that is and a lot of these things sound extremely petty. I think they were. And again you have egos. One guy says, "I'm the head guy, how come we don't do it my way?" Well, somebody else has a better way than yours. But unless Walt were to come and say, "Hey, wait a minute, I like this the way so and so is doing it better than you're doing it," nothing will happen or nothing would happen in those days when he was alive.

DJ: I felt that maybe that is what happened. Why the character is basically more consistent than she may have been, because if half of her... In very few scenes does she look really cartoony, and I have a feeling that after Grim got to her that Walt may have liked that approach better and may have brought it out of Ham's drawings more.

MD: I don't know if it ever got to that point. It may have been in sweatboxes that I was not privileged to be in, but I was in a lot of them, and it was a matter of Walt looking at something and saying, "Yeah, yeah, yeah, yeah, that's OK," or saying "Nah, something wrong here, let's do this."

DJ: Were these sweatbox sessions mostly roughs, though, or were they actual cleanups? Because if they're roughs it's mostly animation you're talking about rather than details of character.

MD: These things were done pretty clean. If you remember the book of mine you looked at there, the drawings... There's no way that anyone knew how to do her rough, because of the crutch of the rotoscope that was used at that time. And try to do drawings and here's some boy that traces this film on a moviola, which was really what it was.

DJ: Yeah, Ken O'Connor.

MD: Well, there were a lot of them doing it. That's a rough thing. So then here you have all these pencil drawings that are ungainly, out of proportion, and you put a line around any photograph and it's going to be lousy. So then, you work from that. So by the time you're working on this thing you're doing a pretty clean job to begin with. Grim was inclined to be more rough than anybody else, I think, in regard to that. Although Tytla and Fred Moore were very rough in their animation of the dwarfs. And the vitality of Tytla's drawings, and of Fred's drawings, too, was done rough. They were also not depending upon live action as we had to for the girl and for the Prince and, I guess, the Queen. Of course there was live action for the Witch, too, but Fergy was the roughest animator around. Drawing was not something that gave him any pleasure, but he liked to move things around. He was awfully good at it. Tremendous at it.

DJ: The reason I was bringing this up again, about the conflict that you mentioned, is because Grim doesn't really recall anything. And I don't think that he is trying to be nice.

MD: No, I don't think so, but this was a tough period.

DJ: I always had a feeling that he felt... Here's a man of immense ability and experience in animation who created Betty Boop, etc., etc., who was only at the studio maybe two years, and who left. Now I know he went to Florida because he was a Fleischer person to begin with and Fleischer wanted him. But I think if he would have been treated differently, he would have stayed on at Disney's.

MD: Oh, I think so, but again, as I say, for lot of people, here was a man that was a lot more mature than a lot of the others. He was older, and I asked somebody when I was working with him, "How old is Grim?" At the time he said he was fifty, but he must have been in his late forties. So, here was a man a lot more mature in age than a lot of others and he had studied drawing and painting in Europe and he was very dedicated to what he thought. He was a tremendously skilled draftsman. He wasn't very consistent always in what he drew, but he could sometimes do some drawings that'd just knock your hat off. But you know, as I say, this was different. And every guy there was different, and at that time there were guys from Europe. They were from all over. Like Albert Hurter and [Gustaf] Tenggren who was a marvelous illustrative artist. He had a great deal to do with setting the style of the picture.

DJ: I don't think he's ever been given very much credit either.

MD: No, Well how do you give credit on the thing? You know, this was the first and I think Walt was grasping at straws.

DJ: Everybody mentions Albert Hurter, but Tenggren did a lot of stuff, too.

MD: Oh yeah. Yes.

DJ: Ken O'Connor keeps saying that he was very much influenced by Tenggren's inspirational water-color sketches. ... Grim did say about Milt Kahl that he did some of the early scenes of the Prince. And then I know he eventually did redo the Prince, the scenes that were redone. But he worked as an assistant for part of it with Grim, because Grim told me that Milt at the early stage would do the

rotoscope perfectly, exactly the way it was, but he said there was no life to it, because it was difficult to convey how to do that.

MD: That's what I say: nobody knew how to make a picture like this until it was half done. Nobody had done a Snow White, nobody had done a Prince, nobody had done these animals. Nobody had done the dwarfs; yes, that was a lot more understandable, but doing the animals and the human characters there, this was a first. I was very pleased and I was very surprised when I saw it. It had been many years since I'd seen it. And to see it with a full audience at the Paramount Theater, and to experience the reaction of the audience… God, they all cheered when the Witch went off of the mountain. As I say, you have to remember that these things were being done for the first time. There had to be conflicts between people feeling, "I have the right way to do something." There were two groups of people at the studio. There were those who had started out here on the West Coast and there were those that came from New York. And there was a strong division between these people. Like the North and South, in other words

DJ: One was more intuitive and one was more…

MD: No, it wasn't anything like that at all, really. It was just the fact that "I'll stay with my friends over here."

DJ: I was speaking of artistic background. Weren't the ones from the East Coast more art school-trained than the ones from the West Coast?

MD: Well, I think there are yeses and nos. I think that some of them had no training at all. I don't think that Ham had any art school training. On the other hand, neither did Norm Ferguson who came from New York.

DJ: Ham came from New York?

MD: No, he came from out here. As far as I know, he worked with a newspaper in Oakland. As a matter of fact, I think that Milt Kahl said that it was because of Ham that he came down to the studio. Milt did a lot of newspaper advertising work up there for the theaters, beautiful stuff. And I could be wrong, but I kind of remember that it was Ham who encouraged him to come down. This was such a low point in the Depression, the mid-1930s, and there wasn't work for artists. You know, you need something to eat, some pants to wear, and a place to sleep, those are the important things. So you had a choice of people from all over the world literally that came to this one spot that was down here on Hyperion and Griffith Park. Literally hundreds and hundreds and hundreds of people went through there or at least submitted work and were turned down. Some very good people were in there and for some the business wasn't for them.

Marceil Clark Ferguson (1914–2000)

Interviewed on February 28, 1990.

Les Clark's sister, Marceil, joined the ink and paint department on August 8, 1932.

DAVID JOHNSON: A little bit about your background and [your brother Les Clark's] background: Where did you guys come from?

MARCEIL CLARK: We lived in Venice.

DJ: Oh, you're local Californians?

MC: Californian. And went to Venice High School.

DJ: How much older was he than you?

MC: Nine years.

DJ: He started at the studio in 1928 or '29?

MC: I should remember… His art background was only art in high school. Mine was the same.

DJ: Did he go to any college at all?

MC: No, he didn't. It was the Depression. Nobody had any money. Very bad Depression.

DJ: Now were your parents in the arts?

MC: No. I don't know. We just both were interested in art and I had two majors: art and business. I figured that when I got out of high school I planned to get a job and I'd probably be in a business, like a secretary or something. We just loved art. We were attracted to it.

DJ: Are there any other brothers and sisters?

MC: There were twelve of us. That's why we didn't go to college. Twelve of us during the Depression.

DJ: Was he the oldest?

MC: Yes, he was the oldest. I was the oldest girl. I was the fifth in line.

DJ: OK. So he got started there right after high school.

MC: I graduated in June and I went to work in September and he said, "Maybe when you graduate I can get you a job at Disney's." I didn't think much about it. I thought, "I'll continue with all of my business subjects so there will be something there for me." And three months later after I got out of high school, he got me a job. I started as a painter.

DJ: Do you remember the woman who actually hired you?

MC: Yes. Hazel Sewell.

DJ: I know she was head of the department.

MC: Yeah, she was head of the department. She was the one who hired me.

DJ: Ward Kimball just described her to me as being kind of a frightening person.

MC: I think sometimes those boys fantasize.

DJ: It wouldn't be Martha Rose Body?

MC: Martha Rose Body. I never thought of her as being formidable. They always were older than I and used to call me the baby. It might have been Martha Rose.

DJ: Who was Martha Rose Body?

MC: She was just an inker at the time.

DJ: But she wasn't in charge of anybody.

MC: Not when I was there.

DJ: [Showing some photos to Marceil.]

MC: Kaye Valejo. She was quite young. She was younger than the rest of us.

DJ: Not younger than you.

MC: Yes. She was younger than me.

DJ: But you were seventeen when you started and this was only three years later, so you were twenty and she looks more than twenty, doesn't she?

MC: She worked in the paint lab.

DJ: Isabelle Wheaton was in charge of the bonuses and things.

MC: Except, we inkers and painters didn't get bonuses.

DJ: Oh, you didn't.

MC: No.

DJ: But you did for *Snow White*, I think, didn't you?

MC: We got overtime. We didn't get bonuses. Only the big shots, the animators and the rest.

DJ: So you went in as a painter. Did you have a training period?

MC: No.

DJ: So you just went right in.

MC: They sat me down and handed me the paintbrush. It was only black and white at that time. I remember they gave me a scene with lots of splashes of water all over the place. Zip. And they handed me another set and I was on my way!

DJ: You were on the payroll immediately.

MC: Yes, $16 a week.

DJ: Did you do inking subsequently?

MC: Oh yes.

DJ: I knew that some of the inkers actually worked for several weeks and months with no pay. They had a training period.

MC: It was a necessary period for inking, because it involves more. Anyone who had any art background could pick up a paint brush and paint those cels. But inking was different. I had a training period when I went into Inking. But I was still on the payroll, because I could still paint.

DJ: How long after you were a painter did you move into inking, and why?

MC: I guess they felt I was skilled enough and I'd be able to do it. But I was a very fast painter. They didn't really want to lose me as a painter, because I was one of the fastest at the time. But I guess they felt I might be a fast inker, too.

DJ: Did you go into inking during the color transition, or was it before?

MC: Oh, it was color.

DJ: Because color came in in 1932. So you started that year.

MC: I started in black and white. I painted black. The first few days all I painted was black.

DJ: Well, the color was reserved for only the Silly Symphonies until 1935. Were you doing painting for several years before you did inking, or was it just more like a year or so?

MC: I was only there seven years all total. I left in 1939. So, not very long. I was in Paint a couple of years, maybe a year or so.

DJ: Now, when you started inking, what were the training procedures for an inker?

MC: I think one of the inkers who'd been inking for some while would sit down and you'd watch how she did and then she would watch you ink and paint, point out what you might be doing wrong or what would be an easier way for you to hold your paint brush or whatever. And that was the way we learned, the way I learned.

DJ: I think it was Helen Nebovig MacIntosh who said that everything was from the arm when you did it.

MC: Yes.

DJ: You couldn't use your wrist.

MC: Yes, the technique was your arm movement. You couldn't do it this way [use your wrist] because you're handling a pen point on a slick surface and it didn't work that way. You held the cel with a pointer and you held the pen and then you would...all arm movement.

DJ: I think *Snow White* was actually the first time they used colored ink.

MC: Yes.

DJ: Because before that they used black and white.

MC: Yes, right.

DJ: And the man who told me this, Maurice Noble, said he was the one how suggested it. ... Now in 1934 they did "Goddess of Spring" and I know you modeled for Persephone.

MC: Yes, for my brother.

DJ: You were studying ballet at the time.

MC: I had fancied that I wanted to be a ballerina. I started a little late. And when my brother was working on "Goddess," he would ask me to strike a pose, a ballet pose, and I would.

DJ: Would this be done at the studio or at home?

MC: At home. Some days it might have been in his room after work hours. It certainly wasn't at the studio while I was supposed to be working. Then he'd say, "Strike a pose," or this and that, and I would and then he'd quickly sketch it.

DJ: And you were dressed up in a Grecian outfit?

MC: No. I might have had a bathing suit on. I don't think I had a tutu on. But I think he added the drapery and so forth.

DJ: This always reminded me of Isadora Duncan.

MC: I don't think we were dressed that way at the time.

DJ: Did you do a lot of modeling for him for this movie?

MC: No, not a lot. Not a great deal. He seemed to get what he wanted right away.

DJ: Did they ask you to do any modeling for Snow White before they got Marge Belcher?

MC: No.

[Changing the subject]

MC: You see, that was a pretty tight-knit group, Les and all the rest of them. They all were very conservative thinking, politically. And Art [Babbitt] and Bill [Tytla] were not. I could see where they disapproved of those two politically.

DJ: Were those the only two that…

MC: Well, that were, yes. There probably were others that I wasn't too much aware of.

DJ: What were your impressions of Walt?

MC: He'd come through the room in the department and we'd all be very impressed with him. I think that we all respected him a little bit, looked up to him. See, he was the king. He was. And I think most of the guys felt that way too that worked with him. With the exceptions of a few, like Art Babbitt. But I know he was like a father to my brother. My brother just revered him.

[Changing the subject]

MC: You know what I had to do on Snow White? They used transparent shadows and it was very difficult. The thing is that it was very hard to get that paint on without it streaking. And one batch was never the same as another one and often it varied in color. Somehow I managed to do it and they liked the way I put the shadows. So they made me do them all. They gave me a department and people to work with me and I sat there and did this. They weren't opaque. They were the transparent ones. It was a transparent paint for underneath them, where they're standing. A gray-blue transparent solution, kind of like a gelatin, a gelatin kind of thing. It was very hard to get on evenly. Maybe at the end I wasn't painting them, I was checking them to see if they were all the same and I'd have to flip them to see that they didn't…

And when they're walking, those shadows animate and the paint was just a messy job. I painted and inked, too. We had a different way of inking and we did shading. When we inked, we would do what they call shading, and later on everything was just one fine line when they inked on. I don't mean at Disney's, because I wasn't there, but at the other studios they just do one fine line of ink. At Disney's, like on Mickey Mouse and all, on the rounded heavy areas, we'd make the line heavier underneath it. The pens used were 290, 303, and 170. And then we used another, heavier pen for the colored ink line because it was a different consistency than black India ink. 290 was a great one.

Marge Champion (b. 1919)

Interviewed in September 1987.

Born Marjorie Celeste Belcher in Los Angeles, California, on September 2, 1919, to Hollywood dance director Ernest Belcher and Gladys Lee Baskette, she began dancing at an early age and became a ballet instructor at her father's studio at twelve. She was hired by Disney as a dance model for *Snow White and the Seven Dwarfs* and later modeled for the Blue Fairy in *Pinocchio* and the hippo Hyacinth in *Fantasia*.

Marge Champion's first marriage was to Art Babbitt. That marriage was short-lived. In 1947 she married Gower Champion. As a dance team, she and Gower appeared in such MGM musicals of the 1940s and 1950s as the 1951 version of *Show Boat* and 1952's *Everything I Have Is Yours*. MGM wanted the couple to remake Fred Astaire and Ginger Rogers films, but only one, *Lovely to Look At* (1952), a remake of 1935's *Roberta*, was completed.

During the summer of 1957, the Champions had their own TV series, *The Marge and Gower Champion Show*, a situation comedy with song-and-dance numbers. Marge played a dancer and Gower a choreographer.

The couple had two sons, Blake and actor Gregg Champion, before divorcing in 1973. Her third marriage, to director Boris Sagal, father of actress Katey Sagal, lasted from January 1, 1977, until his death on May 22, 1981, when he was killed in an accident during the production of the miniseries *World War III*.

In the 1970s, Champion, actress Marilee Zdenek, and choreographer John West were part of a team at Bel Aire Presbyterian Church that created a number of creative worship services, later offering workshops and related liturgical arts programs throughout the country.

Since retiring, Marge has worked as a dance instructor and choreographer in New York City. In 1982, she made a rare television acting appearance on the dramatic series *Fame*, playing a ballet teacher with a racial bias against black students. In 2001, she appeared as Emily Whitman in a Broadway revival of *Follies*.

DAVID JOHNSON: How exactly did you come to model?

MARGE CHAMPION: From my dad's studio.

DJ: Did you audition at the Disney studio or did you audition at your father's academy?

MC: No, at the studio. The scout for Disney came around and watched a couple of my dad's classes of the older teenagers and the people who were eligible for this kind of a job. I don't remember who the other two girls were, but he did pick three of us out of the class. And at some point, not very long from that (I think it was an evening class he watched), he picked me out. He asked my father to bring me to the studio. I can remember in high school telling my high school dramatic teacher whose name was Arthur Kaytchel that I had to go for this audition. It was for the modeling of Snow White.

DJ: Was this a three-year high school?

MC: Yes, this was Hollywood High.

DJ: So you had to be fifteen then.

MC: Well, no. I graduated when I was sixteen. I went in when I was thirteen.

DJ: You were really precocious.

MC: Not really. In those days you started earlier. I was just fourteen when I went into high school. Then when I graduated in June 1936, I was not yet seventeen.

DJ: You told your drama teacher you had to audition for Snow White.

MC: I told my drama teacher Arthur Kaytchel about this and he started having us do some sort of fanciful improvisations in class. I can remember him making up some kind of a story that he wanted me to do about picking daisies and stuff like that. I think just to get me loosened up in case I had anything to do... He didn't know what I was going to have to do. I didn't know what I was going to have to do.

DJ: Had you done any acting before that time?

MC: Not very much. I'd gone to a woman near my dad's studio in Wilshire Boulevard and her name was Marta Ottmann and I had taken maybe like nine months of some sort of drama training. But that was it, really. I didn't know anything about... And they didn't want me to know anything about acting because they didn't want me to act. They just wanted me to be free enough, because I was a dancer, to move. They didn't really want a trained actress. That's why they went to the dancing schools. They were actively looking in the dancing schools. I think there had been a model for "Goddess of Spring." They had tried once before to have a model so they learned a little bit from that. And because of the singing and the dancing with the dwarfs and all that, I had to be a dancer. But they did not want an actress. That I remember was quite clear.

DJ: Do you remember anything about the audition?

MC: They showed me storyboards for a scene; which scene it was I don't remember. And they had me audition with some material from the picture.

DJ: You were probably so excited that you were doing this.

MC: I was very excited. I just wanted to get the job because they were going to pay TEN DOLLARS A DAY. And I hadn't made ten dollars a MONTH before. And I really was excited about that. Little did I know that I would do enough in one day to keep them busy for over a month. So if I worked one day a month I was lucky. That's why I worked for two or two-and-a-half years.

I remember my father driving me over to the studio on Hyperion. I remember making friends with some people there, a young couple that were twenty-one years old. They were married and he was working at the studio. Hal Adelquist his name was.

DJ: Do you remember where the outside scenes were filmed?

MC: They were all filmed on the soundstage.

DJ: They were? Because this is one of the few photostats that I was able to find with the Prince. Do you remember that at all?

MC: Now that you do mention it, I think that was done outside.

DJ: This looks like you're a little bit older than thirteen.

MC: Oh yes. By the time we got to this sequence I must have been maybe fifteen.

DJ: When you say your father drove you to the studio: can you remember the first time when they called you and said it would be nine o'clock the next day, and your father would drive you that day?

MC: Yes.

DJ: What exactly was it like? You had been to the studio before, but now you were coming to really work. How did you feel?

MC: I think I was very excited.

DJ: Were you far from the studio?

MC: Yeah, We lived in Hollywood. We lived right near Hollywood High School. Hyperion was farther east, quite a bit farther east. It was almost Glendale. I guess it took about three-quarters of an hour to get there.

DJ: You probably didn't sleep the night before.

MC: I don't remember ever being really nervous on a performance as I think I was to even know what the import was. And I had been around my dad's dancing school and *teaching*. I was already teaching when I was thirteen.

Don't forget, I was a child of the Depression and my dad couldn't afford assistants after a while. So I had been through his teacher's course at least three or four times by then. I had been assisting him in classes with the tiny little ones. By the time I was thirteen or fourteen I was teaching young kids and I was getting them ready to come into his classes. That gave me a certain sense, a certain maturity, which other twelve- or thirteen-year-old girls didn't have. He really depended on me to help him. That's why I say I didn't make very much money. My allowance, I think, was twenty-five cents a week. And when I worked as a teacher I got maybe a dollar or two a week. Don't forget money was totally different then. You could go to any restaurant in town and for three dollars eat all you could...and good restaurants. And breakfasts were like twenty-five cents in those days. So the whole concept of money was totally different. As I say, ten dollars a day really seemed like a fortune to me. I think I was more interested in the money.

DJ: You wouldn't have known it was going to be a world-famous film.

MC: We all knew about Walt Disney. And it was a thrill to be around there but it didn't seem so impressive. At least from where I sit now, I don't think that I felt there was any more than going to a terrific junior college and meeting all these artists, just little bit older than I was, and being treated as an adult...I mean, as a performer.

Don't forget also the other thing was that my father had never let me perform professionally. I didn't perform professionally till I was out of high school. He had a very strict rule about that as far as I was concerned. He felt that I must complete my education. But he didn't mind my going to the studio because he knew Walt Disney and he knew what he stood for. He knew that I would be looked after, that I wouldn't get into any trouble.

DJ: So he just drove you there and then picked you up when you were through?

MC: I don't even think he picked me up. I think either my mother or somebody else picked me up, because he taught from nine in the morning till nine at night. So that he could drop me off at the studio at eight or eight-thirty and then go on to work. But he couldn't have picked me up in the afternoon, because he was always at the dancing school.

DJ: Did you meet Walt at when you first came to the studio?

MC: Oh yeah. And he was Uncle Walt.

DJ: You had known him before?

MC: Yeah, my father had known him. I don't think his daughters had taken dancing at my dad's school, but for some reason I felt more family than... Maybe it's just my over-optimistic outlook on everything, but I felt much more family than I was. And as I say I met these young people who were not that much older than I was, who had been at the studio for a couple of years. People started there when they were eighteen, nineteen years old. And the animator that I eventually married, a year after *Snow White* was released... I had stayed on at the studio to do the Blue Fairy in *Pinocchio* and the whole dance sequence in *Fantasia*, the "Dance of the Hours." I staged that with eleven other girls and we did all that galloping around, for those ostriches and the hippopotamus and all that stuff. So I stayed there until I was what I thought was quite mature and I met Art Babbitt there and fell madly in love with him and got married a month before I was eighteen. I had already completed my career at the Walt Disney Studio. And that marriage didn't last very long, because I was certainly not ready for marriage.

He was always doing wonderfully funny things at the studio at lunch hour. He was an amateur hypnotist. And he leaned hypnosis from some traveling hypnotist in Sioux City, Iowa, where he came from. He learned to do this and he was always giving little demonstrations at the studio at lunch hour and putting everybody out and then giving people post-hypnotic suggestions and all of that.

DJ: Did he take it seriously?

MC: Not really, and he would never do anything that was... Well, he did some things that were like practical jokes that were sort of funny. He was quite good at it. Because he would put somebody under a trance and then he'd give them a post-hypnotic suggestion that... Say, if it was one of those boys that were like gofers at the studio, he put one of those under once and he gave him a suggestion that everywhere he went in the afternoon after that he'd have to say, "Have you seen the oranges?" And he'd go into somebody's office who had called him to come in and he'd come in and say, "Yes, sir, have you seen the oranges?"

DJ: [Laughs] It really worked.

MC: And he'd say, "Why did I say that?" It really did work. And he got one of the gofers into his office and he said, "Now I want you to go and get me this..." They had to get supplies. "Pencils are there and a box of stipple dots." [Laughs] There's no such thing as a box of stipple dots. Stipple dotting is when you do it like this. He did things like that. They were practical jokes, really.

DJ: I didn't know he had such a sense of humor.

MC: Oh, he has a great sense of humor.

DJ: What I've read about him is that he was just so intense.

MC: He was intense. But he also had a great sense of humor. "Have you seen the oranges?" Now come on, that's funny. It wasn't cruel.

DJ: Do you still keep in touch with him?

MC: No, not really.

DJ: I know that he and Walt hated each other.

MC: Oh yes. Walt never trusted him. I mean, here was this boy from Sioux City, Iowa, who had all these ideas about what their rights were. Walt loved to give things, but he didn't want to have anybody say that this is what I *deserve* or what my rights are. They were so totally different that they couldn't possibly have even sat in the same room very long with each other. Because Art believed in the rights of the artists and Walt believed in patronage and those are two different approaches. Not that Walt was a cruel man. I don't think for one minute that he was, but he was on a totally different trip than Art Babbitt.

And Art organized the fight for the cartoonist union.

DJ: Yes, I know he was involved heavily in that.

MC: He was very liberal. I think that Art is a fabulous man. I was too young. I was twelve years younger than him. I was too young and too stupid. I had no idea of the world or anything in it. I'd never been outside of Hollywood. I had grown up in a very, very sheltered life, much more so than the average girl there, because I was working from the time I was seven. I was working on my dancing. I was always under my father's eye. He was my teacher as well as my father. So I wasn't allowed to date until I was fourteen or fifteen.

DJ: Do you recall going into any of the animators' rooms while they were actually drawing?

MC: Yeah. Also, Art used to bring a lot of the work… After we were married, he'd bring a lot of work home. So I could watch the process, even though I wasn't terribly interested. You can't help it when it's under your roof. He had an animation table and light and all of that at home, and used to do a lot of work at home.

DJ: Did he ever mention to you about animating the Queen, that it was difficult? Or did they use a model?

MC: For the Witch they used Paul Godkin. And for the Prince, Louis Hightower. Paul did all the stuff. I'm not sure whether he did the Queen or not. I know he did the Witch.

DJ: When you were in the scenes with the Witch, in the movie, when they photographed you for the modeling, did they actually use him?

MC: Yeah.

DJ: In other words, it was both of you together.

MC: Oh sure. And when I did stuff with the dwarfs, the animators would come down to the soundstage and we would dance around. And I remember a lot about Ham [Luske] directing me. Ham I remember better than any of the others. They were all so very kind and very patient, because their work makes them patient. I mean, you sit there in a room and keep looking at yourself in the mirror and drawing and drawing and drawing and looking at yourself doing all that stuff. You've got to have patience. It is one of the prime requisites for that kind of an artist. So they were very patient with me.

DJ: Do you remember the very first scene that you did? Like, for instance, were you in rags at that point, or were you in the actual costume with the starched collar?

MC: I know they had a costume, yeah. They had a costume for me. They always had a costume for me. That was the time when they had that big football helmet, too. They fit it, because the proportion of the head was supposed to be bigger than my normal head. So they always had that, and they had a little mock-up kind of scenery. It seems to me that the first day... I remember a lot of sort of strings and ropes hanging and that was to represent going through the forest. They didn't have any real props. That would give them a chance to see when I push a branch aside or I push something, it would give them the weight that they needed. If I were just miming it, they wouldn't have gotten the same thing.

DJ: Did they use a fan for the wind?

MC: Yes, they had a bunch of fans and also because I was so hot I was nearly fainting from the heat of the lights.

DJ: And that helmet.

MC: And that helmet and that hot costume.

DJ: Now, I remember that you made them take off the helmet finally.

MC: Oh, I couldn't stand it.

DJ: Do you remember if the costumes were the same colors. Did it have a yellow dress like in the movie?

MC: I have a feeling that it was yellow and blue.

DJ: When you did the scene through the forest, did they have a musical accompaniment to that or did somebody play on the piano or were there any kind of sound effects through that scene?

MC: I don't remember any kind of sound effects, and I remember doing everything over and over and over and over. I was not really sure why I did it over so many times, whether they just wanted variations.

DJ: Did they give you your own dressing room, or did you use an animator's studio?

MC: I think I had some sort of a little tented area on the soundstage.

DJ: Oh, so you didn't have your own room.

MC: I don't think so.

DJ: It was rather informal, then.

MC: Oh, very. The whole studio was very informal. Nobody ever called anybody except by their first names and then everybody called Walt "Walt."

DJ: Did they have you go through rehearsals before they actually filmed you?

MC: Oh, yes. I went through a lot of rehearsals and then they would tell me what they wanted more or less or whatever. Ham Luske was the overall director, but each animator would have their specific areas of interest, so that when we were doing a section that was assigned to one or another of the animators, they were always there.

DJ: Do you remember anything particular about one of the other animators asking you to do a piece of business. Does anything pop into your head?

MC: Not really.

DJ: What about when you were going through the forest and you had to look frightened and Adriana Caselotti screams…

MC: That was easy for me. Because I would listen to that voice over and over and over again and then I would just get up and they gave me a certain area to work in and I would just get up and start improvising it. I was very free.

DJ: They didn't say, "You have to move from here to there," then?

MC: If they'd already laid that out in a very set kind of way, but they mostly hadn't.

DJ: So even going through the forest you could do pretty much of what you wanted.

MC: As long as I worked in one linear pattern. And I was forced to do that because of whatever they had hanging there.

DJ: Did somebody come out and scare you to make you frightened, like they do sometimes when they direct movies, to actually make it real?

MC: I don't remember if they did.

DJ: You probably would have remembered, so they probably didn't. I was just curious how they extracted that realism out of you.

MC: I don't know. I was living in a fantasy anyway. Do you know what I mean? I was born in a Disney world. I was living a fantasy. It was all fantasy. It was real easy to be very comfortable there. I don't remember being frightened. I just remember the *fun* of going to the studio and "I wish they would call me more often."

DJ: So, after the first day's shooting, did you come back the next day or did you wait for a while?

MC: I don't remember coming back any two consecutive days.

DJ: So there were big spaces in between.

MC: Sometimes weeks.

DJ: Did you ever think that maybe they had gotten somebody else?

MC: Oh yeah. I was always worried about that. And I was too dumb even to call somebody like Hamilton Luske and say, "Are you satisfied with my work," or any of that stuff. I just went along doing whatever and getting there when I had to get there. Sometimes they didn't let me know until the night before I was going to be there the next day.

DJ: When you did a song, for instance "Whistle While You Work"... When they did the soundtrack for you, when you came in to rehearse it and they said, "OK, now we want you to listen to the soundtrack here," was it complete with the orchestra or did they play it on the piano? Do you remember anything in detail?

MC: I think it was complete with the orchestra. They also had a little set. There was a door and there were little things. They were very primitive, but we had a set and we would have the props and things and I had the broom to work with. I remember working with a broom that seemed like an old-fashioned broom.

I remember somebody playing the piano. They had somebody there and it was probably on the composers.

DJ: Did you meet Frank Churchill?

MC: Yes, indeed. I knew Frank well. That's why I say that he probably was at the piano.

DJ: For the wishing-well scene, did they have any kind of a mock wishing well?

MC: They had a light down there, I remember. I'd look down into this light. It was some sort of a mock-up of a well. And there was a light down there.

DJ: Did you ever meet any of the voices, like Adriana Caselotti?

MC: I met her. There was always that joke around the studio that the complete Snow White was Margie Annabelchelotti. They always used to scream at that. It was funny. It was a perfect composite of our names. I do remember meeting her, but briefly. We never worked together, because her work had been mostly finished. I think they called her back for some additional stuff. But we were never there at the same time.

DJ: Oh, you weren't?

MC: Not really. But I think there was something that we met. I don't know whether it was a lunch or just that they brought her on the set when she was over there re-recording something.

DJ: Did you ever happen to meet the voice of the Queen, Lucille LaVerne, who was an actress at that time? She was an elderly woman, in her sixties. She also did the voice of the Witch who was acted out by this Paul...

MC: Paul Godkin, who was also one of my father's pupils.

DJ: So your father probably knew Lucille LaVerne.

MC: I'm sure he did. He also knew Louis Hightower who was another pupil of my dad's school.

DJ: He was probably much older than you.

MC: No.

DJ: Then he was young, too.

MC: Yeah, he was about maybe a year or two older. He was killed in World War Two, in Sicily. We subsequently danced together. *Life* magazine photographed us a lot. It didn't come out till about 1938, about the models of Snow White and the Prince. They took us out up in Griffith Park or somewhere and we reproduced a lot of the motions for the photographer.

DJ: Oh, I see, they weren't actually used by the animators. This was done after the fact.

MC: After the picture was released, even. Then he went to New York and started doing New York shows. I followed in about 1940 and I got into a show called *The Little Dog Laughed*, which a choreographer named Chester Hale was choreographing. And Louis left *Very Warm for May* and came and danced with me in that show. It never opened on Broadway, unfortunately. That show closed in Boston.

DJ: The voice of the Prince was Harry Stockwell, who was Dean Stockwell's father.

MC: I knew the Stockwells. Mostly through my dad, but I didn't know them well.

DJ: Was Louis Hightower as easy to direct as you? In the scenes when you were together, for instance, at the wishing well, was he a quick study like you?

MC: I guess. I know they had a lot of trouble with the Prince because they hadn't invented, at that time, how to give him weight. Even though they tried copying it, they could not get him to stop flying. If you notice, he just skims the surface. They couldn't seem to give him any weight. It didn't matter for me, because I'm the little girl. But for the Prince, he really flew.

DJ: They had to re-shoot him a lot of times.

MC: No, they released it without ever solving that problem.

DJ: Well, after the movie was released they went back and re-did the Prince. That's why it looks much better now.

MC: It looks better now. But it looked JUST AWFUL. I mean, he really was laughable. It wasn't Louis' fault, because, if you see pictures of him, he was a very sturdy, in fact almost too sturdy a man. There was nothing effeminate about him.

DJ: There was a sequence that was cut from the... I mean it was in the story stage so I don't know if they filmed it, if you can remember: there was supposed to be a dream sequence when Snow White sings "Some Day My Prince Will Come." And, as it is in the movie, you're singing in front of the fireplace. But the original idea was they were going to have a fade-out and it was kind of like an astral scene with baby stars shooting arrows and it was you and the Prince doing a short dance together. Was that ever filmed?

MC: I think it was. Now that you're talking about it, I seem to remember putting together some little kind of dance with him.

I danced with Louis so much and so long. I did a short with him which George Sidney (who was then twenty-one) directed, called *Sunday Night at the Trocadero*. So it's hard for me to remember what we rehearsed for the little short movie and what we rehearsed for Disney. I may have gotten that confused in my head, but I seem to remember something about that.

DJ: And of course the scene with the soup eating, that was cut, that must have been shot, with you sitting at the table showing them how to... You remember that?

MC: I remember ladling whatever we used for soup, and it wasn't soup. [...] I became such good friends with Bill Tytla and his wife subsequently... I know he was great friends with Art and they used to come up to our house all the time. But I don't remember whether I ever worked with Bill on the set or not. We were very close friends and I'm still very close with his widow.

DJ: What was he like?

MC: Bill and Art are the ones I remember the best, because I knew them subsequently, too. Bill was a Slavic man with a funny sense of humor. He was always pretending to be a dirty old man. That was his whole image, and he'd sort of leer and he'd sort of twirl his moustaches. He was, of course, making jokes all the time, but that was sort of his image of himself. It was a cartoon image. And he never lived up to it, that he was just this dirty old man. Art used to talk about himself as an old man, too, and he was only thirty. He was thirty when we were married. He always said things like... Somebody'd say, "How are you?" "Pretty good for an old man." And he was thirty years old. It was a joke. They really didn't consider themselves old; it was all joking. Everything was a joke. They were rarely serious, any of them.

DJ: Do you remember what was for you the hardest thing in *Snow White*? After the day was over, were you so glad it was through?

MC: The hardest part was wearing that damn helmet.

DJ: Oh, that was in the beginning.

MC: Yeah.

DJ: Did you do your own choreography, for instance, when Snow's always holding her dress like this?

MC: There wasn't anybody else to do it.

DJ: Did they tell you they wanted you to hold your dress?

MC: No.

DJ: Oh, so that was you.

MC: Oh yeah.

DJ: You were always holding the dress like this.

MC: Oh yeah. That's what I always did, that was me. I always had my hands like that if I was pretending to be somebody else. It's stuff that I did.

DJ: When you went upstairs with the candle, did they actually have an upstairs? That scene when you go into the bedroom.

MC: I'm pretty sure that they would have a bunch of stairs mocked up somehow, because it didn't do them any good to have me pantomime. I wasn't that good a pantomimist in the first place, to give it any weight. And you can't do that if you don't have the props.

DJ: How did you feel when you were lying in the coffin, and Louis Hightower comes to kiss you... Did you think, "Gee, this is awfully silly," or, "Gee this is fun, I really like this?"

MC: I don't have much of a recollection. I remember Louis leaning over me, but I don't have much of a recollection of that and even what the coffin was. I don't remember whether it was just a board or whether it was a mock-up coffin.

DJ: And the apple. Paul gave you...

MC: With the apple we had a bunch of delicious apples, so we did that quite a few times.

DJ: You did?

MC: Oh, yeah, that I remember. I remember biting into that apple, because they wanted a whole apple.

DJ: Oh, I see, so they had to give you a new apple each time.

MC: They had to give me a new apple each time.

DJ: Do you have any photos of yourself at the time that you did Snow White?

MC: I have myself on the float, because I was on the Rose Parade float.

DJ: Oh, yes?

MC: After it was released, they had a whole new dress made for me with a lot of glitter on it. I was on that float with the Seven Dwarfs. I have pictures of that.

DJ: What was the food there like? They would stop you for lunch and... Was it good?

MC: I think we took our own lunch. We had brown bags.

[...]

MC: [Paul Godkin] did study with my father, but he also studied with a woman named Carmelita Marachi, who was a famous teacher out there. And Paul and I danced together in a show called *Beggar's Holiday*. It was the Duke Ellington version of *Three Penny Opera*. It was at the Broadway Theater. We got to be great friends. This was many, many years later. We remained friends right up until his death.

DJ: Did you start dating Art Babbitt when you were still working on Snow White?

MC: I think it was after I finished it. I think it's when I was working on *Pinocchio*. It may even have been that I was working on *Fantasia* when I met him. I know it was very much because of a woman and her husband and I'm still friendly with her and she's in her late eighties. Her name is Elly Horvath [concept artist Ferdinand Horvath's wife].

DJ: Horvath did some of the designs for the short cartoons and he did some of the designs for *Snow White*.

MC: Elly has a sense of humor that won't stop and she remembers everything. The Horvaths were my closest friends. She just took me under her wing like she was my older sister. She had been a ballet dancer in Hungary. They're both Hungarian. I saw a lot of them, and that's when I started seeing Art, because he was a friend of theirs, too. He adored the Horvaths.

Maurice Noble
(1910–2001)

Interviewed on February 1, 1990.

Maurice Noble's career in animation began at Disney in the 1930s, but he is undoubtedly best remembered as the designer who made so many of Chuck Jones' Warner Bros. cartoons from 1952 onward into some of the best-designed animated films of all time. Noble's association with Jones continued into his later work for MGM and Warner's.

Born in Spooner, Minnesota, on May 1, 1910, Noble moved to California and attended Chouinard Art Institute. He began his career in advertising, designing the famous "red door" for Elizabeth Arden, but discovered his true calling at Disney, where he worked on the Silly Symphonies as well as *Snow White*, *Bambi*, *Fantasia*, and *Dumbo*.

During World War II, Noble was a member of Frank Capra's U.S. Army Signal Corps unit, which created animated films for the Armed Forces. During this period he met his future colleagues Ted Geisel (better known as Dr. Seuss) and Chuck Jones.

After the war, Noble and Jones entered into a partnership that continued on and off for nearly 50 years. Among the animated short subjects Noble created during that time are *Duck Dodgers in the 24th-and-a-Half Century*, *Bully for Bugs*, *Duck Amuck*, *What's Opera, Doc*, and *The Dot and the Line*.

His partnership with Jones continued through the 1960s, when they produced numerous animated versions of Dr. Seuss classics, including *The Cat in the Hat*, *Horton Hears a Who*, and *How the Grinch Stole Christmas*.

Following a leave in the 1970s, Noble returned to animation in the 1990s to contribute designs to Chuck Jones Productions and Warner Bros., and to form his own studio, Maurice Noble Productions.

Maurice Noble died on May 18, 2001.

MAURICE NOBLE: I was born in northern Minnesota, in a little lumber, mining town. My parents told me it had a population of 2,000 and 20 saloons. It was a wide-open lumber town. My father managed lumber mills for Weyerhaeuser and various people like that. And so I have a brother and sister born in Canada and a brother and sister born in United States. There are five of us kids. But we're all American citizens. We left there when I was just a small child and went to Chicago because my father became head of something there. Then he came down with tuberculosis and we went to Albuquerque, New Mexico, where he subsequently died. We lived in Redlands, California, for a long time. I had my first music lessons in Redlands. I used to sing in the church junior choir, and I sang so well that they gave me a piano scholarship. I never could figure that one out. [Laughs]

DAVID JOHNSON: What brought you to California?

MN: We came out here originally to Redlands from Albuquerque. My father was still living then and they suggested a lower altitude for him. Redlands was suggested and we had friends that lived there. Then we went back to Albuquerque for financial reasons, and that's when he died there. But I had my first piano lessons as a scholarship student and learned to play "Baby-by, here's a fly, let us catch him, you and I." That type of thing. The music teacher I studied with, later on, much later, started kids out on simple pieces of Bach. Even as a child, I was bored with that stuff they were giving me. I don't understand why they think children are morons. I never could figure that out. Then I grew up in Pomona where we lived for a long time. I graduated from high school in Pomona. And I got a working scholarship at Chouinard School of Art in Los Angeles.

DJ: Where was it located at that time?

MN: At that time it was on Grand Avenue, near what is now MacArthur Park. We used to call it Westlake Park. Mary Blair and I received the first two full-time scholarships Chouinard handed out.

DJ: So your ambition was to be an artist, full-time.

MN: I wanted to be a doctor and I wanted to be an architect. But somehow I landed on doing art, drawing, painting, and watercolors, and took art all through high school. Then I worked at Pomona College and went there for three years and decided that wasn't for me and I got this scholarship down at Chouinard. It was the Depression and things were so bad that I went on a leave and continued my scholarship at... I had an opportunity to become a designer for Robinson's department store here in Los Angeles. At the time that was THE store in Los Angeles, where all the movie stars shopped and so forth. It was about the time they were building Bullock's Wilshire, which then became the big drawing card for most notables. I designed Christmas departments. I did the sportswear department, the wedding department. I helped design the present building that's still sitting down there, the windows and so forth. I invented the idea of the small window to show a specialized object with one or two objects in it, breaking the big windows down.

DJ: Tiffany's is of course famous for that.

MN: I originally got out here at Robinson's then. I didn't know anything about Tiffany's at the time.

DJ: That came later.

MN: Later, yeah. Oh, among other things, I designed the Elizabeth Arden bright red door that they still use on their big beauty salons. I did the Elizabeth Arden salon there at Robinson's and I put this big red door in there.

DJ: Were you always innovative as a child?

MN: Oh yes.

DJ: Where do you think that comes from?

MN: My father had a great deal of taste. But he was a lumber man and mathematician, and all this and that. My mother was a gal with a lot of imagination, and she should have been a movie star. [Laughs] She was a farmer's daughter, but she was the kind of person that although she had no real formal education, she always had pictures of Michelangelo or Botticelli hanging on the wall. I grew up with a big picture of Turner up over the piano when I was a kid. She had terrific taste and she always wanted to be an artist. Many, many years after, she lived by herself at the old family house, and she had a room that was devoted to oil painting, one devoted to watercolors, one was her autobiography and one was poetry and so forth. She'd drift from room to room when she felt like it. My older brother is a musician. He plays the pipe organ. He's got a number of jazz orchestras that he's played with. One sister graduated from Pomona College, Phi Beta Kappa, as a librarian. It was a family of individualists. My other brother went through Pearl Harbor and was with the Navy for many, many years. Not in uniform. He had something to do with personnel. I grew up in a family that had a lot of curiosity and whoever shouted the loudest got heard. It was a household that didn't have a great deal of money. We were always scraping the bottom of the barrel, trying to make ends meet and everybody seemed to like to come to our house, because something was always going on. We were always dragging our friends home. My mother'd just put another cup in the soup and we'd spread everything out. That was the type of family background I had. I went from Robinsons's... I worked there a couple of years doing everything, even helping to design couturier dresses. I'd draw up sketches and they wanted something very special for a formal party or something like that. I didn't know anything about it, but if you'd ask me, I'd say, "Let me think about it," and I'd go read a book in the library real quick that night and then come back the next day and pretend as though I knew what I was doing. [Laughs] So it was a very creative job. Some Disney scouts saw my stuff that I did for the children's department and one of them had also been in contact with Chouinard and on my vacation I went out there and...

DJ: They contacted you instead of you contacting them. That's a switch.

MN: Yeah. They contacted me.

DJ: What year was this?

MN: Well, it was pre-*Snow White* when they were doing *Water Babies* and some of those early Disney things. [Note: Maurice Noble joined Disney on April 9, 1935.] I worked at Hyperion in the old studio. I tried out and they said they would take me. I think it was $20 a week.

DJ: What were you getting at Robinson's?

MN: At Robinson's I was getting $90 a month.

DJ: Not too much difference.

MN: Not too much difference. But I went back there and I was getting tired being paid $90 a month and I was working sometimes 18 hours a day. I was sleeping in the hospital upstairs. Had no transportation. The streetcars had stopped running.

DJ: 18 hours a day!

MN: Oh gosh, yes. And also you worked until one o'clock on Saturdays, and you had the rest of the afternoon off.

DJ: Yeah. That's the way it was at Disney's, too.

MN: So my boss asked me, "How much did they offer you?" I told him $25 a week. That would be a little over $100 a month. He told me, "I'll double your salary right now." Almost $200 a month. I just said, "You son of a bitch, I wouldn't work for you another day." And I slammed my hand and walked out the door. And so I remember my boss was so mad at me. He just got purple in the face. I'd been doing everything, just everything, working my fool tail off. So I went out to Disney's and I remember the first background they gave me was the picture of an apple with a wormhole in it to render in water color.

DJ: Who was the supervisor?

MN: Mique Nelson was the head of the department at that time. I kinda looked at that and said, "My God, what have I got myself into?!"

DJ: You were hired as a background painter?

MN: As a background painter, yes.

DJ: Why didn't they put you into story development?

MN: Well, they wanted a background painted.

DJ: Did you meet Walt that early on?

MN: Oh, he would walk in and out of the room and look around.

DJ: But you never formally met him, like your first day of work?

MN: Oh no, nothing like that. He kinda got so he knew who I was and nodded to me when he saw me in the hall. That was about it. Walt was kind of a remote character.

DJ: Did you like him, personally?

MN: I had no reason to dislike him. Put it that way.

DJ: Here was this famous Walt Disney. Disney was already famous.

MN: He started to become famous then. Eventually, I was painting backgrounds and I guess I was a little more articulate than some of the other guys because when he had visitors and would bring them through, he'd bring them into my section where I was painting so I could explain what I was doing. I was working there late one day and I heard him: "Hello, Maurice, how are you?" I said, "I'm fine." I was painting and I turned around and looked and there was Walt, H.G. Wells, and Charlie Chaplin all together in my room at the same time. Can you imagine that?

Anyway, I met a lot of people. The famous Mrs. Campbell; she used to be in British society and New York society. I met one of the Rockefellers. It was the period when the thing to do was to come and visit the Disney studio.

DJ: That's what Isabelle Wheaton said. She said everybody was fascinated and wanted to know what was going on there.

MN: Oh yes. I met Constance Cummings. She was a young, kind of sandy-haired, and I remembered she had freckles.

DJ: She has high cheek bones. She's still rather a beautiful woman.

MN: Rather large in stature. I met a lot of people like that. I worked on painting backgrounds and then we did *The Old Mill*, gradually leading up to the *Snow White* opus.

DJ: You must have been aware that they were doing this feature, that they were planning it anyway.

MN: We heard rumors that this was going on. You have to understand: the Disney studio was very compartmentalized. The girls weren't allowed to associate with the boys and so forth. Except we did. So when we painted in the background department we had no reason to go over into the animation department. But when I was working on *Snow White*, they needed somebody, at the tail end of that, to kind of coordinate cel work with backgrounds.

And previous to that I was given a room and my room looked right into Walt's right here. I was working on the last section there, where the Prince comes in there with Snow White, and I was drawing and sketching and painting all that stuff. I guess I must have laid it out and painted it, too. We were working day and night and trying to get the darn thing out. I can remember sitting here and I could look across and here's Walt sitting at his desk over there, and once in a while he'd come and stand at my door. He'd come around this way and stand at the door, and I'd be working late. It'd be 11, 12 , 1 o'clock at night, you know.

DJ: He was there that late?

MN: He'd be there, or he'd be getting ready to leave around 9 or 10 and I'd still be sitting there working. And he'd say, "Hi, how are you doing?" or something like that. I had no reason, as I said, to dislike Walt. I do know that he ruled the roost. There was no doubt of that.

DJ: But you didn't feel an urge to talk to him?

MN: There were no openings for it. There was no reason for it. I'd do my job and that's it. I didn't know him personally at all. About the tail-end of *Snow White*, I was working with the models and I invented the idea of using colored ink lines, which was a big step in the animation business.

DJ: But they used colored ink lines in *Snow White*.

MN: We started to use them then.

DJ: You didn't use them before *Snow White*?

MN: No, everything was black-and-white ink lines.

DJ: But what about with the color cartoons?

MN: They were inked in black and white. The early colored cartoons were all inked in black lines. I remember doing "mirror, mirror on the wall," and using colored ink lines for around the ghost image that came up on the mirror: green, or yellow and blue. Then for some of the props, I innovated, putting colored ink lines on them to help tie them to the background and stuff like that. Ollie Johnston and Frank Thomas were up here and we got talking about it and they said, "According to tradition, somebody, some animator in the studio developed the colored ink line." I said, "You're looking at him right now." Johnston would never give me credit for it.

DJ: Who designed peacock throne?

MN: I have no idea. I did the color model on the Queen and her headdress.

DJ: Did you work on this with Joe Grant? Because he designed the Queen. Did you work with him?

MN: No, I would get the drawings and we would work with the backgrounds and select the colors and finally get the OKs. I would submit them to whoever was...

DJ: Did somebody work with you for designing the colors for the Queen, or was that entirely you?

MN: Walt's sister-in-law, Hazel Sewell, was the head of the ink-and-paint department, and I would get the drawings, and then I would sit down with Hazel and we'd talk about them, to add the color charts, and we'd go through them and we'd make decisions. I would take a piece of animation paper and make watercolor sketches or opaque drawings of it and try different color schemes. Then we'd try to match them up to the color charts and what we thought we...

DJ: What's a color chart?

MN: A color chart was...each color was let down for a cel level.

DJ: Yes, I understand.

MN: We would have a very pale pink and then a lighter pink and then a medium pink and then a bright pink and so forth like that. We'd have 15 different pinks. This would be put on the color chart, and we'd have it let down from the palest color down to saturation. It would be in cards, like this, and then eventually they put them on strips so we could flip them around and compare them and all. I have some out here. That's what the color charts were.

DJ: This is a Joe Grant sketch here.

MN: He might have done something like that, yes, and then we'd have to try and make the thing work.

DJ: So, of course, you would have to change the color and...

MN: Change the color and take them off the charts, and I think we eliminated this and made her [the Queen] into... She didn't have that bright red stripe.

DJ: Yes, she did, on the inside of her cape, bright red on the inside.

MN: I can't remember that. But this is the thing I was talking to you about, selecting the colors for the image that came up on the mirror...

I did a lot of the interiors of the dwarfs' house. I did one of the original sketches of the Witch's dungeon down there, when she goes down the steps and all that.

DJ: Was that a layout?

MN: It was just a painted sketch, an idea sketch.

We worked on Wattman paper with Windsor Newton water colors, and everything was done in transparent wash. We weren't allowed to use any opaques. Trying to match scene to scene with that technique, you became a nervous wreck.

DJ: Why were you not allowed to use any opaque paints?

MN: For some reason or other they had the idea that this didn't reproduce right under the camera lights. On the other hand, we had an old background man who used to use them all the time, and he was considered "oldster." What was his name? A funny old man. He worked all the time with a great big plaid bell cap on his head and a big heavy sweater even in the middle of summer.

DJ: Did he work on *Snow White*?

MN: No, he never worked on *Snow White*. He used to be considered second string. He couldn't do watercolor washes, so he just slopped on a lot of opaque paint.

DJ: Like poster color?

MN: Poster color, yes.

DJ: But originally it was all watercolor.

MN: All transparent watercolor. And many times we would lay out a value sketch underneath it, in Payne's grey. A value sketch and then we would put the color in over it. A wash over wash, and building up so carefully that everything would be matched. You can imagine trying to do that. If you got one wash on that was too heavy, you'd ruin the whole background and have to start all over. Then we had a jury system. A whole crew would come in—the layout men and sometimes Walt—and all of them would look at it. Here are four or five people looking at this watercolor background you've been struggling with maybe for three or four days, maybe a week. And they'd say, "I think that's too light there; that's too dark there," and all this and that, and criticized it. After every period like that you're ready to fall on the floor. It was a terrible nervous strain. Because you work your fool head off trying to render these things and a lot of them are beautifully painted watercolors. They're very tightly drawn, starting from a pencil sketch and traced onto the Wattman paper...

DJ: Brice Mack did that. For *Snow White* he was doing that.

MN: Brice Mack worked on it. And then there was Ray Lockrem. He was working with us on it, too.

DJ: Did all of the background painters work in the same room, when you were on *Snow White*?

MN: Yeah, we were working... See, we had one, two, three, four, five different long desks like this. Maybe there was a sixth one in the corner. We were all in one room.

DJ: Now, Sam Armstrong, wasn't he the key background painter for *Snow White*?

MN: Sam kinda of became the key background painter, yes.

DJ: Because Claude Coats told me that Mique Nelson was the key background painter for the shorts, but for *Snow White* his color was too flamboyant, and therefore he hardly did any backgrounds for *Snow White*, and they had a terrible fight. He and Sam Armstrong were at odds during the whole *Snow White* business.

MN: I was in on it, too, the Mique Nelson thing.

DJ: Apparently, he didn't do much on *Snow White*. That's what Claude Coats said. They gave him credit, but...

MN: Mique, in fact, was kind of eased out.

DJ: That's why he was very angry.

MN And they started to put him over doing publicity and stuff like that.

DJ: What about Sam Armstrong. He was quite a bit older than you?

MN: Yes.

DJ: Did you ever go in and watch him paint?

MN: Yes, at the desk next to me.

[Changing the subject]

MN: I was painting backgrounds along there and then I did a couple of sketches for the Witch's dungeon and all of a sudden I found myself doing model cels. Then they gave me the section to do toward the end of the picture, and they moved me out of the background room and put me up by myself in this room where I could see Walt. So I was painting and doing layout and painting backgrounds and everything up there in that room all by myself. Then from there I shifted down and became head of the [color] model department. I didn't ever go back into Background.

DJ: Why do you think they had you go from doing backgrounds to doing layout sketches for the Queen going down the staircase?

MN: I had no idea. You just went where they told you to go in that studio.

DJ: Was it toward the end of the movie?

MN: It was toward the end of the movie and they were rushing to finish the picture up, because I started to do that tail end of the thing.

DJ: I mean where the Queen is going down the stairs.

MN: The only thing I can remember about that was that I showed that sketch and drawing to Hugh Hennesy. And when the thing was all kinda winding down, Hugh said, "Maybe you'd like to have this for a souvenir," and he gave me this sketch back. That's how I happened to get it back. I didn't ever go back into the background department, because I did the color models and all that, and then they started to develop *Bambi*.

[Concerning live action]

MN: I remember seeing the puddle they put up where… It was Snow White, when she was swinging on a rope and dropped into the water, and she was fleeing through the forest. Remember she's clinging to a vine and all that? I remember watching out the window while they were photographing that and she was swinging on a rope and she kept doing it over and over again and falling into the puddle. It was done out on the parking lot. They put her out in the parking lot and they built up this kind of big thing with the ropes on it, and she'd swing up over the thing and they were photographing this, swinging on the thing. I remember seeing that. You see, in the studio, you did your job. That's where you were. I was a background painter, so I didn't associate particularly with the animators or the storymen or the layout men at all. After all, I was a very junior member of the staff.

[About seeing someone else's work that may have been copied from your own]

MN: It's a very peculiar thing. We were all in it together. We were all putting ideas and effort into the thing. It was a joint project. If something, if they reverse this staircase and it was from my sketch, I didn't feel mine had been stolen. I felt I had contributed this. This whole period of when we were working, we were, in a sense, pioneering the technique of animation. And whatever old-hat things, these days, were things that we pioneered. Like the colored line and different things like that. And the binders in the paint, and stuff like that, were gradually developed in the paint lab to get paint to adhere really well to the acetate and so forth. And they switched from the old acetate to the new type of cels. It was so tricky to get the paint to adhere to those old celluloids. They were always repairing cels.

[Referring to his own backgrounds]

MN: I did this one with the chair. I did the bedroom scene, all the interior here… Hugh Hennesy would come in while we were painting the stuff. This had a door on it. It swings open. And I think this is one of the times they innovated and put some colored lines on some of the doors or something on that scene. But a lot of the stuff looks very familiar to me because I was rendering all this stuff: close-ups of the bed and the end of the bed and the wall and all this sort of thing.

You know the amount of loving care that was given to this and the ideas that were fed into it. We were all enthralled with it. We knew we were doing something very special. Going back to your statement about being robbed: I don' think that type of thing existed, really. There was a certain amount of in-fighting probably, but all this stuff went into the hopper to produce a picture. We were not... From my standpoint I'd always been rather stupid as far as studio work goes. I just enjoyed my work, I did the best I could, and I didn't play politics. Once in a while I'd go out and get drunk with Freddie Moore. Freddie and I would go out on Riverside Drive or some bar there and get pie-eyed.

DJ: I heard that drinking was rampant at the studio.

MN: I tell you, working at an animation studio is a nerve-wracking business. It really is. It's not fun and games at all. It really is hard, hard, hard work.

DJ: And yet they were doing practical jokes all the time.

MN: Most of those took place over in the animation department. In the background department we were all a bunch of nervous wrecks from trying to render all this darn stuff. And then we had the juries.

[About backgrounds]

MN: They are beautiful. When you consider they were all done in transparent wash and built up... I remember doing some trees... This is the type of stuff I painted. All this stuff for the last sequence I was laying out and painting and all that sort of stuff.

DJ: Were you there when they decided they were going to use yellow for Snow White's dress or anything like that?

MN: Oh yeah. We were experimenting with that, I remember, and the final selection of the dwarfs' costumes and all that.

DJ: What were some of the other colors for Snow White that you can recall that were not used?

MN: I remember at one time she was far more colorful than she finally ended up.

DJ: Like maybe she had more red?

MN: Probably.

DJ: Did she ever have a pink dress or a different color dress?

MN: I think she always had that little dark bodice on her and light stuff here. I don't recall if we ever had any different color combination. We probably did. You know when you're sketching, you do two, three, half a dozen or a dozen sketches, watercolors, in tones like this. And then you have to make them work. So all of a sudden you throw all those things away and you say, "We're going to go with this one." And you forget all about the rest of them. Having gone through years of selecting stuff like that, I don't recall.

I remember we gradually selected these colors. At one time I had the only existing cel that had all the Seven Dwarfs on it. I represented the animation industry [at the Smithsonian traveling exhibition] and that was the only piece of animation art, the only cel, they had in the show. Gordon [Legg] was very good at designing, at lettering the titles. I wouldn't be surprised if he designed that [the Snow White lettering at the beginning of the movie]. He probably worked with Albert Hurter on this. Albert had an awful lot to do with it, the total overall appearance of *Snow White*.

[Break in tape]

MN: Who wrote the "Lord's Prayer"?

DJ: Alfred Malotte.

MN: Well, that was being composed up there. Then there was some kind of ruckus that went on, and Malotte left because he had... You see, I had a contract eventually at Disney which gave them control of everything creative I did. I couldn't even do a postcard that they didn't own. They call them "yellow-dog" contracts. I tried to look at this thing and I said, "Gee wiz, I may want to do some watercolors or something like that." So I went and asked an attorney. He said, "Go ahead and sign it. They can't make it hold up in court." On paper they owned every creative idea, anything you did.

DJ: What about this Malotte?

MN: I remember vaguely hearing this "Lord's Prayer" being composed and played upstairs there [by Malotte]. And he left sometime around about then.

Paul Smith once was playing me little fugues and stuff that he had composed. I said, "Why don't you go ahead with it?" And he said, "Who's got time for it?" You get involved in the studio work and if you really are into it, you don't have the energy to come home and burn the midnight oil and try to do something creative on your own.

DJ: What do you think was the best background you did for *Snow White*?

MN: Most of the stuff I painted was the interior of the cottage and also the stuff at the end of the picture. And that was all kind of gray and hazy, and then we had the blossoms falling down and that sort of stuff. But that was not much of a punch; it was grayed down.

DJ: Funny that you're not sure.

MN: Everybody worked so hard and was so punch-drunk to get it out. We had to get it out. And we kept hearing rumors, "Gosh, he had to borrow some more money from the Bank of America to get through another week." We were all really working to get this picture out, because as we saw little bits and pieces of it, we knew we had something. Then it was the satisfaction of knowing it was such a smash hit. I still think it's a gem.

DJ: Did Walt come into your room while you were working and check your work personally?

MN: He was in and out of the room. Sam [Armstrong] had a tendency to keep everything under his coat tails. Chances are he took the backgrounds and took them in to Walt and showed him. Because Walt would be in and out of the room unless, as I said, he would come in and bring visitors in and stuff like that, and I'd see him then. I do recall him coming in and poking his head in the door when I was working up there on a sequence.

DJ: Is Sam Armstrong's wife still living?

MN: Sam was never married. Ray Lockrem did a small amount of painting. He died an alcoholic. Phil Dike didn't paint backgrounds. He was, in the sense, a talent scout. In fact, he was the one who got me started there at Disney.

DJ: Was Sam a nice person?

MN: I didn't like him.

DJ: Tell me why.

MN: Because he was a selfish, ambitious person.

DJ: How much older than you was he?

MN: Oh, he probably was ten years older.

DJ: So he was in his mid-30s and you were in your mid-20s, late 20s?

MN: I hope I don't hurt your feelings, but he was a very proselyting Christian Scientist. He would take stuff and take it out of the room and come back and wouldn't tell you what he'd done.

DJ: So he was a sly one.

MN: He really was. I don't think Sam was generally well-liked. One time, many years later, I was working at Warner Bros. and that's the last time I saw Sam. They were considering hiring him for something, to do some layout work or something like that. It turned out that he was too ingrained with the Disney snob. And he couldn't fit into what we were doing at Warner Bros. He came in and saw me in my room a couple of times. Then all of a sudden he disappeared and that's the last I ever saw of Sam. The general impression was that Sam was gay. As the studio grew, these various key people began collecting treats around them. We were segregated into... When they built the new studio, each wing had a locked door and a secretary, and you had to check in and out. And everybody was under lock and key.

DJ: What about Albert Hurter?

MN: I remember going in and trying to tell him how much I admired his drawings. But one didn't circulate in the studio. If you were in this department, that's where you were, that was your job. If you're on layout, that was your job. If you're ink and paint, that was your job. If you animated, that was your job. As I recall, there wasn't a great deal of circulation.

Harold Miles was a wonderful draftsman. Gustaf Tenggren: I worked with him on *Bambi*. He was a concept artist.

DJ: So you would say that some of these sketches were done prior to the actual layout rather than the other way around?

MN: Oh yeah. Tenggren was a concept sketch artist. Chances are that he was probably doing ideas like this [*Snow White* sketches] and Philippi put them into working order. See, I did a lot. I worked on *Fantasia* and *Bambi*. [Shows drawing of forest by Philippi] This undoubtedly came out of the original sketches by Tenggren, the concept sketches of the woods. And I always thought that Tenggren was a follow-up of Rackham. I have a hunch that Tenggren did a lot of this stuff and Philippi as he got the sequence of going through the forest and all that probably had these sketches of Tenggren up on the wall. All this material was all being fed into the hopper to produce the picture. I sketched a year and a half on *Bambi*, for instance, and there's no direct sketch of mine in the picture.

Albert Hurter was the concept artist for the cottage and the general feeling that you got, all the detail and the carving and all the tables and chairs and doors and all that type of thing. The castle and all that might have been Harold Mile, because this was the type of thing that he drew. He worked on Cecil B. DeMille's *King of Kings* and all these big, dramatic, live-action pictures that had castles and things of that kind. He was very well-known in the industry. I was floored when I met him. Of course, I was kind of bowled over when they put me in there and I worked with Gustaf Tenggren. I never did go back into the background department after I left it. They put me over in the concept sketching after I did this drawing for the staircase in *Snow White* and a couple of other things. I think I did some sketches for *The Old Mill*. That's when they decided that maybe I'd do better as a concept artist. And more or less that's what I did from then on in all the studios.

The animators were the ones that became a closer-knit group. The background people didn't socialize a great deal.

DJ: Did you design or work on the color for the mask?

MN: Yes, very much so.

DJ: How did that come about, the colors for that mask? I do know that Hugh Hennesy himself made his face up in a mask and was photographed and Woolie Reitherman animated that and used his model. But as far as getting the color scheme…

MN: I think I probably worked the color scheme out myself. Because I knew what the setup was, and what we had to do. This was when we started to employ colored lines around the color separation. No black-and-white lines were used on this.

DJ: The light looks like it's from down below.

MN: That's the way we… The black and white indicated that they were to use a lower light. And then we had to break it down to make it work for flat tones of color. Chances are I selected the colors and everything to contrast with the bright warmth of the flames here so this would come out.

DJ: You worked on the color of the box. Did you look at any crib sheets, like pictures out of old art books that you could recall to get the idea of using such a thing?

MN: That stuff is all pre-determined by the original. Maybe Albert Hurter or somebody did the original sketch of the box.

DJ: You mean he knew what color he wanted?

MN: He didn't know what color he wanted, but the design and everything comes down from the model department.

DJ: Were you ever influenced by, for example, Persian miniatures or anything like that for the color scheme of anything you did in _Snow White_?

MN: I have a hunch that the colors and everything on this box were selected so that they would work well against the Queen. In other words, one prop had to read against the other and so forth. So colors were always carefully selected so that they would read well on the screen. And this would have to always work: these warm colors would have to work against the tones of her costume. This is what usually were deciding factors in selecting colors.

DJ: And this medallion that she has there, were you involved in the color scheme on that, too?

MN: I was working with all the models and I don't recall specifically any particular one. I worked on the dwarfs, I worked on Snow White, I worked on the Queen.

[Changing the subject]

MN: When I finished working in the studio, the last thing I did was some of the Dr. Seuss TV shows for DePatie-Freleng. In a sense, when I got through with the animation business, I was through with it. I'd had it. I was fed up with it. And really I have never had an urge to go back into it, because I became interested in doing serigraph and watercolors and portraits and stuff like that. In other words, all the things you put aside because you're busy earning a living and paying the mortgage. Then when you put that behind you... I always say and have said before that I fell over the retirement line on my face. I was ready for it. The studios are very complicated and sometimes very sticky places to work. And Disney particularly, the studio cliques... And I'm not a joiner or a clique person. I'm a person that did the best I could with the job and got it finished. I didn't play politics. I was young, yes, but I was fired because I went out on strike. I didn't think $13 a week was a living wage.

DJ: But you weren't making $13 a week.

MN: My goodness, I was up on the third floor, I was making 56 bucks a week.

DJ: You knew Art Babbitt.

MN: I knew Art Babbitt. I was there the day the cops dragged him out of the building and threw him off the lot.

DJ: He was and still is a very angry man.

MN: Very feisty.

DJ: Did you socialize with any of these people?

MN: No. I knew a few of them. I was too busy making a living, and then I'd do my own art work on the weekends. I guess I felt the responsibility of... These were Depression years.

DJ: Were you married at that time?

MN: No. I wasn't married and I was taking care of a mother and a brother and a sister, sometimes a brother-in-law and a niece. When I was through at the studio I went home and was exhausted. Also I didn't have any money to socialize.

DJ: But you socialized with Freddie Moore, you went drinking with him.

MN: Once in a while, sure.

DJ: Now it was always WASPy-oriented, wasn't it, wouldn't you say in retrospect?

MN: In retrospect, I think so.

DJ: There were no black people there at all.

MN: Otis Williams, I think. He was a cel washer. But nobody creative. No black people and a few Jewish people. It was pretty WASPy. Of course, what made it such a terrible crime for anybody, shall we say, to go out on strike against Walt, because he was... I've always given Walt all sorts of credit for what was accomplished in the studio. But I can't whitewash him for what happened regarding the strike. Because I do think that the prime movers of the whole thing were his brother Roy and Gunther Lessing who was the attorney and a big stockholder in the thing.

DJ: Walt really wasn't a businessman.

MN: Walt in a sense wasn't a real businessman, but I'm quite sure he knew exactly where every buck was.

DJ: Possibly; but I think he genuinely felt betrayed. I think he couldn't understand why they would be going on strike. I think he had that kind of a mind.

MN: I think probably he did feel that way. But he just couldn't understand why people couldn't live on $13 a week. And yet I've talked with guys... They had five guys living all in one little old shack to make ends meet and doing your own cooking and everything. They'd have one automobile so they could go back and forth to the studio. They were living hand to mouth. I was painting backgrounds and working there and working my ass off, and yet I was walking to the studio. I was within walking distance of the studio. And I didn't have a spare cent; I very seldom had any money to spare or throw around.

DJ: That's because you were supporting a family.

MN: Like various people, yes. But on the other hand, there wasn't enough money to spread around. I remember when I bought my first car, a little old Plymouth sedan.

DJ: How old were you then?

MN: We were working at the Hyperion studio. I got tired of walking two-and-a-half miles each way to work. There were no bus lines out there in Hyperion, no bus lines that came out to the Silver Lake district out there. I could have gone downtown and rode on the streetcar and come out to Glendale and then walk across the bridge back into the studio. There was a reason for the strike to happen and a very firm reason for it. Because the living conditions that a lot of these guys were living under...

[Going back to *Snow White*]

MN: I remember we all crowded in on the soundstage and as I recall it wasn't completed. Some in color, some in line, and all this stuff.

DJ: And Grace Godino said some of them would get up and speak the lines because some of it hadn't been edited.

MN: I remember going in on the soundstage.

DJ: What was your reaction? Were you thrilled with it?

MN: I was thrilled with it, yes. And of course we were given seats according to our seniority at the studio. So I was way up in the balcony for the premiere. I remember I was very thrilled with it when I saw it. In fact, creatively, even many, many years afterward when I got a film all together, I would still get a hoot out of seeing how the thing gelled. Sometimes it would gel beautifully, sometimes it wouldn't. Other cartoons I worked on… In other words, creatively I think that animation is a real art form in itself. And it's the first time that graphics moved on the surface since the time they drew the cave drawings, way back.

You realize that dialogue was one section and sound effects was another section and the music was another section and all this and that. And of course, there's a master exposure sheet and everything had to be coordinated. But everyone worked in their own little section, as it were. So if I'm painting backgrounds, I don't necessarily talk to the musicians.

DJ: But you remember talking to Leigh Harline?

MN: Yes, talking to Leigh Harline, and I vaguely remember something being said about his working so late and trying to get the stuff together.

DJ: You said he lived in a Spanish house?

MN: Oh yeah, he lived there in the Silver Lake district up the hill. He was one of the original builders up there. My primary memory of the music is Frank Churchill thumping his foot on top of my head.

DJ: And then you mentioned something about Paul Smith.

MN: I remember talking to Paul Smith and he played some original fugues and stuff that he had composed and we were talking about that. I was taking piano lessons at that time.

I always had the feeling that Walt ran that studio by the seat of his pants. Intuitively, he knew in a sense what he liked. If Walt would break it down and do a critique on a section of picture, these guys are all sweating: "Walt's coming! Walt's coming! Walt's coming!" like this. And everybody was running up the wall. He could walk in and look over a thing like this and say, "This isn't working," and they probably had worked six weeks or two months on it. So "this isn't working" and take another tack on this and walk out of the room. No other producer, in the animation business, would ever do that.

Sometimes at Disney they over-polished it and they lost the spirit of it. And this is the thing that made the Warner Bros cartoons so fresh and vivacious. You designed the thing and you turned it out and that was it, period. But the Disney way was constant over-polishing. And they reached a point that they polished it so much that they lost the spirit of the thing.

DJ: Of course that didn't happen in *Snow White*.

MN: No, it didn't happen in *Snow White*. I don't think it happened in *Dumbo*.

DJ: The studio was never the same after the strike.

MN: It became in-grown. I always say that after the strike Walt fired all the really creative people. And I was one of them that he fired.

Ruthie Tompson (b. 1910)

Interviewed on April 21, 2001.

Born in Portland, Maine, on July 22, 1910, Ruthie was raised in Boston, Massachusetts. Her family moved to California in 1918, first arriving in Oakland on November 11, Armistice Day, which marked the end of World War I. As she later recalled, amidst the end-of-the-war celebrations, she and others wore masks over their faces to guard against influenza, which was epidemic at the time.

Later, Ruthie attended Hollywood High School, and at 18 took a job at DuBrock's Riding Academy in the San Fernando Valley, where Walt and Roy Disney frequently played polo. Walt offered Ruthie a job as a painter in the ink-and-paint department, where she helped put finishing touches on the studio's first full-length animated feature, *Snow White and the Seven Dwarfs*, which premiered in 1937.

Soon after, she was promoted to final checker, reviewing the animation cels before they were photographed onto film. By 1948, Ruthie again transferred to animation checking and scene planning. Her technical mind led her to be named supervisor of Disney's scene planning department, where she helped establish the camera mechanics used to photograph animated scenes and background art onto film.

As Bob Broughton, former Disney supervisor of special photographic effects, recalled: "Ruthie was mechanically inclined. She was excellent at figuring out the mathematical and mechanical logistics of camera moves."

As a result of her adept skill at guiding camera movement for animated films, Ruthie was invited to join the International Photographers Union, Local 659 of the IATSE, in 1952. She was one of the first three women to be admitted into the Hollywood camera union.

After dedicating nearly 40 years to Disney and working on virtually every Disney animated feature up through *The Rescuers*, Ruthie Tompson retired in 1975.

DAVID JOHNSON: When was the very first time you saw Walt.

RUTHIE TOMPSON: I guess that it was at the little studio on Kingswell Avenue in 1923.

DJ: You must have been like a teenager.

RT: I was. He and his brother Roy lived two doors down from where I lived.

DJ: Was that on Lyric Street?

RT: On Kingswell Ave.

DJ: Oh, that's when he was staying with his uncle.

RT: Yeah, Uncle Robert.

DJ: So you probably knew Uncle Robert, too?

RT: No, Uncle Robert's son was maybe six or eight months old when I first...
I don't remember Walt there, at that place, but I do at the studio. Because
I was more nosy, I used to look in on my way home from grammar school.
And I think he's the one that invited me in. There were a lot of guys there
and they were doing their animation and stuff. They just turned me loose.
I wandered around, asked questions, and I ended up sitting on the bench
with Roy while he was shooting these animations. He had a blue light that
made my fingernails all purple. You know, that fascinates kids, things like
that. I think they call it a black light.

DJ: Where's the black light coming from?

RT: Above. That was the light they used. It was an antiquated thing and
I was just fascinated with that light. I used to sit on the bench beside Roy
until he'd say, "It's time to go home. You must be hungry." At five o'clock
or something.

DJ: So you did this on several occasions?

RT: Oh yeah, almost every day.

DJ: Why did you take the first step to even go there?

RT: It's on my way to school. And in the window, the two women are
painting the cels, putting the color...the grays, in those days. So first I'm
watching them through the window like that and then somebody comes
out and says, "Hey, why don't you come inside, see what we're doing?" Walt
was always very enthusiastic about everything that he did. He was like
a little kid with a new toy and he just enthused anybody that wanted to
listen to him.

DJ: Including you.

RT: Probably, yeah.

DJ: When did you first come to California?

RT: That was 1921 or 1922, something like that. We lived with my aunt
and uncle.

DJ: You were, like, ten.

RT: No, I was eight when I came to California. We landed here in Oakland on the day that the armistice was signed.

DJ: 1918.

RT: Yeah. I got to stay up after five o'clock for the first time in my life. Kids always go to bed early in our family. We rode all over Oakland in an open-air taxi-cab and I sat where the top was folded back and they threw confetti. Boy, it was an excitement. We all had to wear masks because of the flu epidemic. They met us at the station with this mask.

DJ: Where were you coming from?

RT: Boston. I was born in Portland, Maine. We had a farm up in Vernam, Maine, about two hundred miles north from there. The family had two farms that my grandfather still owned. There was a lake. They used to call it Dodge Pond. But after I was born we lived in Portland to be near my grandmother. And we lived in Boston. So I lived in Boston, goodness knows where.

DJ: Until you were eight?

RT: Yeah.

DJ: And then the family moved out to California.

RT: No, just my mother and I came out. My sister went into a Catholic convent.

DJ: And your father had died by then.

RT: No, my father was quite alive. He lived until his nineties or something. They were separated.

DJ: Oh, I see. So she took you.

RT: And left my sister.

DJ: But she came out with her sister, too?

RT: Her sister was already out here.

DJ: OK. So she came with you. How did you come out, in those days?

RT: Union Pacific.

DJ: Oh, on the train. And that's the day that you arrived, during the armistice?

RT: Here in Oakland, yeah.

DJ: And then you moved to southern California.

RT: It was a roundabout thing. I stayed in Oakland with my grandmother's twin sister, and Mother went on down to Hollywood.

DJ: Was she trying to get into the movies?

RT: I don't know whether she was or not. They knew a lot of the people. I remember while I was living in Oakland at my great aunt's, Mother wrote a letter and said that my aunt was in this movie, but she was sitting at a cocktail table. So we went to the movie. And the minute my aunt came on the screen I jumped up and yelled, "That's my Auntie Irene!" and she was gone. I saw the movie I don't know how many times and each time I pointed to that and nobody ever saw her. But I did! So that was my first acquaintance with the movies, too.

DJ: So that was about when you were ten or so.

RT No, I was about eight or nine. I lived with my great aunt and her son in Oakland for four years with a couple of years mixed up when he got transferred to Dunsmuir and we lived in Dunsmuir a couple of years.

DJ Where's Dunsmuir?

RT: Mount Shasta.

DJ: North.

RT: Yeah, and we lived there awhile and then we came back to Oakland until Mother came and picked me up and we went back east. Back to Boston.

DJ: How long were you there?

RT: Well, we went up to the farm in Vermont. We were going to meet her intended new husband, supposedly. He was a commandant from the Argentine navy. But he never did come to the West Coast. So we went east to join him. Mother got an elopement and we jumped right on the train and came back to California. That's when I was in Los Angeles for the first time.

DJ: This was when you went to the Disney studio?

RT: No, no. This was when I was ten or twelve.

DJ: Oh, so they hadn't even started yet.

RT: No, they just had the little place, on Kingswell. And when I graduated from high school, I was horse crazy so they allowed us out. I could earn some rides by working in the office of the DuBrock Riding Academy. And while I was there, after two or three years (I was with them almost ten years), Walt, Roy, and a bunch of men came out to learn how to play polo. They were all riders. It was Walt...

DJ: Bill Cottrell.

RT: Bill Cottrell, Walt, Roy, Jack Cutting. That was Bud and Wilma and Dad Dubrock. They ran the riding academy. They used to rent horses for a cent a minute, sixty cents an hour. I don't know what they charged them to play polo. It was probably was a couple bucks or more. When Walt and Roy came up to the window to pay I was sitting there. And Roy said, "Ruthie Tompson, what are you doing here?" "Working, of course. What do you think?" [Laughs] Then Walt comes and does the same routine. They both remembered my name from the time I was twelve or thirteen, until I'm in my twenties. They remembered me, they recognized me: first name, last name. "How's your sister? How's your brother? Dorothy and Junior." And Junior's my cousin, not my brother, but they thought he was my brother. We all worked in this thing, played games, and stuff.

DJ: In the Alice series?

RT: Yeah. And they gave us money to play up and down the street and have us run and stuff and do things like that.

DJ: I want to go back to Kingswell, because there aren't very many people that were there. Can you talk more about that? You would just sit there and watch?

RT: Yeah. Roy's the one I remember the best of all. I've always been real fond of Roy. He's my favorite fellow. I was a little leery of Walt because he was a smart guy and running the whole shebang and everything. When I first went to work at the studio we had a lot of fun. I worked in what they called the nunnery.

DJ: What year did you come?

RT: Well, first I was there about 1932. And I worked on the very tail end of *Snow White*.

DJ: Oh, you did. That was in 1937, though.

RT: I know. But I worked there first in 1932. We went to school and then we got hired and then we got fired because we were hired to finish a picture.

DJ: Let's go back. When you were at Kingswell, when they moved to Hyperion in 1926, you had stopped visiting them at that point.

RT: That's right.

DJ: So you would go every day for a long time and then you got in the Alice Comedies and they would take pictures and you would run down the street.

RT: All the kids in the neighborhood. All of us. No separate individuals. And he probably knew the names of all these kids. Just like he knew mine.

DJ: And then suddenly you stopped going there because you got interested in other things.

RT: Moved away.

DJ: Oh, you moved away? Where did you move to that time?

RT: It was in the area.

DJ: Where did you go to high school?

RT: I went to Belmont High School and I went to Hollywood High School. I went to so many schools that I never made any friends, no school friends or anything like that. I had no favorite teachers or anything. Because first I'm in New York, I'm in Boston, I'm in Maine, I'm in California, I'm back in New York, and so forth, back and forth...

DJ: A gypsy.

RT: I went to Roosevelt High School in Oakland.

DJ: Why did your mother keep moving?

RT: I have no idea. She married John Roberts in 1922.

DJ: That's not the Argentinian.

RT: No.

DJ: He went out of the picture.

RT: He's out of the picture because Mother got sick and we came back. That's one of the reasons we came to California was her health. She was the puny one of the two and she lived alone.

DJ: And she's the violinist?

RT: Yeah. She was on the concert stage.

DJ: She was practicing all the time when you were moving?

RT: Yeah. When we came out on the train she practiced every night on the train. They had a concert in the club car.

DJ: Did she have a manager?

RT: I don't think so. But she right away made arrangements to take teachers or to have a teacher when she came out. And her twin's husband loved violin and he took lessons from the same guy. This fellow told her one day, "You, I won't charge anything. Him, I'll charge. He'll never know how to play the violin."

DJ: So you remember her playing all this violin stuff?

RT: Yeah, always. My sister and I used to sit and listen to her practice. They made us sit on the chair and not even waggle our feet. We could sit there until we got so restless we couldn't stand it anymore and we'd go out. She'd call somebody to come and get us. That's how we used to sit and listen to her. She'd parade back and forth playing and we'd sit there.

DJ: Was Lillian Disney at the Kingswell, do you recall?

RT: She and her sister were the two...

DJ: Hazel Sewell.

RT: Yeah, Hazel sat at the window and painted. They were the ones that were doing the painting.

DJ: What were they like?

RT: Oh, very gracious and lovely. And friendly, warm people. Hazel was great.

DJ: Did they have much of a sense of humor?

RT: I thought so. But then I'm not going around cracking jokes very often. And the kids were great. Diane was a little snooty, but the other one...

DJ: Sharon. She was adopted.

RT: Yeah. I know. Now she was very friendly with everybody. Diane was polite, but she was not as affectionate. Sharon was very warm and she used to come down to shows with Walt.

DJ: So in 1932 you were about twenty-two, I guess.

RT: Yes.

DJ: And you got a job at Disney's, in 1932.

RT: When he played polo, one day he was paying his bill and he said, "Why don't you come work for us?" I said, "I can't draw." He said, "You don't need to. We'll teach you what you need to know. You come to night school." Evie Parsons' father kept the horse in the private barn and she used to be out there almost every day. And we became quite good friends. I said, "But my friend Evie can draw." He said, "Bring her along." So the two of us went in there and we went to night school twice a week.

DJ: For no pay.

RT: Well, no, of course not. No, it was free. They said if can cut the mustard we'll hire you. So the time came for us to graduate, and we both got hired. It was, I think, late November or early December.

DJ: And this is 1932?

RT: Yes, and we were working on shorts, finishing a bunch of shorts. I think they were about ghosts.

DJ: Oh, no, that came much later.

RT: Did it?

DJ: Yeah, *Flower and Trees* was 1932.

RT: No, it wasn't that. We did something with a bunch of green ghosts… It was 1937 when I went back. See, they kept us to finish whatever it was.

DJ: Why did you quit?

RT: They laid us off.

DJ: Oh, they laid you off. Well, how long were you actually working there?

RT: I don't remember.

DJ: Was it more than a couple of months?

RT: Probably just about that much.

DJ: And then all of a sudden they laid you off.

RT: What they hired us for was finished and we were gone about Christmas time, I think. And two weeks later they called us back. In the meantime, there was a family that came out to the riding academy. The guy opened an office and I offered to help him. They called me back to the studio and I said, "I can't leave him in the lurch." I'm just sitting there answering the phones, but I'm getting a pittance. And I couldn't do that. So I didn't go back for about two years, more or less. And that's probably why they got me down like 1935, probably, when I went back.

DJ: Tail end of *Snow White* was 1937.

RT: Could have been 1936 or '37, something like that. Yeah. So that's when I went back.

DJ: Now, when you went back, did you go in as a painter or as an inker?

RT: I went in as a painter. I wasn't good as an inker. When we went to school, the first time, the first place they put us was in inking. You know how fragile those lines are. You do not go this way with those pens [upwards], you only draw from [like this, down] or they just spread ink all over everything. Of course, the first thing I did was I'm drawing Mickey and everything is splattering. I spent the whole evening there trying to do one Mickey. The second night… Evie and I both went into inking the first night. She stayed, but I didn't.

DJ: Who was the supervisor? It wasn't Marie Henderson, was it?

RT: Yes, it was.

DJ: I understand that she was quite formidable.

RT: Oh yeah.

DJ: Big woman.

RT: Not too big.

DJ: But she was very firm and stern.

RT: Yep, yep.

DJ: And people were frightened of her.

RT: [Laughs] I wasn't afraid of her. No. But anyway, she comes up to me and she says, "Honey, I think maybe you'd better go into the painting department." And of course I didn't know I was being demoted. The inkers were the top dogs. Boy, and what a clique they were. Grace Baily was one of those inkers.

DJ: Evie Coats, too.

RT: Anyway, I went in and they sat me down beside one of the faster students. And this kid, she just floored me at it. I'm sitting there painting, she picks up all her paintings and runs up to get some more to do, and I'm still on number three. So it's a wonder I got hired. I know it wasn't because my name was Ruthie. Because Evie and I made a pact that we would never, *ever* mention how we got in. Because everybody has to give a drawing, they have to submit their artwork, but we didn't. I had a friend who was a real good artist and she tried and tried and tried. Finally she made it. Her name was Vivian Brian and she was an inker. She was one of the better ones. She was so conscientious, she'd work during tea time, she'd work through her lunch hour. I kept saying, "Vivian, when you get used to doing this, you're going to be sorry, because you can't keep up the speed you've been doing if you take a proper lunch, if you take a proper rest period of fifteen minutes. You've got to stop it." Finally she did, but…

DJ: What finally brought you back in 1937?

RT: They called me again.

DJ: Oh yes, they needed people for *Snow White*.

RT: Yeah. Evie called me. I'd just been on a trip up to Yosemite and seen the opening of the Bay Bridge or something. She called me and said that: "You want to come back to work?" I said, "Really, after all this time?" She said, "Do you or don't you?" I said "Yes, yes, yes!" So I went back.

DJ: Who was Martha Rose Bodie?

RT: She was an inking supervisor. And I think she was over the supervisors. Others were just plain supervisors.

DJ: So she was underneath Hazel who was really the head of it all?

RT: Yeah.

DJ: How was Martha Rose Bodie in relation to Marie Henderson?

RT: Same as.

DJ: So she and Marie Henderson were the two supervisors under Hazel and Marie was the more formidable of the two. I understand she was built like a truck driver.

RT: *No.* Who told you that?

DJ: I think it was Ward Kimball.

RT: Well, don't believe him. He didn't like her, I betcha.

DJ: No, I'm sure he didn't. So Marie Henderson was very stern, but not…

RT: Yep, she was. She took her work seriously. But she wasn't any more buxom than I am right now. I don't remember that at all. She'd have scared me if she was like that and she didn't scare me.

DJ: And none of the supervisors were like that?

RT: I don't think so.

DJ: OK. And Martha Rose Bodie was much nicer.

RT: Yes, she was. We were the low-class nuns and the inkers were the upper-class nuns. And we didn't fraternize too much with the inkers.

DJ: Oh, you didn't?

RT: No. Betty Ann Gunther was a supervisor, too. And she worked on *Snow White.*

DJ: So when you went back, they were working on *Snow White*. Can you talk a little bit about the studio at that time?

RT: Frenzy.

DJ: It was.

RT: It was. They were working around the clock. Like Evie worked… She's the one that came off at 8 o'clock in the morning when I arrived at 8 o'clock. She worked all night, I expect. Twelve-hour shift or whatever it was. And I came in at eight. I can remember one morning I got in there… Evie's left handed… She writes right-handed and erases with her left hand. She could also draw with her left hand. And I'm walking in and here's Evie on the desk like this and she's painting on the Queen. "Who's the fairest one of all?" She's painting on the Queen. I say, "Evie?" She's fixing the cel. When we worked, we got the finished stuff and if anything was wrong with it, we had to fix it. She's fixing it. [Laughs]. "Evie! Go home!" "I can't, I've got to finish this because we're late." "Sit up!" I said. That was a couple of weeks after I came back. When I came the second time I moved in like I belonged and of course, that's my nature. I don't just sit back and say, "What do you want me to do next?" I get in and do it if there's something to be done. And so I'm a pretty good fixer-upper.

DJ: So that's what you did, you fixed up the cels?

RT: Anything that was wrong.

DJ: Oh, you were a checker then? I thought you were still a painter.

RT: I wasn't a checker. I came in to help. Then I became a checker at that time.

DJ: So you didn't go into painting again?

RT: No. I went right into checking. I had to learn how to read the exposure sheets and all that stuff, but there was no time for that. You get here and do whatever they tell you to do. I was cleaning cels, I was doing everything.

DJ: Oh, cleaning them, too?

RT: Oh sure, we had to clean them several times, always.

DJ: You mean wash them off and reuse them again?

RT: No, no. We wiped the dust off the cels. Full of electricity and stuff.

DJ: Could you describe a little bit about that?

RT: Whenever you finish a scene, in Checking you do everything the camera department does except shoot. So in doing that you can tell if everything works. You compare it with the instructions on the exposure sheet. You count the cels, see how many cels are called for. Then go through them like this to see if they painted the right spots in the right places, and after you get through you stack them and then you unstack them and you clean them. You're supposed to wear either a new [garbled] or a soft cloth and you clean the cels with it. A cloth, real fine, like a handkerchief almost, made of cotton, but it's very, very fine. And you get fingerprints off it. When you're working with cels you're going to leave fingerprints if you've got any oil on your fingers at all.

DJ: I thought they always wore gloves, though, to prevent that.

RT: No, we did wear gloves, but only at certain times. I never did wear gloves. I've got real dry hands. We had a period when we had blowers in the hall and we had something to keep our hair. We wore sleeves and things like that, to keep dandruff off. We did everything trying to keep those cels clean. And we ended up by cleaning them and stacking them and sending them to Camera absolutely pristine clean. But then the guys had to handle them and you never pick the cel up like this [with your hand], because when you pick it up this way you make a dimple and the lights in the camera are on the side and they pick that dimple up and shoot it right up into the camera. You'd see the flare. So you always pick them up like this and put them down like this [with the tips of the fingers]. But you never, never pick up a cel this way so that you pinch it and make a dimple in the middle, which is so easy to do.

DJ: Well, was it nerve-wracking knowing that you had to...?

RT: No.

DJ: Now was the atmosphere quiet or did somebody have a radio going at the time.

RT: We had radios at the new studio.

DJ: I mean at the old studio.

RT: Some started at the old studio, they did have some radios.

DJ: Do you remember Helen Ogger?

RT: Oh yeah.

DJ: Now tell me about her cause somebody said she was an ogre.

RT: There were some people that she liked and some she didn't. And she was a little austere. She was a talented lady. I liked everybody as a rule, you know. And I know that Katherine Kerwin decided she wanted to learn how to drive and she got a Model A coupe, I think from Evie. She was a checker. So Evie sold her car to Katherine. Katherine had never driven before. And Evie bought a Studebaker from Helen Ogger. And Helen got a new something.

DJ: A new motorcycle. I understand she came dressed in leather.

RT: I never saw her do that. Anyway, Katherine learned how to drive and right off the bat she started going on trips. Palm Springs, places like that.

DJ: That was a long way, in those days.

RT: She lived up in Atwater district, somewhere on top of the hill. It was about that time we had the strike, when Katherine got her first car. Walt was friendly with everybody in the studio. He knew us all by name. He would see us in the hall and call us by name. And we had that strike and he became a different person. I think he realized at that time that he *was* the boss. He was one of us before that. Because they had that big party out at the Norconian. It was wild in areas, in sections. I got a little tipsy. I tried to ride the donkey. I didn't fall off, but I came close to it. Somebody got a picture of me with one foot up in the air. [Laughs] And we'd haul them out of the pool and put them to bed, wherever we could. It was really quite a party. That was the party to end all parties, too, because it was so wild in parts.

DJ: So you really feel that the strike turned Walt into more of an autocrat?

RT: That's a good word, I guess, but I don't think it was that bad. He learned that he was the boss. He was it before, but it was a friendly it. Because I can remember coming in from driving through the gate, parking the car and… The first day of the strike he's sitting on the big things in front of the animation building and his hat's turned up and I said, "What are you going to do now?" He said, "I don't know." It was awful. I mean friends became enemies and you just dislike this person and that person because they went on strike. I mean a lot of them I lost faith in…

DJ: Well, do you remember Maurice Noble?

RT: Yes.

DJ: He went on strike and he was fired. But he felt that there was good reason to go on strike because he said that they didn't get a living wage, the people who started at that time.

RT: I know that's the reason for it. But they worked at Disney's and they *stayed* at Disney's and they were paid when there was no work, to do something else. In other words, you didn't lose your weekly check.

DJ: But you did, in 1932, when you were laid off.

RT: That's different. That's when I first started. And I was hired for a reason: to finish a picture. OK, the picture was finished. Two weeks later I was called back.

DJ: Then you couldn't make it because you already had another job.

RT: Yes. Then when I went back, we went through a lot of sour periods where we had nothing to do. We started making these cel set-ups, making the frames and all that just to be busy. We made those so Walt could give them to friends. And we were paid our weekly salary. We had no animation or anything going through and we weren't laid off. We stayed. We were paid. Where can you work day in and day out, year after year, you're working every day, not laid off? In the picture business, the minute the picture's finished, off you go! They're laid off and they're gone until they're called back and that's what the picture business is today. I was grateful for what monies I got because I went through the Depression. And of course my step-father was a commercial artist, and at that time commercial artists didn't get nothing for nothing. So we were without money quite a bit of the time. And what I first earned at the studio helped pay the rent and do a few things like that. So during the Depression I worked in the riding academy. I didn't cost anybody any money. They gave me $5 a week and I was happy for that, and breakfast, lunch, dinner, whatever, or gas. And if I ran out of gas, I'd give the gas station guy a ring and say, "Can I have five gallons?" I'll come back and get it.

DJ: He was your local pawn shop.

RT: Yeah.

DJ: But you didn't do that very often, did you?

RT: I bought a lot of gas with that ring. I've still got it. The guy'd see me coming in and I'd say, "OK," and I'd get some gas, I'd get five gallons.

DJ: Now you were living with your mother at this time.

RT: And my step-father.

DJ: He was was a musician?

RT: No, strictly an artist.

Thor Putnam
(1911–2001)

Interviewed in 1990; transcription by Ed Mazzilli.

Thorington Caldwell Putnam was born on October 14, 1911, in Berkeley, California. He graduated from Stanford University in 1932 with Frank Thomas, Ollie Johnston, and James Algar, and all four men shared apartments while studying at the Chouinard Art Institute in Los Angeles. He studied illustration with Pruett Carter from 1932 to 1934, and joined the Disney studio in 1934 in the layout department. He served as assistant layout man on *Snow White* and *Ferdinand the Bull*, then became head of layout on *Pinocchio*. He worked on all subsequent productions in that capacity until 1942, when he joined the U.S. Navy for active duty (June 1, 1942, to October 2, 1946).

In the Navy, he supervised the production of thirty-seven U.S. Navy training films and photographic reports. This work covered a wide variety of naval subjects, both technical and dramatic. Putnam was often responsible for all phases of production, including in many cases the writing of the script.

On November 4, 1946, Putnam rejoined the Disney studio in the layout department and worked on all animated features, from *Melody Time* to *Lady and the Tramp*, and on many shorts.

Thor Putnam left Disney on March 13, 1959, and died on January 26, 2001.

DAVID JOHNSON: Is there anything you can recall about those days, particularly about *Snow White*?

THOR PUTNAM: I can recall the wishing-well sequence in the castle. We did indeed do an incredible amount of research on that castle. You couldn't do something like that from memory.

DJ: What kind of research?

TP: As I recall, the one in Segovia, the one there is an Alcazar that is very much like the one that's in the picture.

DJ: In fact, they used that for *Ferdinand the Bull* if I remember, for the opening.

TP: I think it is, yes. One thing I was going to say about the Disney architecture and this includes *Cinderella*: it's almost an architecture of its own. In effect, it's almost a non-period architecture. The castle in *Cinderella* is new. John Hench did an awful lot of the design on that and he just did it out of his head.

DJ: But you recalled some research being done on the castle.

TP: Oh yes, I know I did my share. Like the turrets.

DJ: And the one you can think of is the one in Spain.

TP: That was done just for the distance shot.

DJ: Then what about these close-up shots?

TP: The close-ups I don't specifically remember by name, just what that would be.

The studio did indeed have quite a good library and a lot of good reference in it. It was just down the hall and you could always go there.

DJ: Now for this wishing well, did you draw anything for the design of that?

TP: I remember really struggling on an up-shot or a down-shot. I was trying to get depth in this thing. In other words, bigger stones here and as they went down they got smaller and smaller and smaller. I remember working really hard at that one, because it's a hard thing to take a flat surface and get a feeling of depth.

DJ: Did you have photographs to assist you with that?

TP: Possibly stones, just the appearance of stones may have been used in that. But other than that it's pretty much [Charles] Philippi leading the way, the way he wanted it to look.

DJ: Including the vines and the buckets?

TP: Yeah, things like that. And just as I think about it again, I was appalled at how he could pull this out of his head and his ability to do that.

DJ: Do you recall using any sketches by Albert Hurter?

TP: Yes, definitely. I'll tell you another thing: after having made a layout to go to camera or to go to be painted, there was a policy at that time to take the layout, the finalized sketch and to send it to Hurter for him to work over. And he would; and very often he would take your sketch and not like something—it wasn't old enough or didn't have the feeling that he was able to impart—and he would work over your sketch.

DJ: Do you remember him working over yours?

TP: Yes, I do.

DJ: And what did he have to do about it?

TP: Very often he would make something more aged than it was or than you had made it; more textured, possibly, than what you'd put into it. He had that certain touch and they wanted that. They wanted his ability to do that. And it was important.

DJ: Can you recall anything specific in your designs that he changed that at the time you didn't like, but then realized that he was right?

TP: I would say specifically making stones look older, more character, maybe more rugged. He would actually just work right over your drawing with putting that kind of work on it.

DJ: And what about in the trees, the flight through the forest?

TP: Yes, he worked on that.

DJ: Do you recall anything that he changed on that?

TP: Branches sometimes, certain things that he just wanted to put his touch to. I would definitely say that Albert Hurter contributed a lot to *Snow White* and *Pinocchio* later on. For example, the way he visualized the Prince. You can see his influence there. As a matter of fact, he would be the first visualization of a sequence; he would come in with stuff like that.

DJ: Tell me about Perce Pearce.

TP: [Laughs] I remember him arriving at Disney's. He came from New York and I saw him go up the ladder. I saw him do just that, one little step at a time, until he ended up being top story man. And he was good. He had a good sense of humor. And it was very important for a story man to be able to talk, to be able to get out there and really sell his story. To do that he had to almost be an actor himself.

I remember one time on *Pinocchio*, we had a story meeting with Walt. We're in a room with a hallway on this side and a hallway on that side and the room was in the middle and there was a man named T. Hee, a very talented guy and a good artist, a very good caricaturist. T. Hee ran out of the door here, went around the hallway and came in through the other door while he was telling a story. I don't know why he did that, but everyone will always remember that. Everybody died. [Laughs]

DJ: Would you say that Perce Pearce stole a lot of the ideas?

TP: No, no, I wouldn't. People might have thought that he did, but he had Larry Morey, the lyricist. They were very good friends and I just happened to go on a quick one-week or so vacation to Honolulu and they were both on the ship. So, I got to know them quite well on that trip. After *Snow White*. Larry Morey was a strange talent: he really could put those words together in the way Disney wanted them. They were not the greatest lyrics ever written, but they fitted perfectly for what Snow White was supposed to be saying and doing and thinking. And I was interested in how he could do that.

DJ: Did he mention anything about writing the lyrics?

TP: No, I don't think I ever talked to him about that.

DJ: Do you think Larry Morey worked hard on these lyrics?

TP: Yes, yes, he did. I think he worked pretty darn hard.

Now Churchill, the musician on *Snow White*, you would always hear him banging away on the piano and you'd hear these things develop. You'd actually hear them grow and that was one of the real thrills.

DJ: Can you recall anything from *Snow White*?

TP: Oh yes, certainly, "I'm Wishing," it just seemed to me you could hear it evolve next door.

DJ: So it wasn't overnight, then?

TP: No, he seemed to sort of build it as he went along. Tremendous talent, Churchill, and he had the same problem that Freddy Moore did. He was an alcoholic. He'd be pretty well smashed by about noon.

DJ: Do you remember him composing any of the other songs for *Snow White*?

TP: Yeah, there were others being worked on, like "Whistle While You Work." They were playing that again and again. I don't know why he'd keep playing them over and over again, but he might have been working with Morey. They might have been working together on the lyrics.

DJ: Do you remember seeing a rough cut of *Snow White* before it was finished?

TP: Oh yes.

DJ: Can you recall if anything was changed drastically or things that were altered?

TP: I think that Huntsman scene was added. I saw that added after the fact. It might have been a shadow at first.

DJ: It says in here, in this storyboard meeting in 1936: they wanted the feet of the Huntsman as Snow White is talking to the bird.

TP: I think that's right.

DJ: They actually animated that and it didn't look very good so then somebody thought of just showing the face coming...

TP: Then they show his back, too. They show the whole Huntsman and that was added, I saw that added.

DJ: How was it originally?

TP: It did not seem to play: the menace wasn't there. Now he has a knife and he comes in and there's a real menace to it. Then it didn't, it didn't have it.

I had nothing to do with the dwarfs, nothing to do with the forest or the little animals and the only two sequences I really identify with are the one where she is running in the woods and the wishing well, because those were my two sequences. Ham Luske was the director on both those sequences. Philippi was the layout man.

DJ: So, in the wishing-well sequence, when you saw a rough cut of that, that was pretty much it?

TP: That went pretty easy, not too much trouble with it. The one thing that you always noticed on almost all of the Disney pictures as you worked on them was how loose and how wonderful the pencil tests looked and how it stiffened up as it got traced on cels. The movement would just become stiff and wouldn't retain the flow that the pencil tests had.

DJ: Marc Davis told me that part of the reason for that was the heat and the humidity. They didn't have air conditioning at that time and it would be hot during the day, because this was during the summer when a lot of the inking was done on *Snow White*. It was the summer of '37 right before the premiere. And at night it would cool off so the cels would contract. They would expand from the heat and contract from the cool weather at night, so when they were photographed some of the cels were contracted and some were expanded, and they gave kind of a jitter.

TP: I think Marc's comment is very plausible. And he incidentally was a very talented artist.

DJ: When you saw these rough cuts they were all white line over black?

TP: Oh yes, that was always a negative.

DJ: How can you see a layout drawing like that? If they were photographing a pencil test over the layout, how would you see all the...?

TP: There would be a tracing of it sometimes showing the contact points and the path of action, but I imagine on occasion they would go to a positive test. I'm sure they did, but I don't recall how often.

DJ: Like when you saw a rough cut of the flight through the forest...

TP: That would have been a negative.

DJ: How would you see all the trees and the background? That would be all white.

TP: You had a tracing. The animator would make a line tracing. That would be a negative, too, but you'd see an outline of where the trees were, a registry point. That was pretty much routine, all during my period anyway. We saw a negative test. This is how the thing worked. You had your whole picture in negative, then as the dailies came in they take out the negative test and cut in what they call a daily. So, by degrees the thing became in color. Finally, you had a rough cut of the whole picture. It was added as they came in.

DJ: Oh, I see. So, you recall seeing some of the scenes in color.

TP: Oh yes, sure.

DJ: What was your reaction when you saw the flight through the forest with all the yellow eyes of the trees?

TP: It built more, it got more effective.

DJ: Were you happy?

TP: Oh yes, I always feel good about that sequence. I didn't feel so good about Snow White generally, because I felt she was stiff and did look traced and didn't really become a factor as, say, the dwarfs did. She was pretty much a puppet. I think most people feel that, too. She was the first of her kind, and incidentally the Disney pictures preceded it, where they attempted to do live action and humans were not good at all. "Goddess of Spring," particularly. They were just awful. No question about it. When you attempted Snow White and you've got "Goddess of Spring" in the background you wondered how this was going to come off.

DJ: You went to Stanford?

TP: Yes. Ollie and Frank went to Stanford. We were all there at the same time. We knew each other.

DJ: Did you all start at the same time at the studio?

TP Yeah, pretty much at the same time. Frank and I started the same week. Ollie came in just about a week later. And Jim Algar was another one from Stanford. One of the top background painters at Disney's was a guy by the name of Art Riley and he had to have his arm amputated. I heard the other day it was cancer. He had to lose his whole painting arm. Best painter I've ever seen.

DJ: Is there anything else from *Snow White* you recall?

TP: The thing that is so interesting and is part of the story and is something to bear in mind is the appearance of the old studio. It was built like a rabbit hutch. It had different levels and had different small rooms and the music rooms were sorta small. The individual animation rooms were real tiny cells. Nothing of the splendor of the Burbank place now. There was only one soundstage. Just one. You were in such proximity, you knew everybody in the hall and it was like a family. There was a lot of interplay and inter-trading of ideas between the animators. They did a lot of this. They would exchange ideas, they would ask advice. Ferguson was almost the senior man. Everybody respected Norm Ferguson for his experience. So, in other words, there was a lot of trading off between animators. More in the old studio than the new, because they were all sort of together.

DJ: I think that's one of the reasons why *Snow White* came out to be so good because it served just having a flow...

TP: Yes, and the similarity of movement: you didn't feel that when one music room stopped and another one picked up. You could never tell when it happened, because it flowed very well.

DJ: It was certainly a remarkable achievement. ... Did you know Walt very well?

TP: Everybody knew him quite well. He was a distant person. He never, at least to most of the people, he didn't share too much. At a story reading he pretty much walked in and did it and walked out. I only went up to his home twice. When I was in the Navy in uniform he invited all of us on active duty up one time on a Sunday. And once I was invited up to his home in Holmby Hills where he finally lived.

DJ: What was it about Rackham the layout men would like to use?

TP: I think it's the stylization and it's a linear quality that was strictly his, but again, I think Tenggren could almost be a Rackham.

DJ: Yeah, it does have that feel to it.

TP: One layout man made a whole library of about 50 copies of Rackham and we all bought them at that time or got copies of them.

DJ: You got copies of them?

TP: To study.

DJ: For a scene in *Snow White*?

TP: Just a general study of style. ... Kay Nielsen came just a little later. I worked with him on *Fantasia*. I worked with him quite a bit.

DJ: Did Tenggren have his own office?

TP: Yes, he had his own little room, sort of like his own little studio. All these extra artists did that: they worked by themselves.

DJ: So Harold Miles had his own studio?

TP: Yeah, more or less. I didn't work on *Bambi* at all, but he had an awful lot to do with *Bambi*.

DJ: You were Philippi's assistant?

TP: Yes.

DJ: So you were in his room?

TP: Yeah, right with him. They kept us together.

DJ: And Ken O'Connor was originally with him and then he went off and did his own scene.

TP: I don't recall Ken being with him...

DJ: He said he remembered you in the same room with Philippi, but he was only there for a short time.

TP: I was with Philippi for about year, at least.

DJ: Was Hennesy's room right next door to yours?

TP: No, because you were always with your director and our director was Ham Luske. Ham directed that whole run-through-the-woods sequence.

DJ: In other words the room wasn't set up so that all the layout people were together.

TP: No, the layout people went with the director. The director was the glue that held the whole unit together. It was called the music room, of course. There was the director, the assistant director, the layout man, the assistant layout man, the gofer that was running around, and a secretary. That was the typical "music room."

[Changing the subject.]

TP: Sam Armstrong painted that?

DJ: Yeah. I understand he was a proselytizing Christian Scientist.

TP: Yeah, that's right. He lived with his mother.

DJ: I don't think he ever married.

TP: Never married, that's right.

DJ: He was a thin man. And Claude Coats told me it was his influence that toned down the background so they had this beautiful antique

look. Because **Mique Nelson, who was the shorts specialist, wanted brilliant colors and they had a terrible fight and Mique Nelson was taken off** *Snow White* **and put on some other film.**

TP: I think it's probably a true story. I would abide by that.

[Talking about the Magic Mirror]

DJ: Hugh Hennesy modeled this and Woolie Reitherman animated it...

TP: Isn't there some live action of Hennesy made up doing that role?

DJ: There might be. It was filmed but I have not seen any photographs of it yet.

TP: I remember seeing it [the film of the live action].

DJ: With him in the mask and all that stuff?

TP: Yes, yes.

DJ: And it was lit from the bottom, I guess?

TP: Yes, and you wouldn't recognize that it was Hugh Hennesy, but it was.

DJ: Did he have an actual mask on, or did he just have makeup?

TP: Makeup, as I recall. I think it was black and white.

[Looking at drawings]

TP: I would say that was Hennesy without question: that typical cross stroke he had for shading. As a general rule, Hennesy's drawings had more shading then Philippi's. Philippi was more linear.

DJ: These are yours.

TP: I did the scene of the alligators. ... [Ken] Anderson and [Tom] Codrick did this sequence.

DJ: Codrick and Anderson did these of Snow White going up into her room.

[Changing the subject]

DJ: That wouldn't be Harold Miles, would it?

TP: No, because Harold Miles...I don't think did much on actual production scenes. He did a lot of what we call clean-up work on *Bambi*. Scenes that were already done, he cleaned them up.

Volus Jones (1914–2004)

Interviewed on February 21, 2001.

Volus Jones was born on November 17, 1914, in Fort Worth, Texas, the son of Mr. and Mrs. William and Mayme Jones. The young cartoonist-to-be left with his parents for southern California when he was seven years old, and the family remained in the Los Angeles area ever since.

He attended Compton Junior College in Los Angeles, and at one time contemplated a football career. When Volus gave up football, he took up archery as a recreation and became one of Hollywood's finest archers.

In 1934, Volus joined the Disney studio as an animator. Little is known about this early part of his career at Disney. On September 12, 1941, he left the studio and joined Columbia Pictures-Screen Gems where he tackled, among others, two animated shorts that were nominated for an Academy Award: *Dog, Cat, and Canary* (1944) and *Rippling Romance* (1945).

On August 20, 1945, Volus Jones came back to Disney. While he worked on some of the features like *Song of the South* and *Cinderella*, his claim to fame at Disney lies in the work he did on Donald Duck. From the mid 1940s to the late 1950s, he worked on virtually every short where Donald Duck appeared, often under the direction of Jack Hannah.

Volus' career was far from over when he left Disney in the late 1950s. He went on to work for such animation studio asUPA, Warner, Hanna-Barbera, and even Ralph Bakski. He retired in 1982 and was awarded a Golden Award by the Motion Picture Screen Cartoonists in 1985 in recognition for his entire career.

Volus Jones died on May 3, 2004, at age 90.

DAVID JOHNSON: Where were you born?

VOLUS JONES: In Texas. I was ten years old when we came out here. I had to go wherever my folks did. We were starving to death then. My step-father drove out here. It took us ten days from Oklahoma City. And that was quite an adventure. It was like the old wagon days with the round covered wagons and the Indians attacks and everything. It was dirt roads, all the way.

DJ: What did your father do?

VJ: He was a barber. He just had a pair of scissors and comb and a razor.

DJ: You were living in Oklahoma City then?

VJ: Oklahoma City at the time.

DJ: And he couldn't find work there?

VJ: No, he had a bad thing. He ran for county sheriff there. Four of them had to be elected. The four highest in the votes. And he was fifth. I'm sure, looking back as a kid, he didn't want to be a barber all his life. He was the fifth one and finally left and came out here.

DJ: Why did he choose California?

VJ: In those days the top places to live were the southern parts: orange groves and all that stuff, paved roads. So we came out here and I went to 22 different schools. About 18 of them were grammar schools, then I finished. My father went from one job to another.

DJ: So you moved locations?

VJ: The first school I went to was in Redondo Beach. I won't go into all the other schools. Some of them I only stayed a couple of weeks. But I finally finished two years in Inglewood High School. That's the longest I stayed in any one school. Then I went to what we called then junior colleges, in Compton, right this side of San Pedro. I went there one year and I had no schooling or background in artwork of any kind. The only thing I had as background was that I just loved to draw when I was a kid. Then when I was in high school I did go to art classes. But that's the first time I ever had formal training of any kind. At Inglewood and Compton. This was probably the height of the Depression, 1933 and '34, and the only thing that saved us all was Roosevelt and World War II. Otherwise, we wouldn't be in the position we are now. And you got a job, the Civilian Conservation Corps, the CCC. I just had finished that year from college. Most of my income was from caddying on a golf course. There was quite a little course there in Inglewood, Inglewood Country Club I think they called it. In those days, I didn't make but two or three dollars, which would last me the whole week. I lived with my folks and they were starving to death, too. That's why I joined the CCC. I had a brother two years older and he joined also. He stayed in a couple of years, I guess. I stayed in about one year and I got a job at Arden Farm's dairy. I was always drawing and I was going to see my girlfriend and her mother. After six months or so, she said, "Did you ever think of trying over at Walt Disney's?" I had never thought of it. I hadn't thought of very much then but girls, I guess. I was 19 and this is when I was working for Arden. So I went over there one day and just walked in the door.

DJ: What was it like when you first went in?

VJ: They had a little front office.

DJ: And who was there?

VJ: The only one that I remember that I saw first connected with the production was Clarence Nash.

DJ: Oh yes, Ducky Nash. I understand he interviewed people in those days.

VJ: Yes, he did. He interviewed them and passed on their artwork. He couldn't draw a straight line. But anyway, he said, "Where's your portfolio?" I thought for a minute. The only portfolio I ever saw a lawyer had. "Where are your drawings?" I said, "I forgot them." He says, "Well, go get a portfolio and come back." So I went home.

DJ: How did you go? Did you have your own car?

VJ: No, I had to thumb. I'd been thumbing since I was 14–15 years old. Anyway, I went back and as fast as I could I drew a lot of sketches. So I finally went to a store and got a regular portfolio. It had about ten or fifteen drawings in it to look at.

DJ: How long did it take you to make these drawings?

VJ: A couple of days. I went back to Clarence and got to see him again.

DJ: Were other people in the office besides you, I mean, waiting to go in as well?

VJ: Yes, there were other people.

DJ: It wasn't just you by yourself?

V.J: No, there were two or three others in there at the time. And he said, "You want to leave them. We'll give you a buzz in a few days." So I waited almost a week and then I got a letter. I recall it said that "although your portfolio wasn't acceptable," they were good enough so that "if you'd like to come try out..." Inbetween, that's the lowest in the animation field.

DJ: Do you remember who signed that letter? Could it have been George Drake?

VJ: I didn't know George Drake at the time. So I was anxious to get over there.

DJ: So each time you went over, you thumbed?

VJ: Thumbed, or I could have gotten there by streetcar. Streetcars went everywhere, but it would take a while. And there I went into a little... Not far from the office there were three other fellows, newspaper men. They were probably in their late 20s. I didn't recognize anyone. And they gave us two drawings of Mickey Mouse. It was a large head, and we had a glass disc. He said, "Put a drawing in between those two."

DJ: Who told you this?

VJ: The fellow who told me this was the head of the assistants then, Eddie Strickland. This fellow went on, he left the studio and he invented the nose cone on the first returning capsule.

DJ: So he showed you how to do this?

VJ: He told the three or four of us sitting in a room. I must have done three or four and taken the best one, of course, to show him. One fellow barely finished one and the other two fellows, I think, each made one inbetween. It only took me about five minutes or less. All I'd ever done was pencil work anyway. So I was familiar with the pencil. He told the other fellows that they'd have to go, but he said to me, "You can stay for a while. In a couple weeks we'll get you into production and see if we're going to keep you or not."

DJ: Do you remember the month?

VJ: Yes, it was September of 1934.

DJ: Oh, that's when Frank Thomas joined, in September.

VJ: I can name you several that I remember seeing in the inbetween department within a few days one way or the other: Frank [Thomas] and Ollie [Johnston], and did you ever hear of Jim Algar?

DJ: Oh,sure. He worked on *Snow White*. And Ken [Anderson] had been there just before.

VJ: Ken Anderson. George Drake was going to fire him.

DJ: Yep, I know.

VJ: He was going to fire several good men that went on to stardom in that studio, you know. In September, I don't remember the day. Fred Spencer was the first animator I worked for.

DJ: As an assistant?

VJ: As an assistant.

DJ: How long did you work under George Drake?

VJ: Fortunately not long. He was worse with me, because I didn't do anything and he was going... He called in a couple of other fellows that went on to be good animators. I think he almost fired Milt Kahl one time.

DJ: When you were under him, how many were in the room?

VJ: Oh, at least fifteen or twenty in rows. He sat behind a big glass window and I don't know what he did.

DJ: Probably read magazines.

VJ: I saw him years later when Disney let him go. He was married.

DJ: To Ben Sharpsteen's sister.

VJ: I knew it was a family relation, that's all I knew. He came to the studio called Screen Gems, owned by Columbia; I worked there during the war. Evidently Disney had a lot of people that were in the armed forces that left and I guess George went with them. He came over there looking for a job. I was twenty when I started there. Yeah, so he was about 30. I worked a couple of weeks and then they said, "OK, you can come in and start inbetweening."

DJ: When you did your trial under George Drake, were you paid?

VJ: Yeah, I think they gave us $10 a week.

DJ: And it was eight hours a day?

VJ: Yeah, and four hours on Saturday.

DJ: Were you in the annex during that period?

VJ: No, there was no annex. It wasn't built.

DJ: When you were under George Drake, where was that?

VJ: That was in the main building. The office was right on the corner. You just walked straight back and you'd get into the inbetween rooms, and then in to the animator's room. I think the assistant was with the animator, and then he had a room next to him with a break-down and inbetweener. That way he could use that big room for more animation space.

DJ: You were in the main studio when you were doing the inbetweens?

VJ: Oh yeah. That was the funny thing about Disney's. Even if you were a great artist, you'd start in inbetweening. And after they discovered that you could draw somewhat, you'd have to ask them to get in to what you would like to do. They didn't ask you if you could draw or anything. "Can you paint?" Some fellows went directly into background and layout work.

DJ: How long were you with Fred Spencer?

VJ: At least a year.

DJ: You were with him during the entire year. What was the daily routine? I understand the walls were painted in different colors.

VJ: I don't remember that, but I remember that an animator, if he wanted a certain color, they'd paint it for him. But I don't remember multi-colored rooms.

DJ: No, the hallway.

VJ: Oh, I don't remember the color scheme.

DJ: And when you were working for Fred Spencer, how many were in the room with you?

VJ: Just Fred and I.

DJ: And what size of a room was it?

VJ: Oh, pretty good size. Eight by ten, eight by twelve.

DJ: Did it have a window?

VJ: Oh, yeah.

DJ: Ground floor?

VJ: Ground floor, looking out on the parking lot.

DJ: How did you come to the studio now? I don't think you would thumb your way this time. Every day how would you come to the studio and back from your home?

VJ: My folks had a car, but they had to use it, too.

DJ: So how did you get to and from the studio when you first started there?

VJ: I took the streetcar after I got started. Inglewood went over to Vermont and Hollywood Boulevard. And there was a bus that came over to Glendale and went up Hyperion. But I had to get up at 6 o'clock in the morning to get there. We worked eight hours and four hours on Saturday. And in 1937 on *Snow White*, we worked a couple of nights a week.

DJ: When you were working for Fred Spencer, what was he like, as a person?

VJ: He married a sister of Les Clark.

DJ: Marceil?

VJ: Marceil. She stayed in the business. She was there before I was. Fred was killed right after *Snow White*. He was a good fellow. He was amiable and had lots of friends and everybody liked him. But he was a speedster. He liked fast cars. I don't know why he didn't get a fast car. He was killed in an old Plymouth sedan, I think. He bought a new Packard convertible when I was working for him and he and Marceil dropped me off. They were going to go to Arrowhead and they dropped me off to pick up my car I had damaged. I remember that distinctly. And they got snowed in up there, the whole weekend, believe it or not.

DJ: But Fred wasn't married when you first started with him?

VJ: No, no.

DJ: Did he live by himself?

VJ: I don't know, but I think he did. He had one whole side of his jaw torn away.

DJ: How did that happen?

VJ: Playing baseball he got in the way of a bat and it just severed the whole bone here. Evidently they got the bone out and sewed the face together. His whole face was a scar. There was no jawbone on this [left] side, lower jaw.

DJ: And that happened to him when he was a teenager?

VJ: Yeah, I guess in high school or younger.

DJ: What a terrible thing to happen.

VJ: It was terrible. But his personality overshadowed it. Finally you weren't aware of it. I wasn't, anyway. Today they could have put the jaw back and put an artificial bone in there. But Marceil married him and I think that was after *Snow White* in 1937, end of '37.

DJ: So he was a likable person?

VJ: Yes, a nice guy. If he wanted to chew me out or any one of the other guys that were working under him, he'd do it in a real mannerly way.

DJ: Now how long had he been at the studio before you?

VJ: Oh, not too long. He never talked about it. I know he was from Kansas. I think it was Kansas City. He knew Walt back there. He knew Ub [Iwerks]. I think he did a lot of stuff in *Snow White*, mostly the dwarfs. He did all that stuff of Dopey swallowing the soap. Afterward, he was the only animator that was sent over to the annex. They had rooms over there, too, around the drawing [art class] room. And I guess it hurt him. I knew he was hurt.

DJ: In what way?

VJ: He was the only one that was sent over there. All the other animators stayed. A lot of us were just breaking into animation at that time. That's why he was sent over there. They wanted to make room for the new animators.

DJ: When was he sent over there? What period are we talking about? Before *Snow White*?

VJ: No, after *Snow White*. I think that's why he was so perturbed that he was the only animator still there.

DJ: Why was he sent there? What did he do there?

VJ: He animated. But it was the fact that he was the only one that was sent there.

DJ: Why do you think that happened?

VJ: Dave Hand was the head of Animation. He must have sent him.

DJ: But he could have gone to Walt, since they knew each other, and said, "Hey, you know..."

VJ: Maybe he didn't want to, I don't know.

DJ: Was he a soft-spoken man?

VJ: Yeah. Jovial in a way and very likable.

DJ: Now, you did mostly Donald Duck with him, or did you work on Silly Symphonies, too?

VJ: I think there was only Donald Duck.

DJ: I know he's responsible for taking Dick Lundy's character and revising it.

VJ: Dick Lundy drew the first Duck, but Fred was the one that really did the animation and the drawings of the animal itself. Lundy's are... I saw some of the old Ducks and he laughed every time he'd see it. It was terrible. He was the first director I worked for.

DJ: So you were doing mostly Donald Duck under Fred Spencer. You would arrive at the studio, let's say, at 8 o'clock?

VJ: Yeah.

DJ: And I know there were no time clocks or anything like that.

VJ: No.

DJ: So you must have been very excited. You were twenty years old.

VJ: That's putting it mildly, yeah.

DJ: So you were happy to get up in the morning and go to work at this wonderful place.

VJ: Oh, for forty some years I was that way. I couldn't wait to get to the desk. Then Dick Lundy, they knew he was a Duck man, so... See, most of the top guys were put into direction so that they could help the younger guys coming up. They did a lot of tests in those days. I don't know if you heard about those.

DJ: You mean the pencil tests?

VJ: Yeah,

DJ: Oh, sure.

VJ: And he liked one of mine and said, "Would you like to work with me?" "Yeah, I'd like to work with you." So, being a Duck man he did most of the

Ducks. No, there was another guy, I forget his name, an old timer... Two directors were doing all the Ducks. And that's who I got stuck with.

DJ: Jack King?

VJ: Jack King, yeah. I worked for a short while with him, just when I was out of work. And when Lundy would get a picture all laid out and everything, then I would go back with him. I did Goofy, Pluto, Mickey, but sporadically. We'd get it when we'd always have a lull after each picture. I'd get it from another director.

DJ: Do you remember your very first meeting with Walt?

VJ: I was still assisting Fred at the time. It would be maybe 1936. And the first time I was ever within the vicinity of Walt was... He handed out gag checks. We'd send in gags, anybody, and a lot of them were accepted, but some were accepted where you'd get paid, and he'd get everybody in there out on the soundstage and pass out their checks.

DJ: I didn't know about that.

VJ: Maybe they didn't know about it. But I remember I got five or six dollars for a gag. I'd never had any direct contact outside of that with Walt. That's the first time I ever saw him. And he screwed up "Volus." When he'd call the name John and Jack, then he'd come to, "Who is this Valernus?" I heard that and thought, "God, that isn't even close." So I had to tell him who I was, and he kind of shook his head again and gave me the check. That was the first time. The next time... I don't think I had anything to do with him until I went on tour for the studio with a group of artists doing quick sketch, mostly in grammar schools and high schools and theaters. I had a little talk with him then and that's the first conversation I ever had with him.

DJ: This was way after *Snow White*?

VJ: Oh yeah. This was back in 1954, the first time.

DJ: But didn't you go to the sweatbox sessions with Fred Spencer since you were his assistant? Didn't he bring you in to see the sweatbox?

VJ: I don't think so. I don't remember going to the sweatbox sessions. We had a moviola in our room.

DJ: But Walt would go over all of them in the sweatbox.

VJ: Oh yeah. But if he wanted to show me something he'd just run it on the moviola.

DJ: So you didn't go along with Fred to any sweatbox sessions on the Duck pictures, then?

VJ: No, just Fred. I don't remember any assistants going in there. But he'd go over everything with the animators.

DJ: You were with Fred, then, through *Snow White?*

VL: Yeah.

DJ: You knew Freddie Moore? Was he from California? Do you know anything about his background?

VL: I know absolutely nothing about his background except from what I heard from other animators. He had relatives out in the east side of Los Angeles. In those days it was an Italian section. He went to Lincoln High School. He lived in a court near the studio.

DJ: When you first met him, did he come in to Fred Spencer's room?

VJ: Yeah, because he was a good friend of Fred's.

DJ: Did the three of you pal around?

VJ: Not pal around. We got acquainted. Fred [Moore] was quite an athlete. He played baseball like crazy. He would have been on my team, any day. We used to play over in a vacant lot across the street there. Noon time.

DJ: I know they did volleyball, but no one has ever talked about baseball. Who else played baseball on the team?

VJ: We didn't have teams then. We had organized teams later on. Just makeshift.

DJ: What was Freddie Moore like? Was he quiet? Was he...?

VJ: No. Talkative and a regular guy, I would say.

DJ: Do you remember any conversations you had with Freddie Moore not relating to art?

VJ: We'd talk about baseball and football. He wasn't much for basketball.

DJ: Were you married by this time?

VJ: I was married in 1936. About the time of *Snow White*.

DJ: Do you remember Freddie Moore ever talking to Fred Spencer about the dwarfs?

VJ: Oh yeah, we all discussed characters, you know. What we were doing, especially something new, like the dwarfs. Yeah, Fred [Spencer] used to go over to his room and get Fred [Moore] to draw them, to make a couple of drawings for him. Then he would occasionally come in and talk to Fred. Maybe they'd be discussing a particular scene or something. I don't remember anything specific.

DJ: When *Snow White* [started] and Fred Spencer started doing the dwarfs, did he have another assistant?

VJ: He had a breakdown and an inbetweener in the next room.

DJ: But you were the clean-up man?

VJ: I was the clean-up, yeah. Fred would give me the rough drawings and I'd clean up on the average maybe one out of every five drawings. The breakdown man, he breaks it down to every other drawing, then the inbetweener takes it and inbetweens.

DJ: As a clean-up man, I thought you have to clean up every drawing. [There was a misunderstanding in that Volus Jones thought I meant all of the drawings when I was referring to all of the *animator*'s drawings.]

VJ: No, just the main drawings. The extremes. Sometimes more. As far as the method of cleaning-up, sometimes you put a whole new piece of paper over it the original drawing.

DJ: You as the assistant would trace on a fresh piece of paper, or would you erase?

VJ: It's according to what the animator wanted. If he was just loosely sketching with a 4H pencil, you couldn't obliterate that, harder thing [harder pencil], you couldn't. So, it was up to the assistant. Sometimes the animator would tell us to make new drawings if he'd want to save it.

DJ: Did Fred Spencer ever draw with that many lines?

VJ: Not that rough.

DJ: When you were working as Fred Spencer's assistant, didn't you go to some of the story meetings on *Snow White*?

VJ: I don't remember.

DJ: Wilfred Jackson told me there was another animator who he called the "creator" of the dwarfs, who did a lot of Dopey scenes. And I thought that may have been Fred Spencer. Did he ever say anything to you that he designed some of the dwarfs?

VJ: I doubt it.

DJ: I'd like to discuss your impressions of some of the other animators. Ham Luske.

VJ: He's a number-two director. It's a toss-up. There were three top directors. Ham, Jaxon [Wilford Jackson], and Woolie Reitherman.

DJ: What was he like?

VJ: Very good. He was athletic, too. He and Freddie were not close, but they were friends. He played a good game of volleyball. So did Woolie, being a tall guy.

DJ: Now do you remember any practical jokes that they used to play?

VJ: I can recall a lot of them. When I first went there we all were very close in the beginning. And we'd go in groups into the art class, mostly life drawings. Anyway the head guy in that was...

DJ: Don Graham.

VJ: Don Graham was the teacher, the instructor. He once said to a group of us that Milt Kahl would never make it. We all looked at each other. Even then we knew his capabilities. Don Graham said that. Anyway, this kid, he thought of a good gag to play on Milt. Milt was...I wouldn't say eccentric, but he was the type of a guy to pick on. His personality, not his drawing. This guy got an old can of smelly sardines, pretty good size, about that long. He took a couple of them out. And the group that Milt went into... We had a second group to go into the art class. He went over to Milt's desk, lifted the board, and put these two sardines right on his light bulb. And we were all sitting there. I don't know if he let the other guys around him in on it or not. But all the guys in the back of the room...there was dead silence. And Milt comes in, strings on the light, puts the light on. It was about three or four minutes, I guess, before the light got pretty hot. And all of a sudden, papers—like a cartoon!—the papers flew up and cuss, cuss, cuss. "Damn this and damn that, if I ever catch you and who did this is going to get it!" Not a word, not a peep out of anybody. Wanting to know who did it. These groups of guys...

DJ: That was in the Don Graham class?

VJ: Then the next best one was with a Japanese boy [Iwao Takamoto] who was Milt's assistant for a while, a long while. He was a crackerjack of a supervising clean-up man. These guys who could draw as well as he could had to come and they appointed him as overseer of Milt's work. He was my third baseman; he was a ball player, too.

DJ: Now this was during the _Snow White_ era?

VJ: No, no, this was after we moved over here, during _Sleeping Beauty_. We had a ball diamond and everything, back stop. They played touch football. So they put fixative over three or four of his drawings. Iwao would take 'em and flip 'em. And he'd put a couple of 'em on the board and he'd erase it, actually erase the guy's drawing. And just leave enough to go over it. He sprayed 'em with a transparent fixative. And Iwao would go like this and the pencil line wouldn't come off. Iwao got real mad when he discovered himself why it happened and told the guy in no uncertain terms to get out and don't ever come back in here again. He was glad that he didn't ever have to come back.

DJ: Do you remember a story artist named Bob Kuwahara?

VJ: Oh yeah, Kuwahara and then Willie Ito. Three Japanese there. And then they had Chinese guy. Cy Young. He's the one who really brought that up.

DJ: I was surprised to find out that Roy Williams was also creative.

VJ: Oh yeah. He thought up the gag of Dopey swallowing the soap.

DJ: He did? That was Roy Williams.

VJ: That was Roy Williams.

DJ: How did you know that?

VJ: We were close, down at Hyperion. Everybody knew what everybody did. He was a regular storyman. He did shorts and he did some sequences on *Snow White*. He was a top gag man. A Pluto short that he did with most of the gags in there got an Oscar. I think we were still at Hyperion. Anyway, I was told he did most of the story on it.

DJ: I thought he was a total idiot.

VJ: Well, he acted an idiot. He took advantage of his size, mostly. He and Jack Kenny went to Freemont High School together. ... Art Babbitt was a born leader, I can tell you that.

DJ: I always thought he had a chip on his shoulder.

VJ: I guess you could call it that. I don't know exactly what, or why. I think what really ticked him off was all these great artists not getting any screen credit or anything. And these other artists that were making movies that you wouldn't show in a bar room were getting credit. I think that gave him the chip on his shoulder. At all the studio parties, Art would be the MC. Walt never did come to any of our parties. Milt Neil was the one who dived off the thirty-meter board at the Narconian Club party after *Snow White*.

Nick DeTolly was a Russian kid, who came over right at the tail end of the Russian revolution in 1917–18, just a little kid. And he grew up 6 foot, 190 pounds. Handsome, real dark, but handsome. He was a powerful thing. He later became head of a ferry command that flew American P63s up to Canada, and the Russians would pick 'em up in Alaska during the war and fly 'em back to the front. He was a lieutenant colonel, head of that group. He was an assistant then on *Snow White*. Burly fellow. We used to have a group of us who lived in the same place and took people's homes: Charlie's house one day, my house the next day, and so and so. You probably never heard of Ray Patterson. He was a great animator. He worked on *Dumbo*. And another guy they don't mention is John Sibley. I'd put him right up there. He did *How to Ride a Horse* with Goofy. He did it just before the strike. He knew animation to a tee. Did it naturally, like Fred. Good draftsman. He was an alcoholic like Fred.

DJ: Do you think that Fred Spencer was one of the better animators?

VJ: Oh, I would say in the top ten. Too bad he killed himself. He went through an intersection going 60 miles an hour against a signal, broadsided one car.

DJ: How long did Fred work on *Snow White*?

VJ: I think for over a year.

DJ: Now were you excited about it?

VJ: Oh, everybody was. And we worked nights at the last there.

DJ: Were there any scenes of Fred's that you remember vividly more than others?

VJ: The soap one. And there's one, the kitchen scene, all seven of them come running down the stairway and then they all pile up down at the bottom. He did that scene. It took me a week to clean the thing up. Yeah, it took him a heck of a time. He'd animate one guy in and then a couple. And then he'd have three. Expose them one on top of the other. It's too hard to draw seven dwarfs all in one line coming down the stairs.

DJ: Did he draw them on separate sheets?

VJ: Separate sheets, yeah.

DJ: So he wouldn't have all seven on one sheet, then?

VJ: They'd be on the film all together. On the exposure sheet, he'd have one level Grumpy, one level Happy, and so on. Then they'd expose them one on top of the other like this in the camera.

DJ: When you cleaned them up you didn't trace them on to one sheet yourself?

VJ: On those, Fred would work pretty clean and then he would sketch sometimes. But on those I just touched them up. I erased so much and made it so that the inkers wouldn't have a hard time with it.

DJ: So you didn't actually re-draw on a separate sheet?

VJ: No. It isn't worth it.

DJ: Did you know Norm Ferguson?

VJ: Oh yeah. He was a nice, quiet guy. He associated with everyone.

DJ: I heard he always wore a vest and was very well dressed.

VJ: Always with a suit. I think he's from New York. His speech.

[...]

Inbetweener, break-down, and assistants, we'd go in and we'd shown whole scenes and sometimes whole movies. It was sort of a training period and a secretary in there taking notes.

The secretary was telling me one day, "You've got to speak up a little more in these get-togethers. Because Walt goes through them." I didn't know that. "And Jim Algar's name came up more than any other person up there. In fact it came up more than all the others put together." And right after... I was working with Algar in the room where the inbetweeners go. Next thing I find out he's gone. I came to find out they'd moved him out of there over to another room, I think with Woolie. And he started animating on the very next sequence of cartoons. I think he animated on *Snow White*. Animals and stuff.

DJ: Tell me about these training sessions.

VJ: We were all just beginners. Just inbetweeners.

DJ: Who presided over it?

VJ: It wasn't George Drake, that's for sure.

DJ: It couldn't have been Don Graham that was doing this?

VJ: No, either a top director group or top animation group. The quickest way, I found out, was to make a good test. And you were allowed any time you wanted to a certain extent, if you were out of work, to do a test yourself so you wouldn't take up the company's time and still be making good for the company. I first started to animate right after *Snow White* when they moved into the annex across the street.

Ward Kimball (1914–2002)

Interviewed in Winter 1988.

Ward Walrath Kimball was born on March 14, 1914, in Minneapolis, Minnesota. In 1934, he joined the Disney studio staff as an inbetweener and quickly rose in the ranks to become a full-fledged animator, working on scenes in *Snow White and the Seven Dwarfs* that were dropped before the film was released. In August 1936, he married Betty Lawyer who was working in the ink-and-paint department. They had three children named John, Kelly, and Chloe, and eventually five grandchildren and two great grandchildren.

Kimball died at the age of 88 on July 8, 2002, of natural causes. During those eight decades, he crammed in at least eight lifetimes of achievements.

Kimball designed and animated Jiminy Cricket for *Pinocchio*, the crows in *Dumbo*, the title song from *The Three Caballeros*, Lucifer the cat from *Cinderella*, and the mad tea party scene and the Cheshire Cat from *Alice in Wonderland*, among other animation credits too numerous to mention.

He directed the first Disney 3-D cartoon (*Melody*); won Oscars for directing the first cartoon in Cinemascope: *Toot, Whistle, Plunk and Boom* (1953) as well as *It's Tough to Be a Bird* (1970); produced the classic outer-space trilogy programs for the *Disneyland* television show; and produced and directed the syndicated television series *The Mouse Factory*.

The Mouse Factory was a syndicated television show produced and directed by Ward Kimball in 1972 where guest hosts like Jonathan Winters and Annette Funicello did comedy monologues mixed in with animated segments of existing Disney cartoons and Ward's wacky montages. It was supposed to be "hip" and "now" for the new generation. Over twenty episodes were done: only one season. The opening was always the Magic Kingdom castle followed by the sound of a factory whistle and then Disney costumed characters clocking in, followed by the guest host. Each episode was themed: sports, outer space, Wild West, etc. There was nothing really "bad" about the show, but it failed to catch the audience it wanted, and it wasn't always respectful to Disney—not mean or attacking, just not respectful.

Kimball also published a popular book of humorous art parodies entitled *Art Afterpieces*, helped design and create the World of Motion attraction for Epcot Center, formed the well-known and respected Dixieland jazz group consisting of fellow Disney animators like Frank Thomas and called the Firehouse Five Plus Two, and collected toys and miniature trains in addition to his full-size railroad, the Grizzly Flats Railroad, which began operation in the backyard of his San Gabriel home in 1938 with a 64,000 pound coal-burning locomotive, a wooden passenger car, and over 900 feet of track. (In 1992, he donated part of his ever-growing railroad to the Orange Empire Railway Museum in Perris, California.)

Walt Disney once described Ward as the only genius at the Disney studio. Ever the iconoclast, Kimball doubted the sincerity of that remark and preferred to believe that Walt said it fully realizing the "ribbing and guff" Ward would have to endure as a result.

WARD KIMBALL: [Discussing "Seagull Swine" music from *Steamboat Willie*.] I know Bill Cottrell took the tune, it was kind of a cliché with music, and he wrote a thing... A bunch of new artists came in, young guys. Some turned out to be animators and some storymen. Stan Quakenbush, which is a funny name; John Lounsbery; and Bob Youngquist. You had Youngquist, Lounsbery, Quakenbush, and Cornet Wood...it's a great first name! These were young guys: some became storymen and some didn't work out. Bob Youngquist and John Lounsbery, especially, became good animators.

Cottrell took Churchill's clichéd tune [in fact, *Steamboat Willie* was done before Churchill came to the studio] and I it was, "Here we go, down the Mississippi, Here we go, Down the Mississippi, Here we go, down the Mississippi, Youngquist, Loundsbery, Quakenbush and Wood!" Which is silly doggerel, whatever you want to call it. That was his first background music and I think it was in some of the early Mickeys. It might not have been *Steamboat Willie*, because they used "Turkey in the Straw" there. That's Churchill's stuff.

[Changing the subject]

WK: Walt was always talking about the characters, and building their personalities. That was the key to the whole damn thing, making Snow White's personality. The Wicked Queen, and the Witch, and all seven of those dwarfs were separate personalities.

DAVID JOHNSON: Did you ever meet Lucille La Verne who was the voice of the Witch and the Queen?

WK: Oh yeah.

DJ: What was she like?

WK: Like all these actors: they're nice people; they listen to you, say, "It's nice weather we're having, but..."

DJ: Was she eccentric like a lot of the actresses?

WK: Clara Cluck was sort of "on" all the time and she played the role, but some of the other professional actresses had to experiment with the tone of their voice.

DJ: Marge Champion said you were one of the dwarfs that she kissed. She remembered that. You would pretend to be Dopey, I think she said. Because you were quite a character at the time.

WK: My wife did a few things. Once they hadn't shot everything they wanted, Betty [Ward's wife] would come in and walk under a bridge or something. And one afternoon Ham Luske asked her to do these rough, crude things. She had to open a door and duck under for the dwarfs' house.

And Bill Cottrell wrote a song. He was great at writing little things and he had a lot of input on some of the songs. He was ambidextrous; he could write his name with both hands, in unison or backwards, one backwards and one forwards.

I was the one who discovered Eddie Collins. I got him over there for the soup sequence.

DJ: Everyone says they discovered Eddie Collins. Art Babbitt says that he and Les Clark filmed Eddie Collins at that burlesque show in Los Angeles.

WK: Well, look, a group of us would go down quite often on Friday nights, and see Eddie and the strip show. I was the one that got him out to the studio because this gag... He was an old guy, which is a pre-requisite for a funny comedian, with baggy pants, and he is this wide and it was almost like he had no teeth in his face. He had this wide mouth that when he did this it'd go from ear to ear. But his main attraction was: if a girl would walk by, he'd drop his tongue out, and god, it must have been 12 inches long and it would do this [waggling] at the end and come back in. I said, "Hey, this guy's great for the soup sequence." So I got him out to the studio. I first took Ben Sharpsteen down there.

So anyway, he came out and he did some funny stuff with his tongue.

DJ: This must have been very early on in the production of *Snow White*, a year before it was finished.

WK: Oh yes, right.

DJ: So the soup-eating sequence was already in the works very early on.

WK: It was all part of the story outline. There was the dream sequence and the soup sequence. After they washed up, they eat and they have bad table manners. Walt talked about that. And Snow White had to show them how to hold their spoons. Then they liked Snow White and so they decided to give her a present, and of course, it's very obvious that she has no bed in that house. She was stretched out across quite a few beds.

DJ: Three beds.

WK: And so that was the obvious thing to give her as a present. Sleepy thought of that, of course. I was working on that sequence also.

DJ: The reason why I asked you that about Eddie Collins is because I read that they had trouble with the character of Dopey; they couldn't make him come to life until they got this man.

WK: Part of it was in choosing voices. Walt would listen in and then would criticize. And as you saw the list of other dwarfs, they had other...

DJ: Oh yeah, a long list. It went on for miles.

WK: And so, if the guy is Dopey, we were thinking, well, maybe we'd ought to use Pinto Colvig. He was the old "a-heulk, a-heulk" [Goofy's voice] guy. Then, because we couldn't decide on it, it was Walt's idea: why not have him say nothing. He does it all in gestures and Doc explains or Happy: "He don't talk none, ma'am." That was a great stroke of genius. And he had these big ears. The crazy thing was that because of those tests on the soup sequence of Eddie Collins... He was discovered by Hollywood and he played with Raymond Massey in *Abe Lincoln in Illinois*, sort of a sidekick. He'd steal the show. He'd walk on... The same thing happened at the burlesque house: he'd just walk on and you'd start laughing. He would steal the scenes without even trying. And then he died right at the... He would have been a great comedian in the movies, and his life was cut short, that's the tragedy of it.

DJ: You would say that he inspired Walt's thinking about Dopey.

WK: Right! It was that tongue. I was dealing with the old guys on the pencil tests which they'd run quite often on the soup sequence and there would be those things with his tongue. Walt would see one thing happen with one animator's work, and say, "Hey, let's develop that characteristic!" He would tell 'em, "Let's add that to some of the other." That went on all the time. That was his way of building a picture. It wasn't cut and dried that you picked up a sequence and "that's the way it was." Then he'd say, "Why don't you look at the way so and so is handling Grumpy." He was always doing that. So all the sequences done by different directors in different music rooms and different animators would have the same characteristics.

DJ: Did you have any good friends in the story department at the time *Snow White* was in the works that told you that they had trouble with this scene.

WK: I think I knew Bill Cottrell better than any of them.

DJ: Was Bill Cottrell on the story team of *Snow White*?

WK: Yes, he was. He didn't draw, but he was an idea man and he started out shooting Walt's Mickey Mouse animation on that homemade Ub Iwerks' cartoon film crane.

DJ: Did you work as an assistant to any animator before you had your big scenes on *Snow White*?

WK: No, I went on *Snow White* as an animator.

DJ: Who was your director? Because there was only five directors: Pearce, Jackson, Morey, Sharpsteen, and...

WK: Sharpsteen didn't really direct anything. He was the so-called producer. He was the guy that Walt put in charge. He was Walt's whipping boy.

DJ: He and Dave Hand, from what I understand.

WK: Who the hell was the director of the soup sequence. Was it Ham? Must have been. [It was Perce Pearce] Ham wasn't animating then.

DJ: He did Snow White, though. He did a lot of animation on Snow White.

WK: Yes, but he didn't really draw it. He would help decide on what she wore and looking at the problems in animation. A lot of people design costumes, but when you have to turn them around you have to simplify them. That's why she has a line down the center. It helps you in keeping track of all her little areas.

DJ: And he worked with Hurter, I guess, on developing...

WK: Hurter was really inspirational sketches.

DJ: Oh, I see.

WK: And he had to change it for... When you got down to the animators, when the informality of making rough sketches was over, you had to boil it down to this is the way it's going to be, because these have to be animated. Like what sort of a hair-do would be easy to turn as she turns her head. Those things influence exactly what she wears.

DJ: So Ham had a lot to do with that.

WK: Yes, but he worked with guys like Jack Campbell and Grim Natwick, especially Grim who had drawn girls before and was a good artist. And the animators would have to find things that weren't working and there would be discussions and finally they had the rules and regulations about drawing Snow White.

DJ: And model sheets would appear.

WK: Yes.

DJ: Now, Art Babbitt told me that at night, after work, he would go into the other animators' rooms to look at their drawings to see what he could learn from them. Did you do any of that on *Snow White* or were you interested in any of the other scenes?

WK: I did it during the day.

DJ: Oh, you did?

WK: Yeah. I would talk to Fred Moore. He was the leading artist on the dwarfs.

DJ: And Tytla, too.

WK: I went in and I'd say, "How would I draw Happy," and he would make a quick suggestion. That's what you did. After all, we all did that. We'd go to Frank or we would go to Fred Moore because he made the best, concise drawings of the dwarfs. They'd come down from Hurter through the story department, but he boiled them down to "this is the way they would be," by animating scenes and trying things and finding out what would work and what wouldn't work. Finally, he would make a model sheet and use drawings from scenes that Walt had liked. Still, if you were also working on the dwarfs you'd be crazy not to make sure your stuff was working. This was the idea here. You weren't trying to be an individualist in your own drawing style; you tried to make it part of a whole team so when the audience looked at the picture they couldn't tell who had done what. You had to be a team player. Your dwarfs had to look to like all the other dwarfs. And so we checked with the guy who was in favor at the time.

DJ: So in some instances the model sheets were out *later* rather than at the beginning to help you guys out.

WK: That's true. They might have. Fred probably sat down and made a lot of rough drawings or even animated...which were maybe half-way there. Looking at Hurter and some of the guys who had made story sketches, and fairy-tale books out of the library, seeing how other people in the past had done the dwarfs. Out of that he would make sketches. But the real proof comes when you start animating, when you have to make that character or those dwarfs move. You simplify things. What sort of shoes work the best and you work out the basic shapes. Doc had broad shoulders.

Dopey had no shoulders at all. That sort of thing. And keeping in mind that you heard the voices and they had to be... Sleepy, you draw a dwarf with half-closed eyes.

DJ: And he would shuffle along.

WK: Yeah. And Grumpy always belligerent. Dopey running around wiggling his ears. Happy kind of nervous, and the way he'd roll his stomach as he talked. Those things came out after you started animating. Fred would define the characteristics besides how they looked, how they acted, which all went into trying to make a model sheet when everyone else was going on the picture. Even so, you were continuously changing little things, afterwards. You would discover, maybe, making Dopey's collar bigger, make it funnier. That sort of thing. It was always building and always with Walt's approval.

DJ: Do you remember any of the early scenes that were animated of the girl?

WK: Before we started animating the girl, the problems of her dress, her coiffure, were worked out with Natwick and Campbell. I used a caricature of Jack Campbell. He was very meticulous and he was one of the good Snow Whiters. Because you had to be one of those guys that... He was great to do small things. Jack would catch flies in the room. And he had tweezers and he would take horse hairs and make a little figure eight no wider than that, almost like termite wings. He would take a horse hair and then he would smear airplane glue across the top of it so this figure eight would be transparent and would make it a wing... And then he'd launch these things and geez, it was beautiful! None of this zig-zag, quirky flight of the fly: they made graceful loops and banks and turns. No quickness at all. I mean, you'd just stand there and he had two or three of 'em flying around the room. They were airplanes. He was able to do that with tweezers and so he was the most accurate of the Snow White artists.

DJ: It's funny because you are about the only person that mentions Jack Campbell. Everyone talks about Grim Natwick and Ham Luske as being the two guys.

WK: He carried a hell of a load.

DJ: I know that he did it because I saw the book that lists all the animators for each scene and he did quite a few of the best scenes, I thought.

WK: Yeah.

DJ: I'm just wondering if you recall what may have been some of the first scenes that were in the movie.

WK: Yes, I have recollections of seeing some of these where she wasn't working just right.

DJ: What scene was it?

WK: I don't know. They'd go back and they'd have a conference: "Maybe you'd better make the collar larger or smaller, it interferes when she turns around." A lot of things like that. Those are mechanical things worked out by the animators that you have to solve. Don't forget, this was the first big attempt at drawing a "straight" girl, even though she was caricatured slightly. And your lines were so subtle, your drawings were so close together and where there's a dwarf... The dwarf's animation is much more active, more spacious. They were seen as broader. But when you get down to doing that with a pretty girl like Snow White, you're in trouble. The width of a pencil line on that mouth... And I know: I've tried some scenes where she collapses and her arms come up.

DJ: Oh, that was yours?

WK: She's sobbing. Boy, I said, "Let me off of this!"

DJ: Oh, you didn't finish it then?

WK: Yes, I did. I did a couple of scenes there and I said, "This is not for me." So that's when I went over and did the vultures.

DJ: Did you have a model sheet?

WK: Oh yeah, they were all set and they were scenes in the picture and you had your photostats that you worked over.

DJ: From the rotoscope.

WK: Right.

DJ: Of Marge Champion falling down.

WK: Yeah, right. With the sobbing with her shoulders. I made the shoulders work too much so...

DJ: Oh, so you had to re-do it then.

WK: Yeah, really it was hard and so that's why I'm telling you...

DJ: That's interesting.

WK: Guys like Jack Campbell and Eric Larson would do little bunnies.

DJ: Yes, I know.

WK: And Grim and those guys, I appreciated the subtleness, but those guys aren't necessarily good at broad humor, the seven dwarfs' animation. And we didn't have the discipline it takes to draw the prince and the horse and all that stuff.

DJ: They re-did the Prince after the film was finished. That's why it doesn't look so bad now.

WK: Nobody wanted to work on the Prince. Nobody wanted to work on the scene where he's on his horse, because you're almost tracing the rotoscope. It worked well in live action on the rotoscope, but if you traced those drawings just as they were with the same timing, they looked lethargic. They had no spark to them. I remember the first drawings that Ferguson did of the Witch. Nestor Paiva did live action and he was the famous villain of a long-running play we had in Los Angeles called *The Drunkard*.

DJ: He did the live action for the Witch?

WK: Yes.

DJ: It wasn't Lucille La Verne that did the Witch, as well as the Queen?

WK: Paiva did that dressed up as the Witch. LaVerne was her voice.

DJ: Yes, I know that. But I'll tell you why I'm asking this. Because in an interview by her that was in the newspaper, she said that she was the only live action that actually modeled one of the characters, and I assume that she meant live-action filming. But what she may have meant was maybe they used her face, because she does look like the Witch except for her nose.

WK: The face was all putty. The whole thing was changed. But Nestor Paiva was so broad and he knew all those old stage gestures.

DJ: Were you ever there when they filmed any of him?

WK: No. I saw the rotoscopes that Fergie had to work with, because I was interested in what he was going to do. He was our top animator and he learned a big lesson. Because as broad as these things were, that Nestor did, he traced them with just a little bit of change and it wasn't working. He had to go back and realize that you can't trace this live action. You had to jump higher, you had to go way beyond the broad action. It may be on the rotoscope, the little things like that which read on a stage actor, but if he had to bend down like this they go *way* beyond. Finally, the Witch started working. Much broader: twice, three times as broad as the rotoscope.

DJ: So it was one of the storymen, probably, at Disney that saw *The Drunkard* and said, "Hey, this guy would be great for the live action for the Witch."

WK: Yes. Because his stage mannerisms were very broad. That was natural. So we photographed him.

DJ: Do you have any idea whose idea it was that the Witch talks to the audience? Was that Walt's idea?

WK: No, those were stage asides that Shakespeare used.

DJ: But she's the only character in all the Disney cartoons, as far as I know, that looks right at the audience and says things like, "But wait! There may be an antidote."

WK: That's Shakespeare. Old-time melodrama. And all through *The Drunkard*, Paiva would say, "Oh, will you come away with me," and then he'd move up to the footlights and say, "Little does she know that I'm really the guy behind this disposing of her father," you know.

DJ: Dastardly deeds!

WK: Yeah, that sort of stuff.

DJ: So it could have been Paiva acting it out that gave the animator the idea to do it that way.

WK: The animators or the story people. Because it was a cliché of early theater. In the Victorian age... "Little does she know that I am planning a party to which his best girlfriend will be there." Things of that sort, filling you in on the story.

DJ: It really works great in that context.

WK: Yeah.

DJ: But they never did it again.

WK: Just happened it worked for that. How many times do you have a villain that's played in the old stock, classical style as the Witch?

DJ: Do you think Paiva's acting influenced the motions, the...

WK: I think it was fifty-fifty. The animators were sitting there and they had something. If they were to sit and do this free hand from their head, if they have exaggerated actions in mind and they would suggest things for you to do... Like every time Buster Keaton comes to a stop sign when he's being chased, he looks right, left, and then takes off. That was a cliché in comedy. That's what the Witch does. It was all in our heads: stuff we picked up from the silent comedies. These are all things that animators, being observers of human action...how people walk, what they do with their heads and hands as they talk. I mean, we have that in our head what is best for a particular character and scene. How to time that, how to plus that mannerism. Ferguson was not necessarily a polished artist and so you can see Walt's thinking. He wanted a gross, broad brush stroke on this Witch.

DJ: That was in Walt's head, from the beginning.

WK: Yeah. He wanted one of his top animators, surely, to do it, because he knew he was going to get a result. So he helped him with this rotoscope. We had rotoscope on the Huntsman and the Queen.

DJ: Who did the Huntsman?

WK: Errol Grey cleaned up the Huntsman. He was an animator of some sort and Ham Luske directed the sequence. [He wasn't given any credit] But you see, this happens lots of times. Like I said, "What the hell did you give Paul Hopkins credit for doing a certain scene here? Paul Hopkins was head of the personnel department. He couldn't draw. He had about as much artistic talent as a brick. He was just a straw boss there." "Well, it said that on the draft." And I said, "He was a schemer, probably wanted people to say he had something to do with it, but he was no artist. He didn't do that scene."

DJ: Even though you went to art school prior to Disney, did you still attend some of the Don Graham action-analysis classes?

WK: Oh, yeah. It was mandatory.

DJ: Did you find him very helpful as a teacher, because I've heard so many wonderful things about him for analyzing action of the dwarfs, for instance.

WK: I found, especially during the night classes, he was more of an opiate than anything else. I fell asleep. He would start talking and his voice would get lower and lower and slower and he hunched down with a cigarette, and it was like a hypnotist going to work on you. Especially in some of the classes in the afternoon, I'd find I was falling asleep. He was very helpful. He had a way of making you look at things a different way. Look for what to accent in a pose. He talked very well. He would talk perspective and his voice went on and on.

DJ: Marge Champion told me this funny story that Art Babbitt would hypnotize people during the lunch hour.

WK: One of the great perpetrators of cruelty to new errand boys was Riley Thompson and he would take a big water jug, five gallons of Arrowhead Water, and would put some black in it so it was gray or black looking and this was "cross-dissolve liquid." He would tell the errand boy, "Take this down to Ward Kimball," and this guy would struggle with this bottle of "cross dissolve," a big five gallon bottle of "cross dissolve."

"No," I'd say, "he's mistaken, this should go to Frank Thomas," and this whole day this guy'd be lugging this thing before he'd catch on. They'd pull a running gag on new errand boys. That happened to Virgil Partch. We did it quite a bit when he came to work as a traffic boy.

DJ: I know that Disney advocated the animators and the storymen to go to see all the different movies. Or go to the ballet or this and that and I'm just wondering if...

WK: We hired Dr. Morkovin. It was so funny, because he sounded like Reverend Fields doing a comedy shtick because of his accent. We'd just sit there and look at each other and ask him "put-on" questions, and he was so naive about the whole thing. He wouldn't know that the question he was being asked was to get laughs from the other guys. Campbell Grant, I remember one afternoon... Dr Morkovin was droning on and on. "Uh, I would like this question be answered by, let's see...um, um, Campbell Grant." We'd all turn and Campbell's asleep and we'd nudge him. "Oh, oh, yes, yes, well, I don't, I can't be very brilliant on such short notice." We're always looking for gags.

Don Graham used to have action-analysis classes. He would run things like *The Great Barnum*. And he had that actor, a big fat guy. He gets off of a trolley car with a shopping bag and walks. And he'd run that over and over and over and we'd look at it, then we would sit down and by our observation do a walk cycle. That's where I got into trouble, because everybody almost traced this damn reel, each animator got to have it for so many hours to play on his moviola. So they all almost went by tracings of this guy. And later on, I did mine which was much broader than anyone else was doing it. Then they wanted us to do a bunch of firemen at a bucket brigade. They had a tent fire and they were pouring water on the flames. And so I did mine: I had a guy run up behind a big crane, and he skids to a stop and... pheeewt... It was much broader and it got a good laugh. I had caricatured the whole idea of the class at that point. It was funny and it was pretty good animation for being in the inbetween department.

The head of the inbetween department was a tyrant named George Drake. He was a relative of Ben Sharpsteen's wife and he was given this job of being the head of Inbetween. He had no training, no background. He was crude, he was a bricklayer. And he ran that department like a tyrant. It was a horrible part of my life because I always knew he was phony from the very beginning, and he played office. There'd be an applicant that he'd made a date for ten o'clock to show his work and he'd not know if it was good or bad. He would ask other people, and say, "Ah, keep him waiting!" for thirty minutes. He played office and all that shit! So he ran the inbetween department. I was an assistant to Ham then, so even though I was under his jurisdiction, George couldn't touch me, because Ham liked me as an assistant. I did all his corrections and everything, and George was a long-faced guy with a moustache. He had big ears and a mop of blond hair that hung down. He was overblown with his own importance all the time. Of course we were all on to him.

So I did my bucket guy, he skids in, throws it... I did it fast and I had time left over. So, at night, on my own time, I did another scene on the problem. I had two skinny arms coming like this "bam!" with the bucket, turned it upside down and like...taps it on the top, one drop comes out, pulls it back in, and then in comes George cut waist high with a straw hat and he does this, wiggles his ears. I sneaked it in.

See, he would look at all of our tests when we finished them. And I told Lou Debney who was in charge of cutting all the things together, to cut it in at the end. So George is sitting back running the machine and Debney comes down and gets all these tests that George is giving and drops down my room and I hand him this thing that George had *not* seen. So Debney cuts it in. Here we are in a little sweatbox sitting there and that particular day it was the day that George had John Lounsbery, Quackenbush, Cornet Wood sitting in the back, impressing them on how he runs the critique. I mean, the guy didn't know anything about it. Don Graham was there, but George did all the talking.

So the guys come there and George starts criticizing, and I spoke, "Hey, George, why don't we just run through everybody's efforts first and then go back and take them one at a time." Everybody said, "Yeah, yeah, let's get so we can compare things!" George was slightly irritated, because everyone joined in with"yeah, yeah!" So he runs through the whole thing. Goes into this tap...drip, and the guy's... I'll never forget this, there was this stony silence and then POW! they started laughing, they couldn't hold it. I can remember Jim Algar, who's a pretty straight guy, kinda stood up and held his side and fell on the carpet, and the laughing went on and on and on. The fact that somebody had the nerve to do it. It was funny and it was a caricature of this guy everybody hated and they laughed and laughed and laughed and George said, "Yeah, yeah, yeah, ha, ha, ha, ha." He was nervous, he was angry, but he had to appear as though he could take a joke like everybody else. And even the new guys were laughing. I would have gotten my ass fired out of there if it hadn't been for Ham.

Interviewed again on February 15, 1990:

WARD KIMBALL: I came to work there in April of 1934, as I remember, about a year later became Ham's assistant, because they decided to push Eric Larson up a notch, to what was called a junior animator. So I went in with Ham and he was working on *The Tortoise and the Hare.* [The *Tortoise and the Hare* was released in early January 1935, so Ward must have gone to Ham no later than early December of 1934] My first animation for Ham I did as an assistant, and that was on *The Tortoise and the Hare.* And I worked on *The Robber Kitten* after that and later on *Elmer Elephant.* I worked on

Jenny Wren in *Cock Robin*. I don't know the sequence of dates on that. I was given little things to animate.

Ham, because they were paying bonuses then, figured out a scheme where he wouldn't have to spend his own time making corrections after a sweatbox meeting with Walt. He turned them over to me and, at first, I protested. I said, "I don't know enough about this stuff." I was just inbetweening his work. And he said, "Sure, just take these drawings and they want the thing to bounce higher; just move them all up an inch and make it work." First I protested and then I realized this is a good way to learn animation. Consequently, because I was doing his corrections, almost immediately after I went in there, he made a good bonus and some of the other animators resented it—especially animators who worked in a style that they had to put their stuff on "ones," like fast action and stuff. Ham seemed to get all the nice personality stuff, a lot of it. Close-ups on "twos" and so forth. Then he gave me outright scenes to do on *Elmer Elephant*. I don't know what the order of those things were.

DAVID JOHNSON: I think that's 1936.

WK: Yes. He gave me a scene of Tilly Tiger running up the spiral stairway to her little tree house. And that was a tough one to do because this camera... The tree is panning by sideways, and I have to time my running up the stairs. Sometimes she'd go out of sight behind the tree and come out again. That was one of the toughest scenes, but through that period making corrections for Ham and his making a lot of money, comparatively speaking, I learned a lot about animation. I sold a story, *The Return of Toby Tortoise*, to the studio, and I really animated on my own for the first time on that picture.

DJ: Now, during that period, could it have been possible that he began his work on *Snow White*?

WK: Yes, because that would be coming up and in '35 you're getting ready to really work on it in '36. And he was sort of put in charge of the Snow White sequences.

DJ: Do you recall discussing it with you at all or saying anything about it, like this is going to be a tough job and the human figure.

WK: Yeah, he was fooling with it when I was animating on my own, and I would go in there and talk to him about it, and he'd say how tough it was for him to do something like this, because he had never really done anything until "Goddess of Spring." He animated the dancing.

DJ: In one of the books it says Les Clark animated that and he used his sister as a model.

WK: He could have done some of the footage. I know it was the long dancing sequence I used to kid him about and I was under the impression that he had done that.

DJ: You were animating on your own at this time. Do you remember if this was your first assignment that you were animating on your own?

WK: The first animation on my own, as a junior animator, was a story I sold called *The Return of Toby Tortoise*. Of course they gave me a chance to work on that, the Hare, this boxing match, because I had been Ham's assistant on it.

DJ: I'm trying to establish a chronology here. So you were working on that one when he was starting to work on *Snow White*?

WK: Yeah, he was getting ready for it and we always worked on shorts in between features assignment. So while we're getting ready for *Snow White* and trying to work out the problem of how to draw [the character of] Snow White... I mean that was a long battle there at the beginning, trying to get that character the way Walt would accept it.

DJ: Now did he ever say anything to you about the problems that he was having with Grim Natwick? Because when Grim Natwick was put on Snow White, Grim had a completely different idea the way she should look, and it's basically because of Grim that Snow White ended up looking like this, instead of like this. Marc Davis was Grim's assistant and he said the problems were unbelievable, the fighting between those two men. Because Luske wanted it a certain way and he really designed it and he resented Grim Natwick coming in and changing the character. But apparently Walt eventually liked it, because most of the Snow White in the movie is more or less that style. She's only in one sequence resembling this and that's when she comes in the cottage, which I think was probably the first one that was animated. Now getting back to Luske: you were on your own and he was beginning *Snow White*. As far as you know, did he stay on *Snow White* from then on out or did he also have to work on shorts?

WK: When he got on *Snow White* he stayed on it till the end and as a director. But he was taking on a responsibility, because he was an animator, helping to develop the feel of it. It was just this coming and going with all the guys, trade-offs and criticisms, and they'd walk into each other's room and, "What if we do this? Wouldn't this help the...?" Always trying to get a depth and believability, which was a technique that was very flat. All the colors were flat. They tried putting shadows and highlights and *Roger Rabbit* is probably the culmination of this effort to make the cartoons realistic. But on *Snow White* it was a battle. I mean, you had three or four people and even so, when they hand in their animation you could tell the difference. I'm just mentioning all these things: the flatness of the rotoscope drawing over the very realistic third dimensional set-up of the live action... You ran into these situations where, all of a sudden, wham! It doesn't look right. The body looks too short, her head's too big. Just before you showed me the one with the leg out I was saying they probably called these back and said, "Change the perspective on the thing." Unfortunately, when they shot it, it looked OK to them, but you could see this foot going away. In a cartoon you have to have slight exaggeration. In the case of Snow White, you had to make that a little more obvious or it would look wrong. All the time, there were angles on Snow White with her head down that you just can't draw.

DJ: But it looked fine on the rotoscope, probably.

WK: Oh, of course, because you're looking at realism.

DJ: Now, when you were coming into the room and you were looking at this new project, you had to be interested, because this was something new for yourself, too. Did Ham have the moviola there, and would he be studying the rotoscoping at that time?

WK: Yes, he would take the animation and he would criticize it as a director would. Those were the days when the organization of a director and a crew and so forth on the pictures were in the formative stages, because it was unlike the shorts. They had different directors take a section of the picture, but Ham was more or less a supervisor with this Snow White effort and bringing all the animators together and getting something that was a model where Snow White would look the same no matter who was animating. And when you're working on a thing as subtle as a realistic drawing—which, relatively speaking, in the late 1930s, was very realistic compared to our regular cartoon style—the width of a line would change the look on her face.

Later, I've seen photographs in newspapers where they decided to put a red coloring along with the black and white on a movie star's face, but the red plate in the printing slipped a little, and the mouth got too close to the nose and... So I made a machine when I was going through my kinetic period, and I had a beauty machine, where slowly the mouth was like an overlay cut out of metal and painted up on a photographic face and it would slowly move up too close to the mouth, then it would start going down, and at a certain point it was perfect, then it would get down too far and the lady would have a long upper lip. She was ugly just by a subtle change, and it was called a beauty machine. I had it fixed so an arrow this whole time would go to NG, NG—both extremes—under the nose and a long upper lip and a buzzer would go off, but when it hit half way it was perfect, you heard a music box behind the thing. It was called the beauty machine. Also, at the same time the eyes were perfect and the mouth was perfect, but as the mouth went down it came in closer—just subtle movements, sometimes 3/8ths of an inch—and then when the mouth came back up, the eyes would start parting again, and when the mouth got up underneath the nose or closer to it, they were too far apart. Beauty was just the width of a line, and that was the thing that animators were fighting—they just couldn't do everything in a rough sort of way, they were tracing a rotoscope and then, after they got a trace, they had to put the new accepted model of her head on the thing and her costume, and then they'd have critiques, and they'd say, "Something's wrong here," and they'd have to sit around. They were learning what to do about this new method of getting realism and believability in the case of Snow White and the Queen. Especially Snow White.

DJ: Do you recall what may have been some of the experimental type of animation that Ham Luske would have done before he actually embarked on some of the scenes? Like, did they do, for instance, work on drapery, specifically for Snow White? Or did he just embark on a scene, let's say, when she goes into the cottage, and just do that several times?

WK: They decided, in order to make Snow White and the Queen and the Huntsman and the Prince and the horse believable, that they were going to photograph it and draw back from caricature. For the beginning they were choosing [Marjorie] Belcher to do Snow White, but they didn't trace her face necessarily. Her face on the photostat would be sort of a guide. The top of Snow White's head would go up so many enlargements and the cheeks would puff out a little more and... So in comparison to Belcher you have an exaggeration, but a very subtle one. Getting back to the problem, it's OK when Snow White was in a normal pose with her head tipped one way or the other, but if she tipped her head down, they tried to avoid those things too much, because they made ugly drawings in black and white. Because when the nose drops down, it cuts over the mouth, right? Looking down from the top? What is wrong is exaggerated when you see only a thin, single line instead of half tone.

DJ: Marge told me that she began the rotoscoping, she thinks, it was fall of '35 when they called her in.

WK: They also did all of the soup thing with her, and believe it or not, they shot a lot of footage of my wife on scenes where she walks some place or she goes over a bridge and down the other side. Because it didn't make any difference: they were using it for the action. That's for something they wouldn't call Belcher to come in and I still have films somewhere of Betty doing these middle distant scenes and walking over a quickly engineered set of steps, which would be a bridge or something else later on, for the live action of walking.

DJ: Now, would these be dated by any chance?

WK: No. They'd have to be in old camera department records. And those things get thrown away. Jack Cutting, I think, had something to do with some of the early... I know he's the one that called Betty in to do these long shots.

DJ: And that was after you were married?

WK: We were married in August of 1936. And these were scenes they either forgot to shoot or contemplated from the very beginning. But they were things that they didn't need Belcher for and they got Betty for nothing when she walked over from the ink-and-paint department.

[...]

When you've got five cels staked on another, the color of Doc's hat and pants, which is on the top cel, is a lot brighter than if he's on the lower cel, which darkens. It's like looking through glass. Finally, you have so many layers of glass it's totally black. If he moves to a position that's behind another character that's just come in and drops down to level number three, all these colors have to be changed, because they're lowering in value. People don't understand this: why are the colors of the dwarfs in this cel brighter than those on this cel. It has to compensate by what level you are, one to five. So if you have a number-two vermillion on top and he goes to the first cel on the bottom, it has to be brighter to balance out in color. A lot of that has to take place and Betty was working on the color and she left the studio in... We had our first kid in 1940 and she was head of the color model. She was in colors, and she'd paint the colors on the back after some girl would trace the lines. They'd take them up to the director and they'd say, "I think Doc's shirt is too much the color of so and so's," and there had to be all those changes so each dwarf as you look at them had different reds—there's a difference between the red used on Happy and the one on Doc. One's a light vermillion, one's a dark red. You can see those things are pretty close. But that's what her job was then. She'd come over on some of the preliminary scenes and do these walking or running scenes with the outfit on so that the animators could get direction. But they used Belcher, of course, for the close-up and the playbacks.

DJ: Fred Moore is given credit for re-designing the dwarfs. Was Tytla also involved in the re-designing of the dwarfs or anyone else other than Fred?

WK: He had to learn. Everybody had to make their drawings consistent with the way all the other animators were drawing. That's why you make model sheets.

DJ: Yes, but the question I'm getting at is was there another influence on the final design other than Fred Moore?

WK: I would say no. He was the dwarfs' man, and the minute he went over and did his preliminary drawings, Walt said, "Hey, that's great!" because it's more of a cartoon style we're looking at. Whereas [Albert] Hurter and [Earl] Hurd and all the rest of them were old-time artists that were based on European fairy-tale illustrations. But they had to start somewhere, and Fred, not having access to all the scraps of old-time German artists and people who'd done Hans Christian Andersen illustrations, Fred, being a very straightforward, not in tune with the history of fairy tales, would take a thing of Earl Hurd's, which is based on the old-time conception, take these and gradually maybe just change a few things. But you keep going back and changing, making the noses bigger, the faces, the heads bigger in relation to the bodies. And the whole perception of the dwarfs gradually changed and Walt, somewhere along the line and maybe the rest of the guys, said, "Hey, that's it!" Tytla would come along and follow that model. I'm sure if Tytla had started he would have been a little more influenced by Earl Hurd or Hurter, but Fred was just an innocent, simple directing animator who wanted them to look—pardon the word—cute.

I was struck in later years, much later, by the way [Hurter] drew the first Dopeys and the way Outcault drew the Yellow Kid. I always say that influenced the way Hurter did Dopey. And he was supposed to be Chinese. Hurter was from back east. He knew all these old-time cartoonists, he was one himself, and worked on newspapers, and that's where he got Dopey.

DJ: Who was [David] Hilberman?

WK: He worked there. I never knew quite what he did. He could have gone around to the animators and merely took the way they were drawing the rabbit and the bird and so forth and put them on a sheet. It was an organizational thing, a model sheet. What he did was trace the drawings from the animation and put them all neatly arranged so that as other artists were coming on after the supervisors had started this stuff, they would be all consistent. He was a great union organizer, and Walt called him a communist. Walt didn't like him when the strike started. I think he came into the animation department. He could have been an assistant or a clean-up man.

[Changing the subject]

WK: Bob Stokes was good on things like the human figure. Better than Babbitt was. And he did very well on *Mother Goose Goes Hollywood*.

DJ: He taught at Chouinard in the late 1940s and that's the last I've been able to find out.

WK: He was a quiet guy, didn't have one of those big ego drives. He'd suffer through them. Didn't say much. I used to go in when we were both working on *Mother Goose Goes Hollywood* and he had slight, droll humor, and not too much comment.

DJ: What did he look like?

WK: He was a tall guy. His hair was kind of sandy blond, grey.

DJ: Was he older than you?

WK: Oh yes, and he wore glasses and was a good draftsman. He was amused. He kept asking me how did I like married life. I had just gotten married. As I say, he was a quiet guy. I don't know if he was married or not. But he was a good animator. He wasn't a flamboyant, wild cartoonist type. He wasn't a pie thrower; I always use that term. Old custard pies. He was reserved. He was conservative. But he did a good job, especially the Hepburn job. Of course, on *Mother Goose Goes Hollywood*, we couldn't miss with T. Hee's caricatures.

Acknowledgments

Many individuals have given so generously of their time and energy to see this project through to fruition. Unfortunately, I know only three of them: my publisher Bob McLain, my editor Didier Ghez, and a Greek friend here in Athens, Christos Mitsios. The rest of you, I can only offer a blanket canopy of gratitude and appreciation for all your dedication and unflagging effort. Blessings to all!

About the Author

David Johnson is an authority on the Disney film *Snow White and the Seven Dwarfs*. A resident of Athens, Greece, he holds a masters (with distinction) in music from the Manhattan School of Music.

About Theme Park Press

Theme Park Press publishes books primarily about the Disney company, its history, culture, films, animation, and theme parks, as well as theme parks in general.

Our authors include noted historians, animators, Imagineers, and experts in the theme park industry.

We also publish many books by first-time authors, with topics ranging from fiction to theme park guides.

And we're always looking for new talent. If you'd like to write for us, or if you're interested in the many other titles in our catalog, please visit:

www.ThemeParkPress.com

- -

Theme Park Press Newsletter

Subscribe to our free email newsletter and enjoy:

- ◆ Free book downloads and giveaways
- ◆ Access to excerpts from our many books
- ◆ Announcements of forthcoming releases
- ◆ Exclusive additional content and chapters
- ◆ And more good stuff available nowhere else

To subscribe, visit www.ThemeParkPress.com, or send email to newsletter@themeparkpress.com.

Walt's People

VOLUME 20

Talking Disney with the Artists Who Knew Him

Iwao Takamoto

Bob Givens

Tom Oreb

Sam Armstrong

Edited by Didier Ghez

Foreword by Alan Coats

SNOW WHITE'S PEOPLE

An Oral History of the Disney Film
Snow White and the Seven Dwarfs
VOLUME I

DAVID JOHNSON

Edited by Didier Ghez

50 YEARS IN THE MOUSE HOUSE

The Lost Memoir of One of Disney's Nine Old Men

ERIC LARSON

Edited by Didier Ghez and Joe Campana

Animator on Horseback

The Autobiography of
Disney Artist Mel Shaw

MEL SHAW

Edited by Andrea Gessell-Severe and Didier Ghez
Foreword by John Canemaker

Read more about these books
and our many other titles at:

www.ThemeParkPress.com

Made in United States
North Haven, CT
23 December 2022

30057991R00124